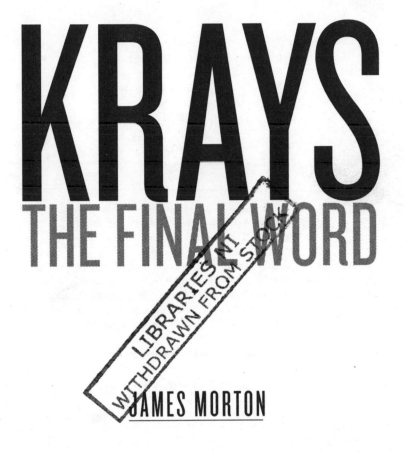

KRAYS
THE FINAL WORD

JAMES MORTON

MIRROR BOOKS

First published by Mirror Books in 2019

Mirror Books is part of Reach plc
10 Lower Thames Street
London EC3R 6EN

www.mirrorbooks.co.uk

© James Morton

ISBN 978-1-912624-68-3

Typeset by Danny Lyle

Printed and bound in Great Britain by
CPI Group (UK) Ltd, Croydon, CR0 4YY

A CIP catalogue record for this book is available from the British Library.

Every effort has been made to fulfil requirements with regard to
reproducing copyright material. The author and publisher will be
glad to rectify any omissions at the earliest opportunity.

3 5 7 9 10 8 6 4 2

Cover images: Mirrorpix

CONTENTS

'But there were other murders too, there were a hell of a lot of other murders. I investigated seven murders myself.'

Nipper Read
Interview with Craig Cabell, December 2001

'Making heroes out of murderers strikes me as both crass and impossible.'

John Pearson
'Ronnie, Reggie and me', *Esquire*, January 19

INTRODUCTION

So, how many was it the Krays killed? Or, how many did they have killed is probably a better way of putting it. They only did two themselves – or was it just two? There was Georgie Cornell, shot in the Blind Beggar of course. Two in the head as the juke box played 'The sun ain't gonna shine anymore'. Dead right. Just like that villain who was reciting the Lord's Prayer as he was about to be topped in a club down Walthamstow way, Valentine's Day it was. When he gets to the bit, 'Thy will be done', the fellow with the gun says, 'It will son, it will'. Cornell had been off his ground after visiting his friend Jimmy Andrews, trying to find out who shot him. Ronnie Kray's was the name in the frame for Andrews as well. Well, that was one story.

And then there was Jack 'The Hat' McVitie, stabbed to death in a basement in Stoke Newington. They were the only two murders the police could pin on them personally. Then there was Frank Mitchell. The Twins got chucked on that one, although years later their mate Freddie Foreman, 'Brown Bread Fred', they called him, went on the box to say how him and Alfie Gerard did it for them.

So that's three altogether or may be four, but there were others. 'Mad' Teddy Smith was meant to be one, but there was a rumour he'd jumped ship and legged it to Australia. Then there was a rent boy picked up in Piccadilly who'd snuffed it during a bit of over-enthusiastic sex. And what about Freddie Mills, the World Light Heavyweight Champion? Then he went on the stage and did telly and had a nightclub on the Charing Cross Road. Star of stage, screen and radio, as they say. But the official verdict was he'd topped himself. That's the best of a contract killing – if it was that even. Make it look like suicide or an accident. Not that poor Freddie hadn't good enough reason to do himself. The official verdict was suicide, but it could have been the perfect contract killing. He had reasons for suicide though – debts, boyfriend gone, not getting any more work on the telly.

And what about Ernie Isaacs, shot in his own flat? That was another that was never solved. There were stories that it was Reggie in person. Did Reggie personally shoot Ernie Isaacs in his flat? And the solicitor David Jacobs? Another who topped himself, apparently? But there was a story Ronnie had him done for not helping him out in the McVitie case. Not impossible. Did brother Charlie on his deathbed tell Reggie to kill the drug dealer Peter Beaumont Gowling because he was a grass? Coming from a grass like Charlie that would have been a bit rich. Whatever Gowling had done and whether Charlie did ask Reggie to see to things for him, he was shot and killed in the north-east a month after he finished his 11-year sentence.[1]

But as they say, 'Where's the evidence?'

CHAPTER I
IN THE BEGINNING THERE WERE THE KRAYS

'This boy has been beaten by beasts', said Thames Court magistrate Herbert Malone KC. The date was 12 March 1950, the time around 11 p.m. and the place outside Barries' Dance Hall in Narrow Way, just off Mare Street, Hackney. The boy in question was Roy Harvey, badly beaten with chains on his way home with Wally Birch, who went on to be a player in the West End escort agencies, and Dennis Siegenberg who, years later as Dennis Stafford, was convicted of the murder of Angus Sibbett in Newcastle.[2] The beasts were allegedly the Kray Twins and their friend Patrick Aucott. Harvey had had the nerve and, for the East End, the bad manners to go to the police. But, when it came to it, he might have saved himself and his friends a good deal of trouble. He needn't have bothered because amid fears of interference with witnesses, the committal proceedings dragged on. By the time the case came up at the Old Bailey, one girl had been threatened with a slashing and Harvey had received a warning letter. The case was dismissed when the witnesses failed to identify the Twins. It was the first of many abortive efforts over the next quarter of a century to pin the Krays down.[3] Laurie O'Leary, a great friend of the Krays, claims in his book *Ron Kray: a Man Among Men* that the Twins were totally innocent in this case.

As the years pass, the truth and legends about the Kray brothers blur and merge just as the men and pigs do at the end of *Animal Farm*. Writers have relied on each other's inaccurate accounts. Dates have been transposed. Names have been changed. There have been so many contradictory memoirs that things have been reversed and the pen has become mightier than the gun. The tendency has been, as the character Maxwell Scott says in John Ford's *The Man who Shot Liberty Valance,* 'When the legend becomes fact, print the legend'.

What then *are* the facts? To begin, it is certain the Twins were born on 24 October 1933, with Reginald a few minutes older than his brother Ronald. But even then some writers have the date wrong. Their brother Charles was seven years older, born on 9 July 1926. In between there was a daughter Violet, who died within a few hours of her premature birth in 1929, possibly because of a beating their father Charles Kray Snr had given his wife Violet during the last stages of her pregnancy.

They came from Jewish and Gypsy stock and were born at 64 Stene Street, Hoxton, in London's East End. They were monozygotic or identical twins, still a comparatively rare phenomenon and, given the high rate of infant mortality in the East End of the 1930s, their survival into adulthood was unusual. However, at the age of three they contracted diphtheria and were taken to separate hospitals. Reggie was home in a relatively short time but Ronnie fretted for his brother and had breathing difficulties for some months until their mother arrived at the General Hospital, Hoxton to take him back to Stene Street.

Charles Kray Snr was a 'pesterer', a man who bought and sold wardrobes and gold and silver door to door. A deserter in World War Two, he spent the next 12 years on the run and so was absent from the family for long periods. Therefore their mother, a flower seller to whom they were devoted, was the greatest influence on them. Violet's father, Johnny 'Cannonball' Lee, had been a fairly well-known boxer and entertainer, who could balance on bottles and lick white-hot pokers. Before the Second World War the family moved to the slightly more salubrious 178 Vallance Road in Bethnal Green – but still with no bath and an outside lavatory – a few hundred yards from Whitechapel tube station. Next door lived Violet's sister Rose, and her other sister May was two doors away. Across the road, her brother John and his wife Maud lived above the café they ran. Opposite was a one-cow dairy.

A different proposition from their father was their uncle Alfie, born in 1909, a high-class receiver who, although never a member of the Firm as such, would work with them during their heyday. 'He warned me against the Twins,' said the dwarf-like 'Little' Stan Davis, himself a noted receiver who also worked with their elder brother Charlie on the racecourse and Point-to-Point pitches. 'Alfie was top class. A good man to work with. Reggie was more sensible [than Ronnie] but that didn't make him any less of a menace.'

During the war Violet and the three brothers were evacuated to Hadleigh in Essex. Billeted with the local doctor, the twins chased and killed his cockerel and defied his wife's efforts to teach them to read and write. Violet Kray missed London, however, and they soon returned. Later they wrote they had enjoyed themselves hugely in the country.

Back in London after the war, their school records were indifferent and they were continually involved in fights, which they usually won. As they grew up they took to wearing razor blades sewn into the lapels of their jackets, so that anyone taking hold of them would have their hands cut, much as the Peaky Blinders in Birmingham and the Sabinis had worn blades in their caps before the war. They also favoured knuckledusters and nails protruding from their shoes.

Until they were young men the pair were identical in weight, height and looks, except Ronnie had a mole on his neck. Then, when their boxing careers ended, Ronnie put on weight, not a matter on which he liked to hear a comment.

Ronnie Hart, their cousin on their father's side, and later their nemesis, who probably knew them as well as any, thought the Twins were both similar and very different in their tastes. As he grew up Ronnie modelled himself on Al Capone, of whom he sometimes said he was a reincarnation, wearing an Albert watch and chain, a fawn camel hair or a dark blue cashmere coat, which he wore over his shoulders like the American Mafiosi. He liked opera and particularly Capone's favourite, the tenor Beniamino Gigli. He kept a stock of around 50 shirts, giving them away when he had worn them once or twice. He would only wear black silk socks – his favourite colour. He drank gin and tonic but moved on to wine, which he thought was the thing to do. He soaked his feet in rose water and milk at night because he had been told European kings had done the same. The only car he could drive was an automatic, and that badly. He hoped that in a film he would be played by Rod Steiger. Once he told Hart, 'I'm a genius, don't you realise it? I'm like Hitler. He was also a genius and he was mad. It's always been like that you know.

Every genius is mad'. According to Hart he unsuccessfully attempted to organise a Kray Youth Movement.

Reggie loved children, horse riding, slow dreamy music – his favourites were Timi Yuro (the little girl with the big voice) and Dean Martin – and writing poetry. He preferred casual wear, owning around 70 shirts, none of which he gave away. His favourite colour was blue. He had his teeth capped. He never forgot he could have been a force in the ring, often shadow boxing as he went along the street. He would drink a glass of hot water every morning and sometimes hot milk and honey at night.

Both had rather effete high-pitched voices and author Bernard O'Mahoney thought that Reggie spoke rather like Corporal Jones in Dad's Army. Neither liked being touched. As a Scorpio, Reggie had a tie clip of a scorpion and Ronnie a charm, both made out of diamonds. Both had a Maltese barber visit them because they feared an attack while in the chair, something which happened to old-time American gangsters such as Albert Anastasia who, on 25 October 1957, was shot and killed while having his hair cut at the Park Sheraton hotel in New York. Both massaged their hair with olive oil and surgical spirit because that was what old-time boxers did. They had a private manicurist and masseuse and used York Town aftershave until Ronnie graduated to Brut. Both were vain and could hardly pass a mirror without straightening their hair, which they claimed was more luxuriant than that of any other member of the Firm. Both feared baldness. They liked having their fortunes told and Dot Brown, the wife of Tommy 'The Bear' Brown (or Welch), a member of the Firm, gave them suitable readings.

As for literature, their detractors said they had read only one book, *How Green was my Valley*. Their lieutenant Albert Donoghue said that Ronnie thought urethritis had something to do with youths. This is probably a bit unkind; the Twins biographer John Pearson told a television programme that Ron's favourite books were *Boys Town* (because it was all about boys) and Anthony Nutting's life of General Gordon – 'He's my hero, gay like me, faced overwhelming odds and died like a man'.[4]

Both collected old weapons, some of which were later hung on the wall of Ronnie's flat at Cedra Court in Hackney. The flat itself had a giant four-poster bed. The lounge was done out in oriental style with Chinese and Persian carpets, an elephant's foot, a three-foot ebony elephant which weighed around two hundredweight and stuffed birds in cages. The bathroom, with a black bath and pink tiles, had a peephole in the door. It was at Cedra Court that Ronnie threw his homosexual orgies, attended by milords Driberg and Boothby.

Their older brother Charlie was unlike the Twins in habits, dress and affability, said Hart. A womanising man who was hail-fellow-well-met, he loved his wife Doris 'Dolly' Moore, whom the family regarded as neurotic and snooty, and adored his children Gary and Nancy. He wore no grease on his hair and little jewellery. His hobbies were his motor boat, caravan holidays and spear fishing in the South of France. After his release from his sentence for assisting in the disposal of McVitie's body, he devoted much of his time to Gary, who had serious behavioural problems.

The Twins had brief spells working as fishmongers, fruit pickers and labourers from 1949-50. After October 1950, neither of them was ever really gainfully employed again.

Charlie was, again, a different proposition. Throughout his life he ran a series of unsuccessful businesses including a theatrical agency and a clothing factory. But most of that was in the future. After his National Service he had worked on the Point-to-Points with Stan Davis, putting up bookmakers' 'joints'. He also helped him with an early form of a package travel company, flying holidaymakers to Beauvais and then coaching them down to a camp in the South of France. That all ended when Davis, who could never resist making a dishonest penny when he could have earned a legitimate shilling, went to prison along with Uncle Alf Kray.

East End hardman and lifelong friend of Charlie Kray, Mickey Bailey, remembered 'Charlie told me a story about little Stan Davis. He was out in the south of France when he was held up by a car--jacker at gun point. He spoke perfect French, did Stan, and he told the man he'd just come out of the nick and hadn't anything. The little bastard got away with it'.

For a time it seemed as though, along with Charlie, the Twins might make a career in the Ring. Boxing, along with villainy, was then the traditional working-class way out of poverty. As kids they had fought each other over three rounds at Alf Stewart's Boxing Booth when it visited Bethnal Green, for which they shared seven and sixpence. Later there were amateur trophies galore. In 1948 Reggie won the London Schoolboys championship and was later a British Schoolboy finalist. Ronnie won the Hackney Schoolboys' championship and the London Junior title as well as a London ATC title. As teenagers Charlie bought them their first boxing boots at Grose's in Ludgate Circus and took them to Bill Kline's professional gymnasium, known as Kline's or The Olympic in Fitzroy Square, where they sparred with top men of the time, including world champion Terry Allen and British light-heavyweight champion Ron Barton.[5]

What their brother Charlie considered a defining moment in the Twins' careers took place on a Saturday evening in October 1950. Naturally his version is biased, but he claims that an officious police officer, enquiring into a fight at a youth club, told a group of youths to move away from Pellicci's café in the Bethnal Green Road. According to Charlie, the officer poked Ronnie in the stomach and in turn Ronnie hit him. Back at the station Ronnie took a bad beating before being charged with assault. Reggie went to find out what had happened to his brother, hit the officer and so, a precursor to the Cornell-McVitie murders, 'did his one' too. Charlie maintains that he was told if the Krays raised trouble over Ronnie's beating then, in turn, the police would cause trouble for the family, starting with their father, who was still avoiding the call-up. Charlie claims the police threatened they'd make life difficult for their draft-dodging father if Ronnie complained about his beating.[6]

In the 1950s assaults on the police generally meant instant imprisonment, particularly since in this case the day before the hearing Ronnie had received one day's detention at the Friends House Juvenile Court for attempted taking and driving away of a motor vehicle. But on 1 November at Old Street Magistrates' Court, into the witness box stepped the chain-smoking Father Richard Hetherington of St James the Great in Bethnal Green. 1950 was a time when people still went to church rather than cleaning their motor cars on a Sunday morning; Anglican and Catholic churches were perhaps held in higher esteem than they are today, and a vicar or priest who came forward to extol the virtues of the defendant was highly sought after.

Hetherington told Harold Sturge, the magistrate, how the Twins were generally good lads, 'apart from their disgusting behaviour on this occasion'. The good Father won Sturge over and this time they received two years' probation each. Over the next 29 years Hetherington and other priests would be regularly wheeled out on both sacred and secular occasions.

The Boxing Board of Control took no notice of their convictions – if indeed they ever knew of them – and now trained by Henry Berry, the father of the very talented Teddy, they turned professional. One story by their driver Billy 'Jack' Frost is that Ronnie had hit a referee and left his amateur club. Reggie had the talent and won all his fights. Ronnie had the aggression. Charlie, who won 18 out of 21 fights, lost interest after his marriage. Finally all three brothers boxed on the same bill on 11 December 1951 at the Royal Albert Hall. Reggie beat Bobby Manito on points. Ronnie lost on points to Bill Sliney, whom Reggie had twice beaten. In the early 1950s the Southern Area of the Boxing Board of Control did not always look after its boxers as well as it might have done. Charlie, who had not boxed for a year, took £25 from the promoter and a bad beating from the then undefeated welterweight and very classy Lew Lazar, who later fought for the British Middleweight title. Outclassed and out of condition, he was knocked down twice for counts of nine but pulled himself off the canvas and, against the advice of Berry, continued until he was knocked out in the third round. That night was the highlight and indeed the end of the Twins' non-criminal career. It was now time to do their National Service.

Not all criminals dislike conscription. The old pre-First World War gang leader Darby Sabini and at least one of his brothers had good war records, and so did the cracksmen Eddie Chapman and Johnny Ramensky. One of Darby's sons was killed during the Second World War and another joined up. On the other hand, London's 'Boss of the Underworld' Billy Hill managed to evade the RAF totally and his friend and later rival Jack Spot obtained an early discharge by complaining that his sergeant was anti-Semitic and that he had been placed in too lowly a position. The Krays fell into the Hill and Spot category.

Had they been separated, things might have been different. Reggie was happy with the discipline of a boxing gymnasium. He might have adapted to army life, but for Ronnie it was impossible.

The pair did not take kindly to the Royal Fusiliers from the moment on 20 March 1952 when, wearing identical blue suits, they walked into the regiment's base at the Tower of London to begin their National Service. After being shown their quarters and equipment, they promptly started to walk out of the room. When the sergeant challenged them they told him they were going to tea with their mother. One of them hit him on the jaw and they headed off to spend the evening at a dance hall in Tottenham.

They were arrested, still in bed, at Vallance Road the next morning. Back at the Tower of London, they were charged with being absent without leave and for the next seven days were confined to the guardroom. For the next few months the army endeavoured unsuccessfully to teach them to be soldiers. At this time the Twins first met Dickie Morgan, who was to become a lifelong friend – until offering evidence against them to the police, that is. He had been sent to the Fusiliers after serving a four-year stretch at Portland Borstal. Morgan's first serious conviction was for robbing Jewish shopkeepers: ironic for a man who worked as a Shabbos goy, a non-Jew who for a few pence fulfilled basic household duties for Orthodox Jews on the Sabbath. Reggie claimed that in their twenties, the Twins and the lantern-jawed Morgan began to steal from lorries, before selling the produce to a farmer. If this story is true, it is one of the few times they actually stole anything themselves.

Five months later on 5 August 1952 Ronnie deserted again, and claimed later he'd boxed at some unlicensed shows while on the run. But Reggie stayed with the regiment until he absconded on 2 October that year.[7] According to Martin Fido, Reggie also boxed on the unlicensed circuit run by their later employee Bobby Ramsey, whom he describes as a Jack Spot man. Ronnie's last bout in a hall in Tottenham earned him £5.[8] [9]

On 2 May 1953 along with Morgan they absconded yet again, were arrested the following day and hauled off to Shepton Mallet to await their court martial. While there they created as much trouble as they could and Ronnie smeared his cell wall with excrement. On 11 June the Krays received nine months for assault and desertion. They were finally dishonourably discharged from the army on 13 November that year but they claimed they weren't to blame for any of this trouble. After all, as Charlie pointed out, things might have been so different had the NCO not rubbed them up the wrong way the day they enlisted. He thought his brothers would have fared far better in wartime and would 'so easily have distinguished themselves with courage in the face of extreme danger'.[10]

Before the end of the year they were involved in a fight in a drinking club in Tottenham Court Road. As with most of their accounts, they claimed they were merely defending themselves against an unprovoked aggressor. This time it was an 'African' who had been pushing and shoving their young friend Harry Abrahams, a man quite capable of taking care of himself. Reggie Kray hit the man over the head with the truncheon he happened to be carrying before Ronnie stabbed him. When Ronnie, but not Reggie, was picked out at an identification parade masterminded by a lawyer, the flamboyantly gay Stanley Crowther, no charges were brought. Being one of identical twins had many benefits.

Given the enthusiasm with which Ronnie Kray used a knife when the death penalty was still in force, he was fortunate not to end up on a murder charge earlier than he did. One early victim who survived was the amateur boxer Billy Roode. Years later Stan Davis recalled:

'In 1954 or 55 Ronnie stabbed a boxer Billy Roode in what was then a poofter pub, the Hospital Tavern in the Mile End Road in Dalston. I knew Billy because we was both members of the boxing club Eton Manor and I tried to straighten it up but Billy wasn't having it. He said Ronnie had taken a right liberty. And so Charlie asked if I would take Ronnie down to my campsite at Boulouris two miles south of St Raphael in the south of France, and he stayed with me for about five weeks until it went away.

I thought I might have trouble with him but he was as good as gold. He offered to pay but I said no.'

While Ronnie was away, it was arranged for the Krays to compensate Roode and buy him a new suit. A fight was also arranged between the old boxer Buller Ward and Roode's brother Joe, but the pair shook hands when they realised they were merely doing the Krays' bidding.[11]

It was at the Epsom Spring race meeting in 1955 that the Twins made their first appearance in what, for them, passed as polite society. The story is that the old gang leader Jack Spot, fearing an attack on his control of the free course bookmaking pitches by the formidable 'Mad' Frank Fraser on behalf of Italian interests, recruited the Twins as his minders for the afternoon. It was easy money. Reggie said:

'It wasn't that we liked him [Spot]. We despised him really. We just turned out with Spotty to show everyone that *we* was the up-and-coming firm and didn't give a fuck for anyone. Old Spotty understood. Whatever else he may have been, he wasn't stupid. He knew quite well that though we were there in theory as his friends, we meant to end up taking over from him.'

In an improved version of the story, a few nights later they heard that Fraser and another Billy Hill henchman, Billy Blythe, were wanting to fight it out in an Islington public house. Armed to the teeth and 'with a dozen of their best fighters', the Twins went looking for them only to find the pub empty.[12]

The fact that Fraser was in a secure mental hospital all that month has never been allowed to get in the way of a good tale. Nor should it. Print the legend.

On the other hand Reggie, at least, was a great admirer of Spot's one-time friend Billy Hill, with whom they went to stay in Tangier and whom they called Crutchie because on one occasion he had broken his ankle and had to use crutches. Reggie looked on him as his mentor and wrote in *Villains We Have Known*:

> 'When I was in my early twenties, the man I wanted to emulate most of all was the former gang boss of London's underworld, Billy Hill. The prime reason for my admiration was that, apart from Billy being very physical and violent when necessary, he had a good, quick thinking brain and this trait appealed to me most of all.'

And:

> 'I like to think that, in some ways, I have come close to emulating him; to be honest, I acknowledge that he stands alone and there will never be another Billy Hill.'

In his declining years, Hill was said to be terrified of the pair.

CHAPTER 2
THE MAKING OF THE 'TWINS'

The incident which some think 'made' the Twins was a fight they and Charlie had in the Coach and Horses on the Mile End Road with 'Big' Bill Donovan and a man named Cooper. Apparently Cooper and Donovan had been saying they were going to see to the Twins, who then slipped out of the door and returned through another entrance tooled up. Donovan, who nearly lost an eye in the fight, refused to press charges and later became one of the doormen at the Twins' Double R club.

The Twins took over Jack Spot's run-down old billiard hall in Eric Street off the Mile End Road. Charlie Kray says they made the manager a proposition. They would take it over, smarten it up and give the manager a weekly slice of the takings. It was an offer he, and many others after him, could not refuse.

Smarten up the billiard hall they may have done, but it soon became a home from home for East End villains and wannabees. The Krays seemed quite happy with this state of affairs, but I once asked Mickey Bailey about it and still recall his words:

'I was spending my time down the snooker hall and mixing with villains. I didn't play, but it was a sort of apprenticeship of its own. It was a meeting place for older villains to talk about crime and pass their skills on to the youngsters.

My mother got wind of what I was up to, and since she'd known the Twins since they were boys she decided to go and speak to them. Apparently it was Ronnie she saw. Whether it was the same day or a couple of days later I don't know, but as me and a couple of friends walked across the waste ground in front of the hall Ronnie was on the steps. He says, "Where are you going?" and I said, "in for a cup of tea and a pie." He just said, "It'll be a long time before you're allowed back here. You're all barred. Your mother's been down." There was no malice from Ronnie. He was just doing what my mother wanted. Even at that relatively early age I knew you didn't argue with the Twins.'[13]

However, the hall was also used as a slaughter, a place to cache stolen goods before they could be sold on. The Krays are said to have fought for control of the hall with a group of Maltese and Ron is credited with chasing his attackers away waving a samurai sword.

The Twins were right when they thought that Spot's empire was there for the taking. On 11 August 1955 he became involved in a knife fight in Old Compton Street, Soho with Albert Dimeo, better known as Dimes, Billy Hill's right-hand man and one of the leaders of the reborn Italian gangs. Both were very seriously wounded and at the subsequent trial at the Old Bailey both were acquitted; Dimes because a Jewish lady who broke up the fight by hitting Spot with a weighing scale pan said Spot was the attacker, and Spot because the bent vicar Claude Andrews and Christopher Glinski, a Polish war hero turned dishonest man about Soho, said Dimes was the aggressor. As a result the incident became known as 'The Fight That Never Was'.

In May 1956 Spot was badly slashed in the street by Frankie Fraser and accomplices. The next month he was set up by Billy Hill and stood trial over a knifing in which he was never involved. Spot was acquitted but he was finished. He set up a small drinking club, the Highball in Lancaster Gate, which was later fired. Reggie would claim personal responsibility, but he was probably acting on behalf of Billy Hill.

The first real sign that the Twins were moving into the West End came in 1956 when they became involved in a drinking club, The Stragglers in Cambridge Circus. Run by docker Billy Jones, before the Twins' involvement the clientele were prone to fighting among themselves, something which reduced the profits. Jones' friend, the ex-boxer Bobby Ramsey, mentioned the problem to the Twins. In a matter of days the club was running smoothly and profitably and they had a share. The Twins' cousin Ronnie Hart claimed they simply moved in and took over the club.

Then came a hiatus. It came about, so the story goes, because one of the Watney Streeters who controlled the Docks at the time, Charlie Martin, had a small scam going with local post office drivers who would re-address parcels to places where he could collect them.

Ronnie Kray wanted 50% of the profits. Martin was a slow payer and Ronnie realised he would soon have to deal with him severely. The opportunity came when Martin had a fight with Billy Jones. In return, the next night, Jones' partner, Bobby Ramsey, sought out Martin and beat him up. Two nights later Martin, this time with help from the Watney Street gang, beat Ramsey unconscious outside The Artichoke pub in Shadwell.

Now Ronnie apparently wanted to make an example of Charlie Martin and to shoot him, but both Ramsey and Jones argued against this. Instead it was agreed that a severe beating would be handed out to the Watney Street connection in The Britannia, another Shadwell pub. Buller Ward claims that the matter could have been resolved with a straightener between Ramsey and Charlie Martin or their respective appointees. Martin nominated one of the bosses of the docks, Jimmy Fullerton, but the Krays decided this was not sufficient and it was time they put their stamp on the Streeters.[14]

Around 9.45 p.m. on 28 August 1956, the Twins, the revived Bobby Ramsey and Billy Jones, headed to The Britannia. The Twins were certainly not brave or foolish enough to go into Watney Street territory with only Ramsey and Jones as back up. The Scotland Yard officer Nipper Read believed that at the height of their powers the Twins could call on up to 200 followers, but on this occasion they looked to Ronnie Diamond and his Diamond Gang for help. Suitably tooled up, they arrived to find only Terry Martin, Charlie's cousin, playing cards. The cowardly, if sensible, Streeters had escaped through a back door. Martin was told to 'come outside or we'll kill you here' and was asked where his cousin was. He was then knocked to the floor, given a kicking and stabbed under the right arm and shoulder with a bayonet. After the Krays and Ramsey left, Martin staggered back into the pub and was driven to the London Hospital.

Ronnie – other pro-Kray accounts put the blame on Ramsey – decided he must now go after the Streeters and he and the others drove off in two or three cars. Around midnight the police stopped his Buick at the junction of Grove Road and Morgan Street in Stepney. He was armed with a gun. Also in the car, which was driven by Ramsey, was Billy Jones along with a machete and a crowbar. At the police station Ronnie handed a loaded six-chamber revolver to DS Walter Cooper, warning him to be careful. It contained four live rounds and the bullets had been filed into expanding dum-dums. Efforts to buy off Terry Martin failed. All were charged with Grievous Bodily Harm. Reggie was defended by the ex-policeman turned barrister William Hemming, who modelled his speech patterns on his hero Winston Churchill, arguing that the witnesses disagreed on whether one or both of the twins had entered the Britannia. The magistrate, Leo Gradwell, replied wittily, 'The difficulty is to know which one to give bail to,' and remanded them both in custody.[15]

Pre-DNA testing, it was easy to argue that the bloodstains on Reggie's jacket might have come from boxers in the gym where he trained, and he was acquitted.

On 5 November 1956 Ronnie was sentenced to three years at the Old Bailey for wounding with intent; Ramsey received five years, and Jones three. Charles Kray Snr then wrote to the Court of Appeal, omitting to mention that the Twins regularly gave him a beating:

'It is my firm belief that he [Ronnie] was intimidated into this brawl; more out of curiosity than any intentions of committing any violence of which he was innocent. If you will at least believe me, sir, they are the most respectful and good-natured lads anybody could wish to meet, so kind to my wife and I and everybody in their thoughts and actions and only do good to everybody, and with my guidance and my wife and son Charles (their eldest brother) they will make good.'

It did not help Ronnie. His mental health deteriorated in Wandsworth prison and believing that that Ramsey was calling him a grass, he gave the boxer a beating. Ramsey sensibly declined to lodge a complaint.[16]

A year later, around 8.50 p.m. on 14 August 1957, Terry Martin's father Stephen left his unlicensed drinker, the Anglo-Pakistan Social Club at 1A Campbell Road, Bow, in the care of 'Ginger', whose real name he did not know, and another man who had come to work for him the day before and whose name and address he did not know either. Forty minutes later, while in the nearby Bow Bells public house Martin was told eight or nine men had smashed up the club, breaking chairs and causing around £35 of damage. In today's terms, nearly £2,300.

Initially Martin suggested that Reggie Kray had been the instigator as a reprisal for Ronnie's sentence, but on 16 August he went to Bow Police Station and said he wanted to drop the matter. Unsurprisingly neither Reggie nor Charlie Kray's fingerprints were found in the club. In his book *Born Fighter* Reggie claims that he later had Martin's club firebombed and that when the Martins left, he eventually took over.[17]

According to Reggie the bad behaviour of Terry Martin caused resentment in the East End and one man, John Hall, offered to shoot members of the Martin family on Ronnie's behalf. Kray told him it did not suit his purpose. Four years later, on 3 June 1961, Hall, an avid gun collector and member of a rifle club, shot and killed two officers outside West Ham police station before shooting himself in a telephone kiosk in Wanstead.

Another story of the fall-out from the incident is that Reggie wanted Terry Martin up on a false rape charge and paid £300 to his friend, fellow Eastender Billy Webb, who was to find a girl strong enough to stand up to police questioning. Later, when Webb realised Martin was an innocent victim, he refused to go ahead with the plan but courageously kept the money.[18]

Meanwhile the more entrepreneurial Reggie, along with Charlie, had opened the Double R club in Bow Road, some two hundred yards from the police station, naming it after himself and the imprisoned Ronnie. Using money obtained from poncing off local thieves – i.e. demanding a share of their proceeds – Reggie had purchased the lease of an empty shop and transformed it into a smart nightclub with a stage and dance area, a real contrast to the usual East End clubs. Kray claimed he 'borrowed' the money from the car dealer John Hutton, of whom it was said 'Put all dealers together and their worst attributes and then you've got John Hutton'. Borrowed may well be a euphemism.[19] If anyone rang, someone would answer the phone with a terse 'Club'.

The 20 stone Glaswegian 'Big' Pat Connolly, with whom Ronnie later enjoyed farting contests, was on the door and troublemakers could expect a beating from Reggie, if necessary aided by Charlie. Later, Reggie opened a gymnasium over the club launched by the great British heavyweight Henry Cooper.

The Double R became enormously popular and a major source of income. It was there that Charlie's wife, Dolly, met George Ince and may have begun an affair with him. She could hardly be blamed, as she was always an outsider so far as the family was concerned. Reggie and Ronnie unkindly called her 'Snotty Nose' and 'Skinny'. Reggie described her:

> 'I have met some really terrible people in my time but
> the one with the poorest personality and looks to match
> is Dolly Kray.'[20]

Ince paid heavily for his devotion. In 1969 he was shot in the leg and two years later a shotgun was pushed down his trousers. This time he received 93 pellets in his left calf.[21]

However, Reggie was not satisfied with just a legitimate income. At the time gaming was not permitted but spielers (illegal gaming houses) flourished throughout the country. First he opened one at the back of the Double R, and then others throughout East London. Rival premises were vandalised if the owners failed to pay over a percentage of the profits.

Some spielers, such as the Green Dragon in Aldgate, were simply commandeered. Gerry Parker, once a Jack Spot man, told me it was owned by another Spot man, the now ageing Moishe Goldstein, known as Blueball because of an errantly coloured testicle:

> 'Eventually the Twins turned up and said they were taking over. Reggie hit Moishe and broke his jaw. He shouldn't have done that. That was a liberty. Moishe was an old man.'[22]

Reggie claims he hit another Spot man, Bernard 'Sonny the Yank' Schack, because he called him 'son' in a disrespectful manner. In his unpublished manuscript, Ronnie Hart claims that Kray had used an axe.[23]

Like so many underworld clubs, the Green Dragon and its sister club the Little Dragon changed owners on a regular basis. Moosa Patel, who had a club at 126 Brick Lane, claimed he had been paying £50 a week protection, and a further £25 for a barman, to Salim Dawood, also known as Angelico, who would in turn pay the money over to Kray men Billy Exley, Duke Osborne or Freddie Bezzina. Patel then became a partner with George Mizel and Matty Constantino in the Green Dragon and he had to pay a third of the £50 they were paying. This time money was collected by Ronnie Bender. Dawood told the police that Bezzina and another man had stolen his fruit machines, but yet another Kray man Cornelius 'Connie' Whitehead had advised him to drop the Krays' name out of things.[24]

The protection racket spread, but the Krays would say people regularly came to them rather than their going looking for things to protect. Charlie also tells the rather touching story of how a tearful club owner Danny Green came to the Twins to ask them to help protect his club in the Kingsland Road, Stoke Newington. Again it is a tale of two stories. In Charlie's version Reggie regretfully declined because it was out of his manor, but in *Villains We Have Known* Reggie says that in return for a half share in Green's profits he put the ex-wrestler Andy Paul in to mind it.[25]

As always with the Krays, there were bends in the road to be negotiated, some of which they created for themselves. The next one was the case of the police killer Ronnie Marwood, a man described by Reggie Kray:

> 'I owed Marwood nothing and I knew he was going to cause me nothing but trouble. But, despite what they say, there is some kind of honour among thieves, a sort of code of conduct. Right or wrong, I took Marwood in and hid him in a safe place until he was ready to make a run for it.'[26]

When the Double R was closed down in 1963, Reggie claimed it was because he had sheltered Marwood, who was wanted for the killing of PC Raymond Summers. Accounts of the murder vary, with Marwood's supporters saying that on 14 December 1958 he was walking home when he saw a friend being pushed by a police officer and went to help. It is more likely that he got involved in a gang fight between the Essex Road and the Angel gangs outside Grays Dance Hall in the Seven Sisters Road. When Summers tried to break up the fight, Marwood, who had been out drinking heavily with his friend Mickey Bloom on his first wedding anniversary, fatally stabbed him with a 10-inch. When Marwood was questioned and released without charge, he went on the run.

According to Reggie, the police visited him and told him that if he gave Marwood up he could have a free rein over his clubs. He declined. Later he expanded the story, telling how he had been to see Marwood in West London where he was holed up in true gangster fashion with a gun and a club hostess. Kray said that on seeing the gun he had, in newspaper terms, 'made his excuses and left'. In an alternative version Johnny Nash claimed it was he who had 'Big Ronnie' stashed away. 'I had him in a flat in Holloway. He never left the place except after dark and even then he did not go far.'[27]

With the net closing in, Marwood did not stay on the run for long and on the evening of 27 January 1959 he went to Caledonian Road police station with his father and, under caution, confessed to the murder.

Marwood's defence was that as he had been drinking he did not realise he had a knife in his hand when he pushed Summers. He claimed his confession had been written by the police and he had signed it without reading it. He was hanged on 8 May 1959, less than five months after the stabbing.

Underworld legend has it that Marwood gave himself up because he did not want to cause trouble for his protectors, and that later the Nashs tried to engineer an escape from Pentonville prison. Certainly they sent wreaths on the anniversary of his death.

The Krays were always keen to claim they had sheltered this or that criminal, but suggestions that they hid the French gangster and killer Jacques Mesrine when he was on the run seem wide of the mark. 'They wouldn't have known how to spell his name,' said one

East Ender disparagingly. In fact the French murderer, bank robber and kidnapper probably did not come to London until 1972, by which time the Krays had been in prison for four years.

Meanwhile, Ronnie Kray serving his three years at first did well in prison and, apart from his fight with Ramsey, his twelve months in Wandsworth passed without incident. He was then transferred to Camp Hill, a lower category prison on the Isle of Wight. Perhaps because he felt he was isolated from London, his mental health began to deteriorate. There had long been a streak of insanity in the family. His great-great grandfather 'Critcha' Lee had died in Claybury mental hospital and his grandfather's brother Jewy died there as well. When, two days after Christmas, Ronnie learned of the death on Christmas Day 1957 of his Aunt Rose, he went berserk and after a fight with a warder had to be placed in a straightjacket for his own safety.

He was moved to Winchester Prison, where on 20 February 1958 he was certified insane and transferred to Long Grove Mental Hospital near Epsom in Surrey, one of a group of hospitals known as the Epsom Cluster, built in 1906 to deal with the overcrowding of inner London hospitals. By this time he thought a man in the bed opposite was a dog who would jump onto his lap if he guessed his name right.

But given proper medication including Stematil, Ronnie's mental health improved and now he began to fret. Time in a mental hospital did not count against a prison sentence and he wanted out. He was, he considered, serving two days for every one he should. If he could stay out for six weeks he could then claim he was no longer mentally ill and could be returned to prison to complete his sentence.

An ingenious rescue plan was then put into operation. As with many Kray stories the details vary – for example, Ronnie says he was in his pyjamas while other accounts have him in a dark blue suit identical to the one Reggie was wearing. Whichever is correct, on Sunday 26 May 1958 Charlie and Reggie, along with their faithful but ill-fated friend George Arthur Osborne, went to visit him in the hospital. Their cousin Joe Lee had already declined the job. Reggie claims the Twins, both wearing navy blue suits and grey shirts, entered the lavatory together and Ronnie then came out first. Charlie Kray said that Reggie merely put on Ronnie's glasses. Ronnie walked out with Charlie and Osborne and, after giving his twin sufficient time to get well clear, Reggie asked to be let out as well, saying he thought Ronnie had gone to get him tea. He was fortunate not to be prosecuted. It was another example of the Twins relying on their almost identical appearances to confuse witnesses.

That night Ronnie was taken to a flat in St John's Wood, which he did not like, and he demanded to be housed elsewhere. According to Charlie, the next day the Hospital Superintendent telephoned Reggie, requesting he bring his brother back with no questions asked, but for the next six months Ronnie remained in and around North London (according to Charlie Kray) or went to Suffolk, where he stayed in a caravan belonging to another Kray associate Geoff Allen while another friend, 'Mad' Teddy Smith, ferried boys up to him (according to Ron and Reg). But despite all this he was lonely, and once again his mental condition deteriorated.

What neither Ronnie and Charlie Kray nor their mother Violet had understood was that Ronnie was a seriously mentally ill man whose health would always relapse without his proper medication. Their doctor Morris Blasker had to come galloping to the rescue or, in practice, Reggie or Teddy Smith had to drive Ronnie down to Millwall to see him. Blasker said that he obtained Stematil tablets at 27/6d a time and charged the Krays a hardly exorbitant 30 shillings. Once Ronnie was stabilised, using the name John Lee he went to see a Harley Street psychiatrist to try to find a cure. Of course there was none; stabilisation was the best that he could hope for.[28]

After nearly five months on the run Ronnie was drinking heavily and beginning to deteriorate mentally once more. He maintained he gave himself up, but Charlie claimed the police arrested him when he paid a visit to Vallance Road.[29] His medication was resumed and on 18 November he was declared sane and returned to Wandsworth Prison. He was released five months later.

However, once out of prison Ronnie was a changed man. He declined to go to a coming-out party at the Double R. He sat drinking endless cups of tea in Vallance Road and because he again failed to take his medication regularly, his mental condition deteriorated once more. Now he began to believe Reggie and Charlie were only pretending to be his brothers. Finally he had a breakdown in the Eric Street billiard hall and was admitted to St Clement's Hospital in Mile End.

On 2 February 1959 Daniel Schai, better known as Daniel Shay and sometimes incorrectly named in police files as Frances Shea's brother, had apparently ordered a leather briefcase from Swiss Travel Goods, run by Morris Podro. Two days later he returned with at least one of the Twins. The prosecution's case was that Shay told Podro he had been overcharged. When Podro protested that he hadn't even been paid, Shay said he would now have to pay £100 or 'he would cut me to pieces'. Reggie and Shay hit him and he agreed to give them the money the next day.

Instead Podro went to the police, and this time officers were hiding in the back room of Podro's shop on Shay and Reggie's return. They were arrested, followed shortly by Ronnie. Reggie said at once that his twin had not been there the day before.

On 12 February their then lawyer Bernie Perkoff produced George Osborne at Marylebone Magistrates' Court, where he did the decent and expected thing and told the police it was he and not Ronnie who had been in the shop:

> 'I can describe the shop and everything about it to convince you it was me. I wouldn't do this for anyone else, but Ronnie is my mate and I'm not letting him get bird for something he didn't do and I did.'

Ronnie told the police he had been at the Regal Billiard Hall in Eric Street, which was now being run for him by Freddie and Vic Bird. Later that day Podro picked Osborne out on an identification parade. Privately paid, the solicitor Ellis Lincoln now acted for Shay and Reggie Kray. They and Osborne were all found guilty of demanding money with menaces. On 10 April 1959 Kray and Osborne, who had received 21 months at the County of London sessions ten years earlier for office breaking, now went down for 18 months. Shay received three years. Cognoscenti in the underworld suggest that in fact the matter had been over an unpaid gambling debt.

Reggie appealed, and because of the delay in obtaining a transcript of the trial, unusually, on 22 September, he was given bail pending the hearing. He was out for nearly a year before his application for leave to appeal was heard and dismissed on 26 July 1960.[30]

At the beginning of June that year two Kray clubs were raided: first the Wellington Way and then the Double R where Harry Abrahams, who, it was said, could have taken over Jack Spot's minding of the Jewish community had he wanted, was now the barman. Ostensibly the police were there over breaches of the licensing laws, but they took the opportunity to search for any stolen property. None was found but prosecutions of both clubs followed and the Double R lost its licence in September that year.

In 1961 the brothers brought off a hat-trick of wins. All were accused of offences of dishonesty, and all were acquitted. The first was in February when Charlie and Ron were charged along with their pickpocket friend Jimmy 'The Dip' Kensit, father of the actress Patsy, with being suspected persons trying car door handles in the Queensbridge Road.

Then in April Reggie was charged with housebreaking. He was apparently seen by a Lilian Hertzberg coming out of her mother's flat in Stepney with another man. She saw him a week later in the street and, she said, recognised him. With the police saying they feared that witnesses would be interfered with, Reggie, again defended by Ellis Lincoln, was remanded in custody until May, when Lilian Hertzberg told the Inner London Sessions that the man she had seen was not Kray. Reggie would have claimed he was actually at an appointment with a Dr Ronchetti, and he was awarded £92 costs.

Charlie Kray says that Mrs Hertzberg was offered the then huge sum of £500 to change her evidence, payable when she failed to make the identification. He justified the Krays welshing on the deal by claiming that her husband was a police informer.[31]

In early May the suspected person charges were dismissed by the stipendiary magistrate John Aubrey Fletcher. They had run an alibi defence and had called a string of witnesses. The Krays represented it as an out and out triumph but Fletcher had thought:

'I don't think it would be safe to convict. I don't know where the truth lies. There is too much evidence that these men were elsewhere.'

But by now the Twins and Charlie had assembled a nucleus of loyal and dangerous supporters. They had also acquired Esmeralda's Barn, a gambling club in Knightsbridge.[32]

CHAPTER 3
THE FIRM

By the middle of the 1960s the Kray Twins, with their elder brother Charlie in a supporting role, had assembled what the press dubbed 'The Firm', but what the police called 'East End Terrors'. They were a gang of thieves' ponces (i.e. making a living from other men's work), hardmen, extortionists, fraudsters and general hangers-on. Just who ranked where in the pecking order inside the Firm is a matter of debate, and much depended on who was trying to sell their story to the public. Tales of merely polishing the glasses before parties do not sell books. Much more saleable is that the author threw the soda siphon at the coffee machine in the spieler, or better still prevented Ronnie from slashing some unfortunate individual.

So while Albert Donoghue was justly described in the blurb for his book as 'The Krays' Lieutenant', the claim by Tony Lambrianou that he was a 'former Kray boss' is more open to question. Other associates suggest Lambrianou joined late in the cycle, and they describe him as a wannabee and gofer. In fact Tony Lambrianou had known the Krays through his friendship with Reggie's brother-in-law Frank Shea, but until shortly before Christmas 1966 he was in prison serving three years for robbing the proprietor of a Wimpey bar. He says that by this time the Krays were looking for new talent and one of his first jobs was to drive Scotch Jack Dickson to visit the escaped Frank Mitchell, who was then being sheltered by the Krays. Chris Lambrianou became involved with the Krays through his friendship with Charlie and the nightclub he ran in partnership in Leicester.

Donoghue's position in the hierarchy did not, however, prevent him from having to clear up messes they had created and do the odd painting and decorating job on their behalf. In later years Tony Lambrianou swung hot and cold. Sometimes he was happy to be regarded as one of Britain's top villains and at others equally happy to say that he had been used by the Krays, such as the time when he was sent to the Regency in Stoke Newington to bring the erring Jack McVitie to the fateful party at nearby Evering Road.

It is now generally accepted that there were in fact two Firms. The first was in existence up to approximately the time of the Cornell murder in 1966 and members included the 18-stone, white-haired Tommy 'The Bear' Brown, who had been heavyweight champion Len Harvey's sparring partner before the war. It was he who cut Kenny Adams in the Stow club in Walthamstow High Street on 16 September 1966. Adams required 70 stitches, and a John Rigbey who investigated the case told me that there was so much blood the forensic officer scooped it up in a teacup.[33] Earlier Brown had received three years for demanding with menaces and was now on the door of the spieler in the Regency basement.

Others included Sammy Lederman, whose history in the West End stretched back to World War Two and who in 1941 had given evidence in the killing by Tony 'Babe' Mancini of Hubby Distleman in the Palm Beach Bridge Club in Wardour Street. Lederman had had a show business agency which the Krays appropriated for Charlie to run. Then there was Connie Whitehead, more a long firm fraudsman than anything else, driven into their arms by the predations of standover man Georgie Cornell; their cousin Ronnie Hart, then on the run; former seaman Ronnie Bender; and the giant Glaswegian Pat Connolly, along with another boxer, Billy Exley. There was also the unfortunate George 'Ozzie' Osborne as well as the equally unfortunate Colin 'Dukey' Osborne, the mathematically talented Alf 'Limehouse' Willey, red-haired Tommy Cowley and Big Bill Donovan, Dickie Morgan from their brief army days and conman Micky Fawcett. There were also non-criminals such as the baths attendant Harry Granshaw, who could be called on to give evidence for members in trouble and have their names placed on the Krays' charitable committees. Wanabees included Lenny 'Books' Dunn, who kept a stall of mildly pornographic books and magazines on Whitechapel Waste and who wanted above all things to be recognised by the Twins, only to find that when he was, he was terrified of them.

Although for a time they shared a club with Jimmy Woods from West Ham, who had been on the abortive 1948 London Airport Bullion Robbery attributed to Jack Spot, the Krays did not actually inherit any of Spot's men. But early in their careers they did acquire one of Billy Hill's right-hand men, and a hard one at that: the dapper ex-welterweight boxer Bobby Ramsey, with a ring record of 26 wins, 33 losses and nine draws. Ramsey, who fancied himself in a black overcoat and pigskin gloves, was a pimp with a predilection for cutting women. He was a pocket-sized version of the ex-world champion Freddie Mills but without his punch, although adroit with a knife.

Then there was the talented fraudster Leslie Payne, said to have become involved with the Twins through the car dealer Johnny Hutton. It was at Hutton's showrooms that Ronnie Kray shot a dissatisfied punter in the leg. Later Payne and the equally talented Freddie Gore ran a car showroom in the East End. In a complicated hire purchase scam Payne had become liable for the debts of a purchaser and was threatened with a visit by the Krays to make him pay up. His version of events is suitably vague but, always a glib talker, he seems to have persuaded them he was in the right, and the matter lapsed. They then began to visit him regularly at the site where Ramsey was now working for him. One day Payne and he quarrelled over a parking place and the next day, which Payne dates as being in the early 1960s, the Twins appeared. Ronnie knocked Ramsey to the ground and when he got up Reggie knocked him down again. The pair then gave him a good hiding and said to Payne that they had heard Ramsey had been causing trouble and they were looking after him now. 'We're friends now, Les, so I gotta protect you', assured Ronnie.[34] Whether the fight between Kray and Ramsey was a contrived *proces d'impressment* for Leslie Payne is open to question. Ramsey certainly does not seem to have held a grudge, and for a time stepped out with their cousin Rita Smith. Ramsey could still be found acting as their bookkeeper when the Twins were arrested at the Glenrae Hotel in Finsbury Park in late 1964, but after that he seems sensibly to have drifted away.

One of their closer friends at the time was George Osborne, who opened Le Monde, a 'bucket of blood' drinking club near World's End. It was there at the end of September 1963 that Ronnie cut the former boxer Johnny Cardew there, for saying he had put on weight. Cardew ran to the nearby St Stephens Hospital for stitching, and at one time it was thought he would need plastic surgery.[35]

Later Ronnie smashed up the Le Monde because, when he arrived with a party, Osborne was not there to greet him and showed no signs of appearing that night. He demanded to speak to Osborne on the telephone and according to another Kray affiliate, Eric Mason, shouted, 'Keep your ear on the phone and you can listen to what's going to happen to your lovely little club.' He then told the regulars that they should stay quiet and, if they did, nothing would happen to them. After smashing mirrors with a soda siphon and destroying the rest of the club he yelled, 'We're going off to drink with real people,' and everyone piled into their cars and drove off.

Mason was summoned to Vallance Road the next day and there he pointed out diplomatically that Osborne was now married, and since his wife had a good deal of influence over him he was no longer his own, or their, man. He was sure no snub had been intended. A penitent Ronnie then told him to get on the phone and tell Osborne to have the damage repaired, no expense spared.[36]

Mason himself had first met the Twins when they all sparred at Kline's gym. Later they became friends and when he was released from Walton jail in Liverpool after serving a seven-year sentence for a series of robberies, they sent Dukey Osborne to meet him off the train and arranged a coming out party at the Cambridge Rooms on the Kingston bypass.

Some others, including the gay Irish ex-jockey Bobby Buckley, with whom Ron fell in love, were acquired when in 1961 the Krays took over the Esmeralda's Barn nightclub in Wilton Place, Knightsbridge.

Some of the original Firm drifted away. Some would not allow themselves to be part of the post-Cornell scene. Others, such as Buckley, went to prison. And around the Twins a much more unpleasant group was formed.

The one-time bank robber Albert Donoghue, the soi-disant 'Krays' Lieutenant', arrived in a roundabout way. When Donoghue came out of prison after serving a sentence for robbery in October 1964 he was told by Limehouse Willey that the Krays wanted to see him. He went to the Crown and Anchor by Vallance Road, where Reggie Kray promptly shot him in the leg. 'It didn't hurt. The pain was when they twisted my ankle at the hospital. I didn't hold it against them. I'd been shot and that was it'. True to the underworld code, Donoghue did not go to the police, and when he came out of hospital the Twins sent word through their Bournemouth-based associate Bill Ackerman that they again wanted to see him. This time the meeting was more cordial. Donoghue, leg still in plaster, went to Vallance Road where he was promptly signed up. It turned out that the Twins thought he had been badmouthing them over the burning of jewel-thief Lennie Hamilton at Esmeralda's Barn. Now Charlie Kray shook his hand and welcomed him to the Firm.

Later Donoghue would recall one of his first jobs:

'I was houseman at the Green Dragon, a dirty little spieler. One-armed Lou Joseph also worked there. I got £40 a
week from George Mizel and he had to pay the Twins as
well. There was just old men playing cards and if one of
them started shouting I would just go over and give them
a tap on the shoulder. It was easy work.'[37]

Another almost odd-job man was Jack McVitie, 'The Hat' worn
indoors and outdoors to cover his incipient baldness after he lost
his mop of black hair. In his early days he had run with Joey Pyle,
seen by some as the Godfather of London crime over a 20-year
span, and bank robber Tony Baldessare, who killed himself in
his attic in Streatham after a two-day police siege. He had been
wanted in connection with the death of police dog Yerba and a
string of robberies.[38]

In 1959 then aged 26, McVitie received seven years at
Cambridgeshire Quarter Sessions for unlawful possession of explosives and possessing a flick knife. In December that year he was
sentenced to 12 strokes of the birch by visiting magistrates at Exeter
prison after he, Mad Frank Fraser and Jimmy Andrews had attacked
the Governor. Because Fraser had been certified insane, the Home
Secretary refused to confirm his birching and, since the rule was 'birch
all, birch none', McVitie was reprieved, so to speak. This was by no
means a popular move. Prisoners sentenced to being flogged could
normally expect a remission in their sentence. Defendants would
often ask to be flogged, but if one was deemed not to be healthy
enough, all were refused.[39] McVitie was also said to have thrown a

girlfriend out of his car. He claimed they were arguing when she fell against the door, which then opened.

One former West End club doorman told me how McVitie had cut a man's throat on behalf of the Twins in a club upstairs from the Log Cabin in Wardour Street:

> 'The Krays either wanted it or wanted money from it, but the Scotsman who ran it wasn't having it. I thought it was rather appropriate when I heard Jack got stabbed in the throat by Reggie.'[40]

According to John 'Scotch Jack' Dickson, he and the much younger Ian Barrie had come to London from Edinburgh to seek their fortunes in 1964. Dickson had fought with the Marines in the Korean War and had later worked for the Scottish Gas Board. Barrie, who had a badly scarred face when a can of petrol had blown up during his time in the army, had worked as a deckhand on a whaling factory ship. In London they lived first in Kings Cross and then Stoke Newington, working as window cleaners and playing cards in local clubs. Playing down in Brick Lane, they met the Krays' uncle Billy, who was then running a spieler for the Twins; he recognised them as likely lads and introduced them to his nephews.[41] Dickson worked principally for Reggie Kray and Barrie for Ronnie.

There were other fringe members who could be called on for help, such as the handsome, immaculately dressed one-armed ticket tout Lou Joseph, who had a conviction for manslaughter. Despite his disability he was a brilliant snooker player. He was another who minded the Green Dragon Club. Then there were the Clarkes, Nobby and Charlie, who were not related. Until he broke his legs Charlie had been a talented cat burglar known as the Cat Man – not for that, but because he and his wife kept cats in their bungalow. His home was used as a safe house where Ronnie kept a rail of suits, staying there with Teddy Smith from time to time. The balding ex-flyweight Nobby Clarke was used in the long firm frauds and as a general gofer.

How close the malevolent dwarf Royston Smith was to the Twins is a matter of conjecture. According to his not wholly reliable memoirs, he was an integral part of the Firm and the close confidant of both Twins. A pimp and a burglar, Smith had once been part of the variety act 'Morton Fraser's Harmonica Gang' and could still be seen in the Double R, sitting on a donkey and singing for the punters. Away from the Krays, he wrestled as Fuzzy Kaye and at one time had a club for dwarves in Gerrard Street, Soho. For a time he also ran the Kismet Club, regarded by the Soho community as 'bilious'. Smith claimed that in the move known as 'noughts and crosses' he had once cut the backside of the former boxer and fellow club owner Tony Mella, who had annoyed him. 'I suppose his bum was all he could reach,' said Mad Frank Fraser disparagingly. 'I don't know if it was true because I never saw it, but that was the story.'[42]

'Former Kray Boss' Tony Lambrianou earlier knew the Krays through his friendship with Frances Shea's brother Frank. However, until shortly before Christmas 1965 he was in prison, serving three years for robbing the proprietor of a Wimpey bar, by which time he says the Krays were looking for new blood. One of his first tasks was to drive Scotch Jack Dickson to visit the escaped Frank Mitchell, then being sheltered by the Krays. His brother Chris Lambrianou became involved with the Krays through his friendship with Charlie, who was then running Raynors, a nightclub in Leicester in which the Krays had an interest. At one time he and Frank Shea had run a short-lived badger game in Paddington.

Both had worked with Eric Mason in Blackpool and had tried to establish themselves in Birmingham protecting clubs, where it was said they had been run out of town by local interests. Tony Lambrianou also claimed he and his brother had taken over protection in both Blackpool and Liverpool, claims generally regarded with some scepticism by the local cognoscenti.

In fact the Krays ran a relatively small area, not extending much outside the E3 postal district − Bethnal Green − and Soho, with outposts in Essex. There was no real attempt to move into the Richardson gang's territory in South London or into West London. Nor was there any suggestion that they might even try to move in on old Millwall families such as the Bennetts. 'They never crossed Bow Bridge', remarked Mick Fawcett derisively. Certainly they did not dare to tangle with armed robbers such as Bertie Smalls and his North London team, who held them in contempt.[43]

Even in Soho there were some people whom the Krays could not reach. These included the club owners Bernie Silver and Joe Wilkins, whose uncle Bert had been convicted of the 1936 manslaughter of Massimo Montecolombo at Wandsworth dog track in a dispute over bookmakers' pitches.

In September 2012, now in an East London care home, Albert Donoghue recalled:

'Joe would have nothing to do with them. He wasn't afraid of them and just before we were all picked up Ronnie asked Connie Whitehead and me how we felt about a kidnapping. Joe Wilkins had been telling us about his daughter doing show jumping at Hickstead, and we thought it might be in an effort to make him come round. It all came to nothing.'[44]

In 1968 the Krays intended to have the Maltese club owner George Caruana killed outside a Joe Wilkins-owned nightclub on Curzon Street, just to show him how vulnerable he was.

Up to the end of their careers the Twins' income could be roughly divided into four sources: first, the protection racket, leaning on shopkeepers and club owners; second, poncing off other criminals – taking a share of their proceeds; third, the Krays acted as an underworld employment agency, hiring out members for a fee and taking contracts from other criminals to carry out beatings on their behalf; and fourth, there were the Long Firm and related frauds.

Neither new nor difficult to organise, the Long Firm fraud has been one of the staple and most lucrative diets of the conman. Back in the 1920s it was estimated that as much as £4 million was cleared annually in London alone. In its simplest form, a warehouse or shop is taken by a front man who has no previous convictions. Goods, usually inexpensive items but possibly wine and spirits, are bought on credit and then sold perfectly properly through the shop. The supplier receives his or her money. More business is done with more and more suppliers until there is one big bang. A massive amount of goods are obtained on credit, knocked out at prices often below the purchase price in a great 'liquidation sale' – that's where the local housewives benefited – and the premises are closed. In those days the beauty of a well organised LF was that goods were bought from the wholesalers over the telephone by a 'blower-man', so identification of the purchaser was unlikely. Managers of the shops knocking out the stuff were changed weekly or fortnightly, so it was difficult, if not impossible, to find out who was actually running the show. A properly run LF could be expected to realise a profit of between £100,000 and £150,000, which was then enormous money. It was sometimes possible to torch the premises, make a bogus insurance claim and double the profits. The problem with the Krays was that they lacked patience and wanted the money immediately, so the full benefits were never realised.

Like Jack Spot, the Krays did not appreciate being approached and then, if a job was cancelled, not being paid. Now in his 90s, Gerry Parker recalled over breakfast one day at Claridge's:

'I was always friendly with Reggie. In about 1964 I was living in Hampstead and I got a call from Eric Miller's mate, Alfie Isaacs; would I go and see him in his office in Regent Street? When I got there he told me there was a problem with Colin Jordan of the British National Party and he wanted him done. Could I see to it?

I went over to Vallance Road in the afternoon and the door was opened by one of the Berry brothers. It was, "Come into the parlour, have a cup of tea." Reggie was there with Big Patsy [Connolly], a huge man. I asked if he wanted a bit of business and he asked who. I said Colin Jordan, and he asked which manor he was on. I said he was the BNP. Did I want him hurt? Yes. Did I want him cut? Yes. He said he couldn't tell me how much it would be because Ronnie was at Brighton races. I was to ring the Double R that night. Reggie came to the phone and said it would be a monkey.

Next day Isaacs rang and said not to do anything because Jordan had been arrested. I rang Reggie and asked if he could hold things and he just said, "Fuck yourself. We know where you are. We want our fucking money."

I thought I was getting too old for this. I had two young kids and so I went to a good friend Steve who had a greengrocery. In the past he'd had a half-hour straightener with Tommy Smithson outside Kearly & Tonge in Bethnal Green, and he lived near the Twins. He said he'd see what he could do. He rang me later and said he'd done something he hadn't done before. He'd gone round and half pleaded with them. They'd thought about it and said for £300 I'm off the hook.

A few weeks later I was buying fruit from Steve, and who walks round the corner but Ronnie and Reggie and Scotch Ian Barrie, who could be a spiteful bastard. I thought, "this looks serious," but it was, "How are you Ger? We're opening a club in Knightsbridge, come and have a drink." It was all pals again. But that was when I went out and bought a shotgun.'[45]

The Twins were also quite capable of extorting money from their associates. On one occasion the late Mickey Bailey and the Jewish hardman Harry Abrahams went to the Regency on behalf of Bill Ackerman, yet another who for a time managed the Green Dragon. Abrahams was no slouch. He was thought to have been capable of taking over Jack Spot's interests in the East End after that man's decline, but it appears he never wished to. Later convicted of a robbery with Albert Donoghue, he received five years and from time to time he managed some of the Kray clubs. At the time the Twins believed Ackerman owed them money from the proceeds of a long firm fraud. Bailey recalled:

'Ronnie and Reggie were going to do Bill Ackerman who'd pulled a stroke and muscled into a long firm. Bill wasn't fully accounting for things and whether Harry's Jewish blood was siding with Bill's Jewish blood I don't know, but he went to see the Twins on his behalf and I went with him.

Ronnie just said, "You can fuck off back, Harry and tell that fucking Jew bastard he's got to pay."

Once we got outside Harry wiped his forehead and said, "At least that's all he's got to do."

Next day I got a call from Ron, who wanted to know why I'd been along. I said Harry was a friend of mine. He wanted to know if I was backing Harry against him and I said there was nothing like that. "Did Ackerman give you a few quid?" he wanted to know. I said he gave us a monkey, and Ronnie laughed and said he should have given us double. Ackerman had to go to the Regency the next day and Ronnie took another £500 from him and gave it to us.'[46]

After the Twins met the hail-fellow-well-met fraudster Leslie Payne, their greatest money spinner and ultimately the man who would contribute greatly to their demise, from the beginning of the 1960s the bulk of their money should have come from long firm frauds.

From the start, while the Twins were enchanted by Payne, other members of the Firm were less so. The first time I met him Micky Fawcett, himself an experienced LF man, recalled:

'At the time the Twins were looking around. Not doing anything much except chinning a few old timers; people were coming to them and they were building a reputation, but then they met Payne who had loads of contacts in a different world. We were told to be in one of the pubs and to be on our best behaviour because we were going to meet someone who was going to be very useful and could do wonderful things. 'Who could this be?' I asked Georgie Osborne. And when Payne came in it looked like he was doing an imitation of the actor George Sanders. "Do you know boys," he said, "I can live on £30 a week." Well so

he should have been able to. It was two if not three times
the weekly wages of a working man. Some of us thought
he was a police informer, but so far as the Twins were
concerned everything he said had to be done.'[47]

In his book *The Brotherhood*, Payne, nine years older than the
Twins, claimed rather romantically to be the son of a solicitor
who after going deaf became a vet and then a horse keeper
for United Dairies. According to Payne, he himself had been a
vacuum cleaner and radio salesman before going into partnership
with Alexander Rapp on a small East End car site. It was there
he met the short, plump Freddie Gore, whom Payne describes as
an eternal optimist, who had been doing the books for Rapp. In
time they bought Rapp out and continued in partnership together
working a hire purchase ramp.

   This account was not quite accurate. In an earlier statement to
the police Payne had been rather more forthcoming. He certainly had
worked for Alexander Rapp, who changed the name of his company
from Rapp Radio to 625 Centre. Rapp wanted to close his business
after several unexplained burglaries and Payne had bought him out.
Rapp stayed for a time but very soon there were visits to the premises
at 181 Dalston Lane by Alf Willey, Billy Exley, Bobbie Buckley and
more significantly by Charlie, Ronnie and Reggie. Bobby Ramsey
was used as a debt collector. It was then that Rapp ceased to have any
connection with what had once been a decent little business.

   Payne maintains the first LF he ran for the Krays was in 1960
when a supermarket owner friend of his who was running an LF

was beginning to lose his nerve after he had been taking too much money too soon. Payne took it over and ran it for the Krays for the last two months before it finally went bust. It was such a success that another end-of-time LF was set up in Brixton, and this was followed by a series of long firms all over London and throughout the country.

Little Stan Davis did not like Payne:

> 'Leslie was a very arrogant man, he would always talk down to you; clever but audacious. He was a self-promoter; people would believe what he said.'[48]

In 1961 Payne came up with the idea of an overseas investment in the form of a development of 3,000 homes and shops for the township of Enugu, the capital of Eastern Nigeria, which had just gained independence from Britain. Just as the idea of the Great Train Robbery was hawked around the country's top robbers for some time before it actually took place, so this scheme had been hawked around the fringes of finance. In theory, the project was legitimate and possibly viable but at the time, doing business in Nigeria was fraught with danger, both physically and politically. Payne claimed that the land was worth £750,000; there was mortgage financing available and, better still, two building contractors had been signed up to do £50,000 of work each before any payment had to be made. They had also paid an introductory fee of £5,000 and Payne thought that, with other contractors coming in, introductory fees would come to £60,000. Ronnie, Reggie and Charlie went out to Nigeria and lorded it over the natives, with Ronnie thinking it would be a great idea to bring a black servant home.

Unfortunately, according to Payne, Charlie later thought the boys at home were short of cash, and he appropriated the £5,000 introductory fees. When Payne, Gore, Charlie Kray and their fellow fraudster the Canadian Gordon Anderson returned to Nigeria, one of the contractors wanted either another contract to build five hundred homes or his money back. He received neither and went to the police. Payne and Gore were arrested and imprisoned. Charlie telephoned to England for help, and now began a frantic whip-round to raise the money. Each member of the Firm was told how much he must raise from his contacts – £100 from X, £500 from Y and so on. Reggie Kray says that both Dolly Kray and Payne's wife declined to contribute, but eventually the £5,000 was put together and telegraphed to a waiting Charlie, who drove with a lawyer to pay the money to a judge.

How much of the money the contractor actually received is not known, but Gore and a very chastised Leslie Payne, said by Charlie to be on the point of a nervous breakdown, were released. As the tale was told and retold the Krays were said to have been on the point of raising a team à la Wild Geese to fly to Nigeria to break their men out of prison.

Charlie maintained the fault was all Payne's, and once back in England, they gave him the elbow but he wasn't actually sacked for another five years. Payne himself claimed Charlie caused the trouble by remitting the £5,000 back to the Twins in England. This may well be true. Would Charlie really have allowed Payne to siphon off £5,000 in front of his very eyes?

At the other end of the Kray flowerbed of fraudsters were much more exotic plants, such as the always immaculately dressed Bobby McKew. Born in 1924 and a member of the breed known by the newspapers as 'West End Playboys', he had earlier on served two years in the Lebanon for a jewel robbery. Then in 1956, along with the playboy and amateur jockey Dandy Kim Caborn-Waterfield, he was convicted *in his absence* in France for the 1953 burglary of the safe of film magnate Jack Warner, which had netted £25,000. He had been extradited from Tangiers in July 1959 and was sentenced to five years, which he served in Les Baumettes prison in Marseilles and then in Fresnes.

At one time McKew was married to the South African Ana Gerber, then the world waterskiing champion, whose brother Robin worked at Raynors, the Leicester club run by Charlie Kray with his partner Trevor Rayner. McKew now lived in a mews house in Swiss Cottage and, during the day, could be found in the company of Leslie Payne and Freddy Gore, and in an evening at the then fashionable villains' and actors' pub, The Star Tavern in Belgrave Mews off Knightsbridge.

Another flower, albeit somewhat faded, was the one-time barrister, and now alcoholic, Stanley Crowther. Called to the Bar in 1949, he began his career brightly, joining the fashionable Derek Curtis Bennett's chambers. However he quarreled with another member of the Chambers, and soon left. But his legal career was already on the wane, and he took to accosting solicitors on Fleet Street hoping for work.

His luck turned, not nessarily for the better, when he impressed two customers, telling them they had the law wrong one evening in the Lord Nelson pub in the Kings Road. As a result he was recommended to various East End clients and was finally asked to help the Twins when they were due to be placed on an ID parade over the stabbing of the 'African' in Tottenham Court Road.

Quite against the code of conduct for barristers, Crowther met Charles Kray Snr and the Twins near the ENT Hospital in the Gray's Inn Road. He then bamboozled the officer in charge of the parade into arranging separate parades for the Twins instead of one large one. At each, wrongly thinking they had to pick out two men, a witness picked out one Kray but also another man, which as a result meant they could not be charged.

After being disbarred and jailed for passport offences in 1959, Crowther worked a number of menial jobs until he was offered a job by Johnny Gamman of A & R Direct Supply Co in Stoke Newington, whose co-director was Alfie Anish. Gamman and Anish later opened the Regency club, allowing the Krays to use the basement as a betting office and spieler before they were legalised. When A & R plunged into financial difficulties the club was sold to John Barry for £1,000 with the proviso that he paid the debts, including £6,000 to the brewers Watneys and the last quarter's rent.

One A & R creditor was David Forland of Oslo Electronics Ltd who then offered Crowther a job. The Krays were regular visitors at Forland's premises in Hoxton Street and one afternoon they brought along Leslie Payne with them. It was no time at all before Crowther was sent to work at an LF at Blenheim Gardens, Brixton Hill under Payne's supervision and later he ran his own long firm, S Crowther & Co in Artillery Passage in the City.

Reggie claimed he met the East Anglia-based arsonist Geoff Allen through Moishe Goldstein, the one-time proprietor of the Green Dragon. Blueball told Reggie he had met a 'mug punter' who lived near Stanstead and was planning to take a few quid off him in a bent card game. He asked if they wanted to come along for the ride, which translated as would they be his minders. If they did, he would give them a few quid. They went with Sammy Lederman. Blueball won £1,100 and Allen told them he would meet them the next morning to pay. When he failed to appear they headed over to his cottage but found him there armed with a shotgun. Later Reggie, recognising talent when he saw it, went back alone and asked if they could do business. Another version suggests it was the great Billy Hill who advised Reggie to do business with Allen.

Maybe Leslie Payne did cost the Firm money in Nigeria, but his biggest coup on the Krays' behalf was introducing them to what was potentially their greatest legitimate money spinner, the night club and casino Esmeralda's Barn, then run by the man-about-town Stefan de Fay.

CHAPTER 4
9-5

Although, as Albert Donoghue wrote in *The Krays' Lieutenant*, the working day for members of the Firm began with a meeting at Vallance Road at 9 a.m., it was by no means a steady nine-to-five job. There was, of course, the usual Friday round of collecting protection money, but there were a host of other duties: LFs to be organised and supervised; new businesses to be brought into the fold; boys to be found for Ronnie; enemies to be shot, or at least shot at or beaten up. There was also often work to be done of an evening.

From time to time members and indeed other East End figures were required to attend meetings away from Vallance Road. Mickey Bailey thought:

> 'A summons from the Twins wasn't to be ignored. Invariably one of the Firm would come round. When they come they'd say, "Ronnie, or the Twins, want to see you tomorrow morning. Get over between ten and twelve." The meeting was always at their house, the Regency or Pellicci's, which was a café in Bethnal Green Road. There was two Pelliccis,

Nevio and Terry and invariably it would be in Terry's. If it was at their mother's or Pellicci's you knew you didn't have a problem, but if it was at the Regency it could be. This was where they held their court.[49]

The best you could expect if you went to the Regency was a bollocking or maybe that you'd have to go and hurt someone. That would clear off the offence, whatever it was.'

Another punishment was for the offender to have to go to a club owner and tell him the Twins were now his partners or even that he was out of the club completely. In one case when they were feeling moralistic, the offender had to go and tell the owner of a porn shop that he was to close it down. Back in the 1990s Mickey Bailey told me:

'The next worst was a beating or a cutting. If you was called over it wasn't likely to come to a cutting. It never took them long of a night to find out where you was. Someone would give them a bell and you'd have visitors in the pub or when you come out.'

The penalty for warning someone brought in for punishment was that instead you would be the one to suffer. When the receiver Tony Maffia refused to give the Krays £400 to help retrieve Payne and Gore from Africa, he was due to 'be hurt'. When his friend Buller Ward intervened and warned Maffia to leave the Regency, he himself was set upon by the Twins, and Reggie cut him so extensively in the face that he required over 100 stitches.[50]

Ronnie, who by now liked to be known as 'The Colonel', had either a high sense of security or the dramatic or both. When there was something to be discussed he would lead members over to the local Public Baths where, he believed, they would be safe from police spies. There was a simple code among members. A successful job would be reported as 'That dog won' and a failed mission as 'That dog lost'. A visit to a business under protection and due to pay money was prefaced by a telephone call, 'Has that betting money come through?' Actual names were never mentioned over the phone. The Clyde was 'The Old Woman', the Crown near Vallance Road was 'The little pub', the Two Puddings was called 'The Fire Engines' because it was next to a fire station. The Lion in Tapp Street was 'The Widow's' or 'Madge's Place', run by the red-haired, stylishly dressed Margaret 'Madge' Jacobs, who allowed the Krays to use an upstairs room as a sort of clubhouse.

The childish code was something which must have taken a listening officer at least fifteen seconds to work out. A gun was 'a book'; a knife was simply 'a thing'. Members such as Dukey Osborne were also required to stash or carry weapons for them. Weapons were kept behind the bar of pubs they used or hidden in the cisterns of the men's lavatories.

The shooting of the enormous, handsome and usually engaging George Dixon was a rather more public affair. With minor variations, the story is that Dixon, barred from the Regency after allegedly causing trouble, returned one night thinking Charlie had granted him permission. Furious, the Colonel headed for the men's lavatory, where he kept a gun. The gun jammed when Ronnie fired it and

Dixon ran out of the club. In an improved version Reggie, seeing what was happening, grabbed the gun, knocking it to the floor before it went off. Ronnie later patched up his quarrel with Dixon and gave him the bullet as a souvenir.[51]

According to Ronnie Hart, the Firm had an arsenal which included Gurkha knives, bayonets, a Limpet mine, a rifle with a telescopic sight and two Sten guns. Reggie had an automatic shotgun and Ronnie a .410 shotgun which was kept for him by Charlie Clarke, the Cat Man, in Walthamstow. His swordstick was carried by Sammy Lederman, who claimed he had gout. Another gun was kept in the bottom of a piano in Lederman's house. Hart claimed they also had a bomb which could be stuck under a car and detonated at a three-mile range. The pair were security conscious, and Reggie Kray's flat at Manor House had a steel plate in the door. Of an evening one of the Firm would be told to leave the pub or club before the Twins to check whether their enemies, the Richardson brothers or others, were about. It seems they were right to do so. One night a certain Albert Nicholls was mistaken for Ronnie and had his leg broken in a hit-and-run outside The Widows.

Their brother Charlie was often used as a middle man. When the heavyweight Fred 'Nosher' Powell retired from the ring he was approached in his dressing room by Jack Isow and asked to act as doorman and take over the cloakroom concession at his restaurant in Brewer Street, Soho. He managed to upset the Twins there by barring them for not wearing ties. He was visited the next day by Charlie, who appeared to accept his explanation. Generally afraid of no one, Powell nevertheless admitted that for the next few weeks, after the restaurant shut for the night, he had walked down the middle of the street and avoided multi-storey car parks.[52]

Friday was generally collection day, something Donoghue referred to as the 'Milk Round'. He claimed it was conducted in a gentlemanly fashion.

The protected ranged from the high to the low. At the upper end was The Colony in Berkeley Square, said to be paying £100 to £300 a week (the figure varies and is anyway disputed) and the Casanova off New Bond Street which paid £50. Donoghue relates:

> 'Ronnie introduced me to Joe Dagle, Pauline Wallace's partner at the New Casanova. He told Joe I was now the collector. After that I called on Joe every Friday to pick up the £50... Dagle was a white-haired man in his sixties. He had a little flat at the top of the club. I'd go up there, have a coffee with him; he'd be having his toast and marmalade, reading the *Sporting Life*. We'd discuss the weather. "Now there's the envelope," just like that. When we'd finished talking I'd say, "Right, see you later! Back next week."'[53]

Franny Daniels of the Mount Street Bridge and Social Club in Mayfair, where the last thing played was bridge, paid £10 less.[54] At the lower end of the scale, scrap metal dealers in Hackney and Poplar paid £10 a week each. There was a mini cab business in the East End from which Albert Donoghue had to pay £10 in addition to the Krays' cut of 40%; Benny's, a spieler in the Commercial Road, anted up £15 a week; the owner of Dodger's in Brick Lane paid over £15, where the collectors were allowed to keep the money as wages. Of course, the Green and Little Dragon Clubs in Aldgate also paid. The Soho porn king Bernie Silver handed over £60 a week for three Soho clubs which the Krays split with Freddie Foreman and Johnny Nash. In return Nash handed over part of his take from the Olympic in Camden Town, the Astor and the Bagatelle.

Members of the Firm worked mostly in pairs guarding each other's backs. 'Scotch Jack' Dickson and Ian Barrie had known each other in Scotland for years. Donoghue and Ronnie Hart teamed up as, naturally, did the Lambrianou brothers. The pairs didn't always get on. Donoghue did not rate Ronnie Bender, whom he considered a bully. Ronnie Kray disliked Connie Whitehead. On one occasion Whitehead put a bottle in Dickson's face and was put on 'trial' by the Twins at the home of their friend Charlie Clarke. After suggestions that the Old Testament law of an eye for an eye should apply and that Dickson should be allowed to bottle Whitehead, he was merely suspended from the Firm and 'sent to Coventry', which meant that his pension was withheld for a time.

The Twins were basically acting as thieves' ponces, but they were good at it. Mickey Bailey recalled:

> 'I know of one guy from South London – he'd had a lorry load of cigarettes and the Twins thought Charlie was entitled to handle the receiving. They had to give Charlie his whack out of the fags. It come to around £2,000,

which was money. The fellow had told a man who was some sort of a relation of Charlie's by marriage, and it got back to them.'[55]

There was a standard tariff. Ronnie Hart recalled:

'They had their ears to the ground all the time. They knew all the good villains in all parts of London and their intelligence services provided them with information about any good jobs villains had pulled off, like major breakings and the hijacking of lorries. When a job had taken place members of the Firm like myself were sent to call on the villain concerned. We had to invite them out for a drink with the Twins. During the meeting the Krays chatted to them about the job they had done. They assessed the overall value and then ordered the crooks to pay up a fairly substantial percentage of their take. Even members of the Firm were not immune. Anyone working for them who did an outside job had to pay up.'[56]

If the Krays knew the thief would get only a third of the value from a receiver then they would take a third of that third.

On one of the rare occasions when they did steal goods themselves, it was a fiasco. Carpets and rugs which the Twins thought were Persian were loaded up and taken to the receiver Stan Davis, then living in Chingford. He took one look and pronounced them as Belgian and worthless. In February 1961 Davis was sentenced to seven years after the police discovered 'a warehouse of stolen property' at his home. It was then the Twins warned poor Charlie, who had been in a loose association with Davis, that, carrying as it did the risk of a prison sentence, receiving was not a suitable line of work for him and he should join with them. Davis did not, however, give up his association with the Kray family, and in August 1967 he was arrested with Alfie Kray and charged with possessing forged American travellers' cheques.

Nor could Firm and fringe members necessarily expect help from the Twins when things went wrong. Their friend Eric Mason tangled with Frank Fraser and Eddie Richardson in a quarrel outside the Astor Club in Berkeley Square. After being hit in the head with an axe, Mason was dumped outside the London Hospital. Mason himself claims that after the Astor fight, Fraser and Eddie Richardson bundled him into a car and took him to Atlantic Machines in Tottenham Court Road, where his hand was pinned to his head with an axe. He was left on waste ground and ended up needing 370 stitches. When he was recovering he went to the Twins asking them to take retributive action on his behalf. They were having none of it and instead they gave him £40.[57]

Once a week the Twins would have a collection for the 'Aways' – locals who were then in prison. Once released, they felt in their debt and would stand at the bar with them in reflected glory: 'I was having a drink with the Krays last night'. It was a way of providing a network of informers who would report back to them of deals or police activity.

The Aways had been founded in a curious way. The Krays were always looking for a spot of good publicity. They had sent money to Oxfam and had a splash in the *East London Advertiser* where they had a contact. One item on the table was the opening of a home for alcoholics in Cheshire Street with Lennie 'Books' Dunn as the warden. The project never got anywhere but Ronnie had made friends with a tramp, James, to whom he gave £1 a night for his lodging. 'We must look after these people and they will look after us if we are ever in trouble', he told Ronnie Hart. One night when the Twins were due to meet Adrienne Corri and Lita Rosa in the Grave Maurice in the Mile End Road, Reggie objected to James's presence but Ronnie insisted James was his friend and 'he'll go wherever I go'. A row followed during which Reggie said, 'You talk about friends but what about our friends in the nick? Who gives them money?' Ronnie replied that they did, but only when they were released. Reggie replied, 'That's fine. You're in the nick for seven years and then you come out and get £50. That's no bloody good'. It was then agreed that instead of handing money to tramps like James it would be more useful to make sure the men in prison were looked after and their families were catered for. A meeting was set for Vallance Road the next day to arrange the details and all the pubs the Firm used were given a pot marked 'For the Aways'. There was also a contributions book kept by Ronnie. At first the scheme was voluntary, but when the Krays saw how much money was coming in they made it compulsory and took half for themselves every Friday. Any money left would be handed to the men's wives to help pay their electricity and gas bills. The rest went on cigarettes, books, magazines and liquor which were made into parcels, known as Joeys, and then sent inside.

Many years later, former Flying Squad officer John Rigbey told me how just before Christmas 1967 he had taken two young Aides to CID (i.e. police on probation to become detectives) to The Horns:

'There were the three brothers along with Sammy Lederman and several Chinese men who I suppose were paying their weekly dues, as well as various people I knew and half knew. I was near the stage when Ronnie came past and looked at me with those expressionless eyes. I had my back to the company when one of the Aides said, "Guv, look behind you." The bar was empty. They had all gone into the other bar. Checker Berry was there that night looking sheepish and I said to him, "Tell Ronnie if he wants to play games he's got the wrong person. I don't mind a joke but I'm not going to be insulted. Does he want his mother's drum spun (house searched) at four o'clock on Christmas morning?"

The following Sunday morning an anonymous bunch of roses was delivered to my home as, I suppose, a sort of apology or maybe they saw it as a sort of warning – "We know where you live." I've always wondered how they found out my home address.'[58]

One of the ways to tie a person to a criminal organisation is to have him or her commit a serious criminal act, which can be held over their heads in case of any potential defection. So, from time to time, members or aspiring members were sent to shoot men who had offended them. When they took in their cousin Ronnie Hart while he was on the run from Eastleigh open prison, he was required to shoot a club owner, who had upset them by claiming that he could send them packing but also that Ronnie's 'little boys' preferred him. Scotch Jack was told to give Hart a .45 gun and a coat to conceal it. Armed with a photo of the club owner and £10 expenses to get to the Horseshoe Club in the West End where he might be found, Hart was told to go with Bobby Teale, find the man and shoot him.

Ronnie gave instructions, 'Don't aim at his head because you might miss. Aim at his chest and pull the trigger three or four times. Nobody will touch you because everyone in the club will be too surprised and frightened.' On the way to the club Hart and Teale thought better of it and instead went to the El Morocco, where they met the Twins' friends Tommy Flanagan and Billy Gentry. They spent the £10 on drinks in the club and went back to report their failure to Ronnie, who was throwing a party in the Balls Pond Road. He did not seem at all upset and told Hart to keep the gun, adding that if they spoke to anyone about the expedition there would be serious trouble.[59]

Then there were businesses to be found and brought under the Firm's umbrella. One of these was Lanni Caterers, which had the Cambridge Rooms, an old-fashioned roadhouse on the Kingston bypass. One story of the acquisition is that Charlie Kray moved in to offer protection after a fight. Certainly Lanni sold 51% of his shares and very soon the Krays moved in, with Leslie Payne being given a share to run it as a Long Firm. Pat Connolly was the doorman, Lederman was a barman and up to twenty members of the Firm were there at night drinking and eating without paying. The former world heavyweight champion Sonny Liston attended the opening night there and the Krays auctioned the useless racehorse Solway Cross, for which they had paid 500 guineas. Stanley Crowther was obliged to find the purchase price. It was finally auctioned when it was bought by the gay alcoholic actor Ronald Fraser.[60] It was at the Cambridge Rooms that Ronnie Kray changed his shirt after cutting Johnny Cardew in Le Monde. The Cambridge Rooms were duly run down and Lanni was the first person on Nipper Read's visiting list when he began his final investigation into the Krays.

When work was done it was party time, often impromptu ones, with women on tap. One woman now long married with children who attended as a young girl told me:

'A neighbour of mine was Winnie Harwood – she was tall and blonde – from Evering Road; she was 12 or 14 years older than me and was always on the pub and club scene. Pat Connolly, who was on the Firm, rented a room from her and that's how I met the Twins. Connie Whitehead, who was also on the Firm, had been a friend from very early days as well.

You would get an invite from Winnie probably about midday for that evening. You would just be told to produce yourself. Most of the time it was Winnie who'd tell me. It wasn't very flattering but you went.

They loved having women around them though and I was with Winnie at the opening night of the Colony

Club. George Raft was the sort of greeter, and I'll never forget he had a lot of make-up on and it looked like he was in a corset. It was really quite funny.

I started to go to the Regency which was just a five-minute walk away. I remember I was at Al Burnett's Stork Club one night and the Richardsons came in. We was told it might go off in a few minutes and we'd be better to go. I remember another night at a party somewhere in Bow, I was dancing with this really gorgeous fellow when I saw Pat signalling at me, but I took no notice. Then he come over and whispered the man was Ronnie's boy. That was a night I made a very swift exit. Everyone knew Ronnie was gay and Reggie was bi. If you saw a boy with a gold bracelet standing near Ronnie you knew he was his.

You weren't required to sleep with members of the Firm. There was plenty of girls hanging around who were happy to do that.'[61]

All in all, it was a busy life being a member of the Firm.

CHAPTER 5
ESMERALDA'S BARN

The East London Advertiser of 28 September 1962 was delighted:

> 'Local businessmen Reggie and Ronnie Kray of the Kentucky
> Club, Mile End Road seem to have a winner with their latest
> venture the Barn Twist Club, opened just recently in Wilton
> Place, Knightsbridge. Attractively decorated, the club is open
> seven days a week from 8 p.m. until two in the morning.'

By the time the Krays came to take it over, Esmeralda's Barn, the once
fashionable gaming club in Wilton Place, Knightsbridge, was in decline.
Once the haunt of Guards' officers, it had had a chequered history.
Originally it was run by society girl, the glamorous Esmeralda, sometimes
Esmé, Noel-Smith but in February 1955 she was found accidentally gassed
on her bed in a flat over a Knightsbridge fashion shop, with a 21-year-old
hostess from another of her clubs. She never recovered consciousness.

At one time, under the protection of Billy Hill, the club had also
been run by the 57-year-old Horace 'Hod' Dibden, sometimes known
as Dibbins or Dibdin, an expert on English antiques and furniture.

The girl whom the officers next came to see was the new Galatea of the middle-aged Dibden, the nightclub queen Patsy Morgan-Dibden, known as Sweetie.

After Patsy ran away from her Pygmalion, the club had lost some of its cachet and was taken over by Stefan de Fay, who at various times had managed Oddenino's Imperial restaurant in Regent Street, was the author of *Profitable Bar Management*, and who had also appeared on the popular Saturday night television show *Café Continental*.

By the beginning of the 1960s there was a lesbian club, the Cellar Club, in the basement, a restaurant on the ground floor and a casino above it. On one of the walls was an Annigoni mural.

There are various tales relating how the Krays acquired the Barn. Part of Kray mythology is that the property developer and slum landlord Peter Rachman was in thrall to the Krays. As a sideline to his property empire, Rachman built up a chain of gambling clubs and in 1956 opened El Condor nightclub in Wardour Street, Soho, under the management of another of his protégés, Raymond Nash of the Lebanese gangster family. For a time El Condor became the in-place. Princess Margaret was seen there and regulars included both the Duke of Kent and the rogue peer Lord Tony Moynihan.

One story is that a fight in the Latin Quarter nightclub, also in Wardour Street, where Rachman was holding a party, led to him giving Ronnie Kray a lift back to his home in Vallance Road. It led to Rachman agreeing to pay the Krays £5,000 to avoid trouble in Notting Hill, where he was leaning on recalcitrant tenants.

Another of the stories is that Rachman had the one-time nightclub hostess, now his girlfriend, Mandy Rice-Davies, with him in the bar of El Condor after it became La Discotheque. One evening Ronnie asked her to get him a drink, and when she said she did not work there, grabbed her wrist. She, not knowing who he was, slapped him. The slap cost Rachman a further £5,000 to avoid the otherwise inevitable trouble.[62]

Yet another version is that to get the Twins off his back Rachman set up their takeover of Esmeralda's Barn. However, it is hard to believe Rachman caved in so easily, as he had three of the most uncompromising men in the business working for him. The senior of these was the former heavyweight wrestling champion Bert Assirati, who came from Islington. Assirati had been part of a music hall balancing act, Mello and Nello, and had close links to the old Italian families. He was a man who liked inflicting pain, and many wrestlers of the period were unwilling to go in the ring with him.

The second employee was another wrestler, the joker Peter Rann, who practised his falls on the concrete in Hyde Park. On remand in prison, when Rann was asked to break a cellmate's leg so the man could be moved to the hospital wing, he obliged by jumping on it from the top bunk.

The third was the half-mad and completely out-of-control Norbert Rondel who, although German, wrestled as the Polish Eagle. Known in the wrestling game as Mad Fred, he had spent long periods in various mental hospitals from which he often escaped. On one occasion, late for a judo class, Rondel apologised and told his sensei he had just killed a man in Tottenham Court Road for staring at him. He had knocked the man's head off and it had rolled across the pavement. Further inquiries showed he had attacked a tailor's dummy. Gerry Parker thought it most unlikely the Krays could get at Rachman because they were frightened of his mad minder. 'Rondel would go down Vallance Road and they would pay to have him go away'.[63]

However, Leslie Payne says it was he who introduced them to the club after de Fay had said he wanted £1,000 for his shares in the Hotel Organisation Ltd, the company which owned the Barn. He says that Peter Rachman initially offered to put up the money but backed out when the racketeer realised how closely the Krays were to be involved. Payne claims he put the purchase price up himself. Other versions include Billy Hill encouraging the Twins in order to get them out of the West End, where he had gambling interests. In mythology the club was purchased following a one-hour meeting with de Fay, but according to Payne's statement to the police there were a number of meetings with a Commander Richard Diamond and Alf Mancini, one of the shrewdest of gaming operators at the time. The first meeting was in the Cellar Club at which Mancini had a major row with Charlie Kray, and the second at Diamond's flat at 15 Hyde Park Mansions, near Hyde Park Corner. Payne thought the price was about £1,750 and was paid at a third meeting.[64]

Yet another version is that the purchase was through Ronnie's boyfriend, the jockey-sized Bobby Buckley, described by the police as 'a dangerous man of effeminate appearance… wears his hair long on occasions' and by writer Min Scala as, 'A pretty leprechaun of an Irish boy with a slight stammer and hard as nails.'[65] Buckley was also a friend of Leslie Payne and had been a croupier at Esmeralda's Barn.

According to Payne, Ronnie spent an inordinate amount of time with, and money on, Buckley, and the Twins came to blows after

Reggie had had enough, saying 'He's only a boy,' but Ronnie replied, 'Yes, but he's my boy'. A fight ensued and they had to be separated. Buckley was also the lover of gambler David Litvinoff, the half-brother of the novelist Emmanuel and the historian Barnet. Litvinoff had been the dialogue coach for James Fox in the 1970 film *Performance* and was said to have contributed to the script, which was loosely based on the Krays. He had also introduced Buckley to Ronnie Kray.

Another story is that de Fay sold his shares on the basis he would continue as manager, but he never set foot in the place again.

It was Litvinoff who was said to have had a sword, or something like it, rammed down his throat by Ronnie over an unpaid gambling debt. Some sort of assault did take place, but there is no evidence Ronnie was directly responsible. The Krays were never averse to having violence attributed to them – for example the shooting of Teddy Berry – particularly when *in extremis* they could show they were not responsible. When Nipper Read, in his first investigation into the Krays, interviewed Litvinoff, he declined to tell him anything. Later Litvinoff would claim that he was in a café by Earl's Court tube station when a man walked up, said, 'Ronnie says hello, and slashed him across the mouth. The writer Min Sala claims the Krays sent some boys round to Litvinoff's Kensington flat, tied him to a chair and razor cut the corners of his mouth.[66]

With the Barn came the sixth Earl of Effingham whom the Twins used as their gofer. It was always desirable for criminals to have an MP or other public figure to ask questions on their behalf and to bring a façade of respectability to operations. For example, Billy Hill had the licence of the Cabinet Club in the name of the Trade Union leader and Labour MP Captain Mark Hewitson, while the Richardsons used Sir Noel Dryden MP in a similar capacity. Effingham fitted that purpose nicely for the Krays.

Mowbray Howard, Lord Effingham, a direct descendant of the man who commanded the fleet which sank the Armada in 1588 and was ennobled for his efforts, had led a louche life. His family motto was 'Virtue is worth a thousand shields', but he rarely lived up to it. He had been engaged for six weeks in 1929 to Kathleen, the daughter of Ma Meyrick, the celebrated nightclub owner, but this had ended when she gave evidence against him following an eighty-man brawl outside the 43 Club in Gerrard Street. On this occasion he was bound over to keep the peace. Two years later a conviction for drunkenness followed and in October 1932 he was extremely lucky to avoid a conviction for manslaughter when lay magistrates refused to commit him for trial after his car had hit a pedestrian. A coroner's jury had already returned a verdict of unlawful killing. In 1934 he bounced a cheque and left the country to work in Canada as a goose farmer, buffalo tender and garage hand. In his absence he was declared bankrupt to the tune of £195. It was not until 1958 that he was discharged after paying his creditors in full.

Described in an MI5 file as 'a weakling and fond of drink', in 1938 and back in England he married the 'worst kind of adventuress', the Hungarian-born Manci Gertler, who was working for her lover, the wealthy arms dealer Eduard Stanislav Weisblatt, thought to be an agent of OGPU, the forerunner of the KGB.

Weisblatt reportedly paid Effingham £500 (around £20,000 in today's currency) to marry Gertler, and promised him a retainer of the equivalent of £1,000 a week. During the Second World War she was suspected of spying on behalf of Weisblatt, and in 1941 was interned for three months under the Defence of the Realm Act. Protected from deportation by her marriage to Effingham, on her release she remained in England until she divorced his Lordship on grounds of adultery in 1945.[67]

Effingham continued to lead his louche life working intermittently as a barman, running a second-hand bookshop and as a haberdasher's assistant. Shortly before he met the Krays he was involved in a business importing electric tin openers. He thought the Twins 'a couple of quiet and rather pleasant chaps. Perhaps a little rough as far as education went.' They continually referred to him as 'Effing' Effingham and, paying him £7 a week to supplement his £4.14.6d-a-day House of Lords attendance allowance, effectively used him as a tea boy when he was not on parade meeting and greeting minor celebrities at the club or at Reggie Kray's wrestling promotions in the East End.

Just as it had been fashionable to visit Charlie Brown's East End pub before the war, so for a time it was now fashionable to mix with these apparently slightly dangerous figures. Gerry Parker recalled:

> 'I was invited to the opening night. All black ties. Fellow on the door Big Patsy [Connolly], so big his suit didn't fit. They thought all you had to do was open a club and take the money.'[68]

However the Guards officers and their friends soon discovered that their gambling debts were not treated in such a gentlemanly way as under previous management. Late payers and knockers (someone who deliberately refuses to pay) could be dealt with severely.

After a redecoration – 'They've turned the place into a fucking Maltese restaurant', said Litvinoff – at first Alf Mancini and Leslie Payne ran the club successfully, making around £800 a week for each of the Twins. Unfortunately Ronnie took more and more interest in being there, sometimes bringing his parents, who did not blend well with the upper class atmosphere. Nor for that matter did Charlie and Reggie, who wore the height of gangster chic light blue mohair suits with white shirts and blue bow ties. At least Ronnie wore a dinner jacket.

Reggie Kray's appeal against his conviction for demanding money from Murray Podro dragged on and he was out on bail on the streets for nearly a year before the application for leave to appeal was heard and dismissed on 26 July 1960.[69] He was sent back to prison and, disastrously, his twin was left running Esmeralda's Barn. If Ronnie had stayed away from the day-to-day running of the club, contenting himself with being a meeter and greeter, it would have provided an enormous income that would have greatly added to the profits, but unfortunately he allowed long lines of credit to punters who were incapable of settling their debts. When they failed to pay he began to threaten them.

One story is that the painter Francis Bacon, whom he admired, and indeed with whom he claimed to have had a short-lived affair – something denied by Bacon – had his gambling debt wiped out.

Another *habitué* was the painter and gambler Lucian Freud who, shortly before his death, told the newspapers he had owed the Krays half a million pounds over his gambling habit. He had once cancelled a show because they would demand more money if they saw what he was getting from his paintings. Lord Rothschild remembered the painter telling him one day, 'I'm in trouble with pressing debts to the Kray brothers. If I don't give them £1,000, they'll cut my hand off.'[70] Rothschild:

> 'I said I'd loan him the money on two conditions. First, that he never ask me for a loan again; and, second, that he didn't pay me back the money. He accepted the conditions, but ten days later a large envelope came through my letter box with £1,000 in cash and a note saying thanks. And he never asked me again.'[71]

David Litvinoff treated the club as something of a private bank, using only some of the money he won there to settle his losses. Finally he settled his £3,000 debt by handing over the lease of his flat in Ashburn Gardens, where Ronnie took up residence with him and Bobbie Buckley.

Alf Mancini began begging Ronnie to stay away from Esmeralda's, even offering him £1,000, but he refused, so Mancini left to set up his own club in Curzon Street. Now Pauline Wallace, a former club owner herself, was brought in to run the tables along with Joe Dagel. This did not prove satisfactory. They were sacked and Uncle Alfie Kray took over. Stanley Crowther recalled having to get the wages for LF workers from him at the club. On 12 March 1962 Ronnie was fined £50 at Marylebone Magistrates' Court for unlawful gaming.

Pauline Wallace nevertheless continued to run Kray-protected *chemin de fer* parties at her flat in Hertford Street off Park Lane. Always involved in greyhound racing, she owned the winner of the Irish Derby and later went to Miami and became heavily engaged in greyhound racing there. Her involvement with the Krays is a good example of the diametrically opposed versions of events concerning them. In *Me and My Brothers* Charlie tells a touching story of how the Twins helped to tide her over a rough patch and declined to take any repayments. Nevertheless she insisted, and so kindly Billy Exley went every week to collect the money. However, Tony Lambrianou says that, weary of paying protection, she made a lump sum payment and vanished from the scene.[72]

It was at Esmeralda's that the jewel thief 'Little' Lennie Hamilton lost his hair. He had been in the Regal in Mile End with Pat Connolly and a young man and his girlfriend when some people from south London sent over drinks. Hamilton asked the girl, 'What do you want, love?' The boyfriend took offence and produced a razor. Connolly told him to put it away and the man then invited Hamilton to meet him in the lavatory. Hamilton agreed, assuming the man would apologise, but when instead he tried to cut him, Hamilton broke his nose, not realizing he was Buller Ward's son, Bonar.

Some days later Hamilton's flatmate Andy Paul, who was then working as a doorman at Esmeralda's, came back at 1 a.m. with the message that he was to ring Ronnie. Instead, foolishly, Hamilton took a taxi to the club, where he met Ronnie Kray, Bobby Buckley, Leslie Payne and Limehouse Willey. Hamilton remembered:

'All the gambling tables were closed down and there were seven or eight people standing on either side. They told me to go in the kitchen and when I opened the door Ronnie Kray was standing opposite. He said, "Nothing to worry about, Lenny." He had a big armchair next to the cooker and he invited me to sit down, asking, "What's going on Lenny? You caused a bit of trouble in the Regal. We get protection money from them."'

He was then told he could go, but as he stood to leave Ronnie told two men to get hold of him. Ronnie picked up a piece of steel used for sharpening knives, which he had had pre-heated:

'The first one Ronnie picked up he dropped because it was so hot, so he went and got an oven glove. Then he picked one up and came over to me, to frighten me, I imagined. He singed my black curly hair. I pissed myself. I was terrified. Next he started setting fire to my suit that I only had made two weeks before. Then he went back and got another hot poker and dabbed it on my cheeks and held it across my eyebrows and burnt my eyebrows off. I'm half-blind in this eye because of it. Then he went back and got another poker and, as he came back, he said, "Now I'm going to burn your eyes out," and he really meant it. As he came towards me, Limehouse Willey called out from the crowd, "No Ron, don't do that!" Ronnie switched, he turned and walked away.'[73]

Hamilton took the cab which had brought him to Esmeralda's back to his friend Harry Abrahams who, along with Donoghue, went to see the Twins the next day for an explanation. George Cornell dropped £200 over to Abrahams with instructions to look after Hamilton and Charlie Kray gave him £100 with instructions not to tell the Twins. Finally the good Dr Blasker came and patched him up.

According to one witness, Bobbie Buckley was so sickened he left the room, but Mad Teddy Smith and Leslie Payne were made of sterner stuff. Hamilton, under treatment at Moorfields Eye Hospital for some years, was fortunate not to completely lose the sight in his eye. Nevertheless, despite everything, he remained with the Firm.

Ron Kray has a rather more romantic version of why Hamilton was burned – unless there were two men to whom he set fire in Esmeralda's. He claimed that a friend in the East End had come to the Twins asking for vengeance (à la Godfather) because Hamilton (whom he does not name) had broken the nose of the man's daughter because she wouldn't have sex with him.[74]

According to Leslie Payne, Hamilton did go to the police, who arranged for the Krays to organise a meeting, telling him to be at the same pub at the same time. When Hamilton walked in and found the Krays with the officers, he knew that was that. In the end, Payne says, he was given some money by the Twins and more money went to the police. Whichever is the real version, the Kray family was righteously indignant that Hamilton made a handsome profit after the incident from two books and various television interviews.

It was not every gambling club which would wish to stage a boxing match, but one took place one morning at 2 a.m. at Esmeralda's between Buckley and Tommy Waldron, known as Chomondley, for a purse of £50 with Lord Boothby and others baying at the ringside. At the end of two rounds Waldron was losing but in the third he caught Buckley on the nose and blood spurted out. Ronnie immediately stopped the fight, throwing the £50 on the floor. When Buckley wanting to continue, saying he was all right, Ronnie protectively replied, 'You ain't, son. You were much prettier than you are now, so you can fuck off home'.[75] After all, Ronnie had said that if Buckley were a girl he would marry him.

Finally the guardsmen and their Sloane girlfriends drifted away to smarter premises. The rump of the club was handed over to the astute Micky Fawcett to run for a few weeks before the shutters went up. The company collapsed, and it was finally wound up with debts amounting to £4,400.

But by now Leslie Payne had already found them another jam pot back on their home territory and they strong-armed their way into the Kentucky at 106 Mile End Road. They kept the name and hired Ben Lipner, who had once run the Beehive Club in Streatham for Billy Howard and who had already decorated the Regency, to tart it up. When it was finished it was a plush crimson-velveted and mirrored nightclub which would bring them their greatest social success. It was at the time of the East End renaissance, with work beginning in earnest to repair bomb damage from the War, and indeed when the working classes were starting to be portrayed on the stage and screen as something other than figures of fun.

One story is that in 1963, Joan Littlewood, the producer of the hugely successful *Oh, What a Lovely War!* and who was then making the film *Sparrers Can't Sing* starring Barbara Windsor, encountered trouble with a group of dockers who, it appears, wanted protection money to allow the production to proceed. Barbara Windsor, who in her early life had a penchant for good-looking, charming villains, including Charlie Kray, now appealed to him for help. Charlie informed his brothers, who saw it not only as an opportunity to appear as white knights acting for oppressed women but also as an encroachment on Kray territory. They spoke with the dockers and the production continued unmolested. Barbara Windsor, in her autobiography, claims there was never any approach by the dockers. Littlewood visited the Kentucky and it featured in the fight scene which ends the film.

When the film was premiered at the ABC in the Bow Road, the after-show party was held in the club. The premiere had been due to be attended by Princess Margaret and her husband, Lord Snowden, and some versions of the opening have them both at the cinema, but with Princess Margaret not attending the after-show party. In fact neither did and she did not attend the premiere either, having unfortunately had a sudden bout of flu.

Nevertheless, as far as the Krays were concerned it was an unprecedented triumph, with the stars of the film Barbara Windsor and James Booth both at the party. The brothers had bought and sold £500 of tickets for the premiere and the local businessmen duly stumped up, as they did for Reggie's charity wrestling, buying expensive advertisements for the programme. It is unclear how much of this cash actually ended up with the charities for which it was intended.

Perhaps the first months of 1963 were the zenith of the Krays' social ambitions. The local newpapers now reported them as being respectable businessmen and there were regular favourable reports on their charitable work.

On 23 January that year Reggie Kray began promoting wrestling at the York Hall Baths. His first bill in aid of charity was supposed to be topped by the ex-champion Bert Assirati, matched with a giant Russian, The Great Karloff, in reality the New Zealander Ernie Kingston, who had taken the name after appearing in the Hammer horror film *The Evil of Frankenstein*. When it came to it Assirati would have nothing to do with the show, and the crowd had to make do with lesser fare in the form of Ed Martinson 'The Docklands Strong Boy'.

Assirati or not, the evening was a sufficient success for further promotions featuring the Kray workhorse, the ageing Bobby Ramsey, and attended by the Mayor of Hackney and Lord Effingham along with a collection of old boxers such as Ted 'Kid' Lewis. On the bill of 12 February Ramsey was in a boxer vs. wrestler contest with Roy 'Chopper' Levaque. The now well out of condition Ramsey was not expected to work for too long and, to the delight of the crowd, knocked out Levaque in the second round. The poor man was later required to go through the same routine in a number of bouts.

The matches were made by wrestler Tony Scarlo, who initially had no trouble with the promotions. That is, until one night at the York Hall when the dwarf Royston French tried to threaten the wrestlers into accepting £2.50 instead of their agreed fees. He threatened Syed Shah with a knife, who took it away from him and explained the rules of life. But that was the end of the promotions.

For a time the Kentucky prospered and was packed out night after night, until the police objected to its licence and the licensing justices agreed. On 7 April 1963 the club, registered on 11 September 1961, closed its doors after just 18 months.

CHAPTER 6
1964

1964 was a defining year in the Kray saga, one which may be seen as the zenith of their careers but also as the beginning of their inexorable slide. Given that for much of the time hanging was still the mandatory sentence for murder, they could perhaps be described as careless with their use of guns and knives. Not only was Reggie involved in the shooting of Albert Donoghue, he was also linked to the shooting of Jimmy Fields in the lavatory of the Senate Rooms, a club in Highbury. Ronnie was involved in a shooting in the Central Club, Holborn, and again when he opened fire while Bert Rossi, who had protected him in prison when he was having a breakdown, was quarrelling with other Italians; he tried to shoot George Dixon, one of the formidable brothers, as well as Russy Bennett from the Upton Park family. Bennett's wounds initially appeared fatal, but fortunately for Ronnie he pulled through. The gun was given to two men to hand to a third for safekeeping, who was not best pleased. 'If the police had come round I'd have grassed him,' said the third man, uncharacteristically.[76]

For once, however, the Twins seem to have been blameless when on 10 January 1964 the 35-year-old ex-boxer Teddy Berry was shot a hundred yards from his home in Bethnal Green. Known in the ring as 'The King of Dynamite', he'd never had much luck in life. Married with three children, he had won all his 26 fights, 18 by knockout, before he became blind in one eye and was forced to retire. At the time of the shooting he was working as a bookmaker's clerk. Berry had been drinking with his brother Henry 'Checker' Berry and was on the Hadrian Estate when he was shot from a passing car. He collapsed and the masked gunman then stood over him and shot him in the left leg at point blank range. The remains of Berry's leg were amputated later that night.

The conventional version of the Berry shooting is that it was a dispute over a car sold by a garage which was under Kray protection, but more likely it was also in part the result of a fight in the Regency the previous year in which an East End hardman had been badly cut.

Ronnie was arrested and taken to Bancroft Road Hospital where Teddy Berry identified him as the man who had shot him. But when the police were about to charge him with grievous bodily harm, he swore he was not Ronnie but Reggie, and produced his driving licence to prove it. His alibi for the time of the shooting was so strong that the embarrassed police at Arbour Square station had to release him. Then, using the services of the East End fixer 'Red Face' Tommy Lumley, the matter was resolved.[77]

It was a question of 'The Lord giveth; the Lord taketh'. On 12 February 1964 the brothers organised a show with ex-boxers playing for laughs, formally promoted by the Spitalfields Porters Association, at Bethnal Green's York Hall to raise funds for Teddy Berry. He used the resulting £500 to buy an interest in The Horns public house.[78]

And then on 12 July that year, it all blew up when the *Sunday Mirror* headlined the story which would signal the beginning of the end of the Kray Twins' empire: 'Peer and a Gangster: Yard Inquiry'. The article reported that a Detective Superintendent was leading an investigation into an association between a peer who was a household name and an underworld thug. He was looking into parties attended by the gangster, his relations with the peer and the peer's visits to Brighton – as well as allegations of blackmail. The unnamed peer was man-about-town Lord Boothby, who was also something of a television pundit, and the unnamed gangster was Ronnie Kray.

The next day the *Mirror* ran an editorial:

> 'This gang is so rich, powerful and ruthless that the police are unable to crack down on it. Victims are too terrified to go to the police. Witnesses are too scared to tell their story in court. The police, who know what is happening but cannot pin any evidence on the villains, are powerless.'

That morning Bernard Black, a freelance photographer, went to the *Mirror* to supply photographs of Robert Boothby and Kray. By the afternoon he had changed his mind and asked for them back, claiming he did not own the copyright. On the Tuesday he applied in the High Court for an injunction preventing the *Mirror* from using the photographs. On 16 July the *Daily Mirror* led with the story 'The picture we dare not print', and described it as one of 'a well-known member of the House of Lords seated on a sofa with a gangster who leads the biggest protection racket London has ever known'.

The MacMillan Government was still reeling from the Profumo affair, in which the War Secretary John Profumo admitted sleeping with Christine Keeler, also the mistress of a Soviet naval attaché. This second scandal might just do for the Government. It was now a question of the top brass conducting an inquiry. What they wanted to know was what Boothby had to say about the matter.

On 18 July Boothby wrote to the Home Secretary, Henry Brooke, saying that by appointment Ronnie Kray and his lawyer had visited him about six months earlier asking if he was interesting in chairing or directing an extensive housing programme.

Kray returned, again by appointment, a week later, this time bringing a friend. Boothby gave them a drink and 'Before he left he asked if his friend could take a photograph of us, as he was a great fan of mine on radio and television'. This was quite usual for Boothby and he claimed 'This is the sum total of my relationship with Mr Kray'.

Boothby denied he was gay and added, 'If I were a homosexual, which I am not, I should not choose either gangsters or clergymen.' He claimed had never met Kray – 'He seemed an agreeable chap' – outside the flat, and then for no more than twenty minutes on each occasion.

The Home Office file noted that Assistant Commissioner Ranulph Bacon (unsurprisingly known as Rasher) in charge of the CID had seen the twelve photographs, none of them compromising except one with an ill-dressed 'beatnik' youth also sitting on the sofa. The police had yet to identify him.

On 20 July Commissioner Sir Joseph Simpson made a public statement that he had asked senior officers for 'some enlightenment' on reports that inquiries were being made into allegations of a relationship between a homosexual peer and East End gangsters. The next day another senior CID officer, Fred Gerrard, took a statement from Boothby essentially reiterating his letter to the Home Secretary. He denied he had been at any Kray parties or to any of their clubs and he explained this strange friendship:

> 'I met Leslie Holt [the beatnik on the sofa] at a boxing match. I took to him right away. He used to drop in a couple of times a year for a chat. We were just good friends and I enjoyed his company.'[79]

In fact the 'beatnik' was the talented cat-burglar and homosexual Leslie Holt, one of six sons of a Shoreditch dustman, a rent-boy marred only by disfiguring warts on his hands and feet, whose favours Boothby, Ronnie Kray and a number of others shared. Some said that Boothby used to masturbate while smacking Holt's bare backside with a slipper. Micky Fawcett one said to me:

> 'The Twins both wanted their picture with Boothby. It was better than money for Ronnie. That's what he lived for. He liked Lords. He was a proper old Queen.'[80]

'Lord Bobby', as the German magazine *Stern* called him, had had an interesting and upwardly mobile career. Fleshily handsome in the fashion of the time, with a gravelly voice, the long-serving Conservative member for East Aberdeenshire was created a peer in 1958. He was bisexual, with a taste for coprophilia, and was rumoured to have fathered a daughter with Prime Minister Harold MacMillan's wife Dorothy, something discounted by Macmillan's biographer D.R. Thorpe.[81]

But, by the end of July *Stern* was less circumspect: 'Lord Bobby in Trouble', it said, 'sitting on a settee with a well-known criminal of degenerate tendencies', naming Boothby and Ronnie Kray.[82]

There was keen anticipation that the photograph in question was of Boothby in a compromising position – with the fuss that was made it had been thought that at least the pair were naked – but when it was eventually published in the *Daily Express* at the beginning of August it merely showed Boothby and Ronnie Kray fully clothed, sitting on a sofa.

Now the government was also making further inquiries and information came from Tory MPs Brigadier Terence Clarke and Barnaby Drayson, of whom one civil servant wrote, '[They are] both gossips. Yet, I do recollect that they were for me the original source about Boothby and greyhound racing tracks etc.'

Another to provide tidbits of information was the louche member for East Thanet, man-about-town and barrister Billy Rees-Davies, the one-armed MP for East Thanet, who had been mixed up in the Profumo scandal when he tried to buy off Christine Keeler.[83] He thought the photographs were 'prejudicial', in other words pornographic. He believed it was all a calculated Labour Party plot to further destabilise the government, but he also reported that the Krays had tried to muscle in on the White Elephant club, a fashionable dinner and dancing place on the river. They had, however, been sent packing by Raymond Nash, the Lebanese partner of Peter Rachman.

There was also a rather sinister note dated 21 July on the Law Office file:

> 'Apparently a Chief Constable knows about this but is taking no official action. It is understood however that he is prepared to sell his knowledge to Conservative MPs.'[84]

The newspapers were being unduly reticent about who was with the Peer until on 24 July 1964 the Krays were named by *Private Eye*. With tongue in cheek, the editor suggested that this might be the last issue under the present management.

The matter was taken very seriously by the Government and three meetings were held in the Home Secretary's office in the House of Commons. The last was held on 28 July at 4.15 p.m. with, in attendance, the Home Secretary, the Chief Whip, the Minister without Portfolio, the Attorney General and the Solicitor General. Now things seemed to be under control. A story about Boothby and his fellow peer Tom Driberg importuning at a dog track had faded away. Boothby suggested it was all an attempt by the Labour MPs Marcus Lipton and Arthur Lewis to manufacture a pre-election scandal. The *Mirror* had been negotiating to publish the Krays' memoirs, as they had earlier for those of the Nash brothers. As for the meetings with Boothby, the information was that the 'Kray brothers have amassed a great deal of wealth by crime in the past and are now seeming to become respectable'.

Driberg was a predatory homosexual in the days before the Street Offences Act of 1957, when indecency between men carried a two-year prison sentence and buggery 14 years. He plucked a handsome boy out of the carpentry division of the BBC and made him his secretary, pursuing him sexually over a long period. He never managed to have sex with him – his ultimate goal – but on one occasion after he had taken the boy out for the evening he sent him a note the next day reading, 'Thank you for almost everything'.[85]

When Melford Stevenson, the judge in the Kray trial, stood against Driberg for the Parliamentary seat of Clacton, he opened one meeting by saying he wished to have a cleanly fought campaign and so would not in future refer to Driberg's homosexuality. Driberg had met the Krays when Joan Littlewood introduced them at the Kentucky Club. He would maintain that he had only a very slight acquaintance, but in reality he was a regular attendee at Ronnie's parties at Cedra Court when East End youths were passed around like parcels.

The next bullet was a letter on 4 August to *The Times* from Boothby re-asserting that he was not homosexual. At least that bit was true: he was bisexual. Boothby had, he said, met the man alleged to be 'King of the Underworld' only three times, and always at his home, which he used as an office. He had no knowledge that the man had convictions. No one had tried to blackmail him. 'Despite advice I have found the best way to treat the press is perfect frankness and telling the truth. This is what I have always done.'

Boothby had thought about bringing an action for libel against the *Sunday Mirror* over the article of 12 July but, on the advice of Lord Gardiner, for the moment he had dropped the idea. Well, not quite. When the newspaper stories appeared, Boothby approached the fashionable, devious, gay, extremely powerful, morbidly obese and ultimately exposed as dishonest solicitor Arnold Goodman to act on his behalf.

The upshot was that Boothby received a groveling apology from the *Mirror* and £40,000 plus his legal costs. In fact, when interviewed for *The Times* on 5 August, Boothby was rather more concerned about his dog than his reputation. His boxer bitch, Gigi Felicity Boothby, had disappeared and had 'pushed the other matter right into the background', he told a reporter. Boothby claimed he donated much of his payment to charity, but one of the 'charities' benefitting from his kindness was Ronnie Kray, who received £5,000.

As for damages for Ronnie from the paper, there were none. He was advised by barrister Eric Crowther (no relation of Stanley) that he was not in the same skiff as Lord Bobby. After all, there was that five-year sentence for GBH to consider. Crowther recorded that the Twins listened politely to his advice and thanked him. A month later Ronnie Kray received an unqualified apology but no money.

The incident did, however, ensure that newspapers were even more reticent about adversely reporting the Krays' activities.

Boothby had been less than frank, if not downright dishonest. Ronnie Kray used to bring him boys on a regular basis whom he would openly kiss and undress in front of him and his friends.

One other problem, so far as the Government was concerned, was that on 17 July 1963 Lord Boothby had reported there had been a clumsy attempt to forge a cheque of his drawn on the National Commercial Bank of Scotland on the Brompton Road. The perpetrator was 17-year-old James Buckley, brother of Bobby. Buckley, who was said to have been working at a licensed club in Knightsbridge, had claimed to be his Lordship's secretary, but the bank manager became suspicious. Three years earlier in June 1960 in the Isle of Man, James Buckley had been sentenced to one month and six strokes of the birch for housebreaking, wilful damage and demanding money with menaces. This time he received a sentence of Borstal training to go with the one he was presently serving for receiving stolen clothing. How Buckley managed to get hold of the cheque was never explained. And indeed few inquiries were made.

Nor was it the first time Boothby had experienced trouble with boys and his possessions. He had had a lucky escape when in 1959 an unemployed 17-year-old Scottish waiter was arrested in possession of half a bottle of champagne, a gold watch and chain and a gold coin given to him, he said initially, after he had spent a weekend at Boothby's flat. He pleaded guilty to theft and was placed on probation. Boothby had been in court to tell the magistrate that because his butler, George Goodfellow, had been away for the weekend, the boy had been doing some cooking and cleaning for him. He had left just before Sunday lunch and had taken the champagne, coins and watch with him. Boothby said:

> 'He is one of several hundred people I have tried to help and he is only the second one to let me down. I was very reluctant to bring the charge. I would like to say in mitigation that he is very young and I think probably the temptation was too great.'

The magistrate agreed with him, complaining that thieving young boys, who thought they could get away with anything they wanted, were the bane of his professional life. Later the boy would tell Sir John Junor, then editor of the *Sunday Express*, that Boothby had indeed given him the items and had also taken him to the fashionable Dean Street restaurant, Leoni's Quo Vadis.[86]

Nor were the Twins being wholly frank with Los Angeles lawyer Harrison W. Hertzberg when they told him they had received £100,000 in libel damages over the affair. Hertzberg had been duly impressed.

The Twins were now being pursued by Francis Wyndham of the *Sunday Times*, who wanted their story. An article by Chester Lewis had already appeared in the newspaper entitled 'The Charitable World of the Brothers Kray', mocking the Twins and including a photograph of their car, a Ford Galaxy, outside their 'ancestral home':

> 'In the clannish milieu of the East End there are many others who have felt the advantage of being friendly with the Krays. As philanthropic fund-raisers their background may not be entirely conventional, but no one can deny their remarkable persuasive powers.'

Lewis also quoted the then Mayor of Bethnal Green, Robert Hare, who said of them, 'They were – and are – nice, able local boys,' adding that local old people such as the Good Companions Club had received a van load of gifts from them.[87]

Others ungraciously point out that the only presents and money received from the Krays were the proceeds of Long Firm frauds or money they had ponced off other criminals.

Wyndham wanted to write an article about their careers and background, but hardly endeared himself to them when he spelled their name 'Cray' in correspondence.[88]

Another immediate result of the Boothby problem was that when on 16 October 1964 Ronnie Kray flew to New York, he was refused admission to the United States and his visa was stamped 'Invalidated'. He was not pleased. He had intended to go to the Joey Giardello vs. Reuben Carter fight for the Middleweight title in December. Ronnie was furious and blamed Boothby. The peer's manservant Goodfellow, wrote to him from the Miramar Beach Hotel, Barbados, saying that he had 'spoken to LB and he says no man could have done more for you than he could have done'. According to Goodfellow, Boothby had also made a statement to Area Chief Superintendent Fred Gerrard:

> '... in the course of which he said he found you [Ronnie Kray] perfectly straightforward in any dealings he had had with you and that he firmly believed you were now successfully engaged in business which was absolutely legitimate.'

He also pointed out that Boothby had obtained an apology from the editor of the *Daily Express.*

But, whether he liked it or not, Boothby was still there to be leaned on when necessary and he would try to prove his worth to the

Twins the following year. One reason for this was that a small suitcase of documents which showed Boothby had been far closer to Ronnie than he cared to admit publicly had been left with Violet Kray. This was used as a stick and carrot with which to goad his Lordship into actions which he must have lived to regret.[89]

The questions put by the Labour MP Marcus Lipton resulted in the Metropolitan Police Commissioner Sir Joseph Simpson deciding that the Krays should not go unchecked. Within a fortnight his instructions became quite specific and on 27 July, Gerrard went to see Nipper Read at the Commercial Road police station and ordered him to put a team together to 'have a go at the Krays', with explicit instructions to investigate allegations of extortion from club owners. Was this a problem? asked Gerrard, meaning quite specifically, did the Krays have anything on him. Read angrily replied, 'No, of course not'.

And so began a frustrating three months which would end in humiliation for the police.

First, Read found that since the abortive prosecutions of Charlie and Ronnie for loitering and Reggie for housebreaking, no one in the CID had seriously tried to tackle the Krays. Read began to realise that the Krays always seemed to be forewarned:

> 'If ever there was a shooting and the overwhelming level of opinion amongst detectives was that this was down to the Krays, the attitude had been that you went along to see them first and they said, "No, we've got an alibi." Then you would go out and look for the evidence. It should have been the other way round.'[90]

Criminals can normally sniff out a policeman at twenty yards, but Read had two advantages. First, he did not look like a police officer, and second, he was not known in the East End. So he went unnoticed in the bar of the Grave Maurice reading the *Evening News* and wearing a cap and raincoat when Ronnie went there to meet the television journalist Michael Barrett. Colin 'Dukey' Osborne, whose hand was in his pocket as if he was carrying a gun, had preceded Ron, checking out the lavatories in the pub before giving him the nod. Read recalled:

> 'For a moment I could not believe what I saw. His [Ronnie's] hair was smartly cut and gleaming and his gold-rimmed spectacles firmly in place. He was wearing a light camel coat which almost reached his ankles, the belt tied in a casual knot at the waist. For all the world he looked like something out of the Capone era.'[91]

Even though Barrett was wearing a neck brace at the time, Osborne and Ronnie's other minder did everything but frisk him. At the end of the interview Osborne again 'swept the street' and Ronnie hurried to the waiting car.

So began a disappointing time for Read and his superiors. He was given a squad with ten Aides to CID. He was also allowed to pick a Detective Constable for himself, Trevor Lloyd-Hughes. A visit to Jack Spot, now down on his luck and away from the West End, produced nothing. Nor did a story that an Italian restaurant near the British Museum was paying protection. There were repeated stories that people had been brought before a court presided over by Ronnie and sentenced to a buttock-slashing – Ronnie commenting, 'Every time he sits down he'll remember us' – but a trawl of local hospitals produced nothing. At the time Read, a stranger to the area, did not know of the good Dr Blasker and no one thought to tell him.

There was one unexpected bonus. 'Dukey' Osborne may indeed have been carrying a gun the evening that Read visited in the Grave Maurice. His subsequent arrest and conviction for possessing firearms came about in an odd way. A man had been brought to Bethnal Green police station after his son had been found in possession of a stolen radio. He told the boy he had to tell the officers where he'd found it. He did so, but when his father left the room the boy said, 'Well, he can have a go at me over a poxy wireless but he don't say nothing about that lodger in our house and all the guns under his bed'. The lodger in question was Osborne, who received seven years in February 1965.

Meanwhile the Twins showed their contempt for the whole investigation by visiting Harrods Zoo and purchasing two pythons, which they named Gerrard and Read. They were proudly photographed with their new pets and told reporters:

'[They] don't give us no trouble; most of the time they're asleep. They're deaf and their sight's not too good either. They just sense vibrations with their tongues.'[92]

CHAPTER 7
A BRIEF LOOK AT THE TWINS' LAWYERS

Criminals are not always the most loyal of clients. They can flit from solicitor to solicitor on a whim. Similarly, for a time, the Krays chopped and changed their briefs.

When the Twins found themselves in trouble they went first to the highly respected, silver haired Welshman T.V. 'Tommy' Edwards who effectively ruled Thames Magistrates' court. Mickey Bailey remembered him:

> 'Old Tommy Edwards was a right old gentleman who got me out of trouble more times than I care to remember and I stuck with him for a few years and then I went to Ellis Lincoln, who everybody used in those days. I think old Tommy Edwards must have been too straight for the Twins.'[93]

Later, in the early 1960s, they moved their criminal business to Bernie Perkoff. Perkoff was another East End solicitor whose father's pub The Windmill had once been wrecked by Italian gangsters looking for Jack Spot. After Perkoff, the Twins graduated to Ellis Lincoln and his offices in Holborn.

Lincoln was the doyen of the solicitors of the 1950s and early 1960s who specialised in crime. Many of the highest class of criminal, including some of the Great Train Robbers, passed through his hands, as did their cash. Reputed to launder money on their behalf, he cultivated a not wholly unjustified reputation for being able to bribe the police, and a wholly unjustified one of also being able to do the same with magistrates and judges.

The Krays turned to Lincoln in 1960. By the spring of that year the Twins, and to a lesser extent Charlie, were so much in the local police's sights that Lincoln wrote to the Metropolitan Commissioner on 28 April complaining of undue surveillance and denying that they were involved in any criminal activities. The letter brought an angry internal memo on 6 May from the detective Tommy Butler saying the Twins were directing protection to:

> 'Club owners, café proprietors, billiard hall operators, publicans and motor car dealers. That they will spread their operations to other districts in due course may be taken for granted.'

Butler also observed that the Lincoln letter was a common tactic employed by what he considered to be the less reputable solicitors of the time, and he compiled a list of those who made use of it. Apart from Lincoln, the list included a man who Butler described as 'the oily Manny Fryde'.

Lincoln, who had had troubles early in his career when he was suspended for five years in 1940, was finally struck off in 1966 over a failure to keep proper accounts and to supervise a clerk adequately. He sold his practice for which he received, he said, £122 to settle an electricity bill, and became a managing clerk before opening a 'law consultancy' in Holborn, passing a good deal of work to a local solicitor. In May 1971 he failed in an application to have his name restored to the Rolls.[94]

In the summer of 1961 the Twins were boating on the lake at Victoria Park when they noticed they were being watched by the police. Somehow they managed to telephone Robert Hare (the ex-Mayor of Hackney) and Father David Evans, who came down, cassock flying, to be with the lads until the police dispersed. Rumours had been rife that the police were 'gunning' for the Krays, and intended to charge Ronnie with 'indecency or some homosexual offence so as to humiliate him'. However it was not until 1963 that the Mayfair firm of T.J. James & Wheater were instructed to write on the Twins' behalf. Their letter concluded, 'We hope you will investigate this complaint and cause this victimisation to cease'. It was supported by letters from Evans and Hare. Both were full of praise for the family. The priest wrote:

'From what I know of the family they are carrying on a legitimate business and from what I have seen and heard it is my opinion that the police are victimising them.'

And from Hare:

'I have known the Kray brothers for the past three years and to the best of my knowledge and belief they are carrying on respectable occupations and I know they do a good deal for charity.'

An inquiry resulted. As for the boating incident, there was nothing in any police pocket books or diaries to suggest officers had been keeping observation in Victoria Park, and so much time had passed that it was now impossible to confirm this story.

As for respectability, the police pointed out that Ronnie had been fined £50 for running gambling at Esmeralda's Barn, where croupiers at *chemin de fer* parties were said to be paid £500 a week. The local police believed the Krays' empire was spreading. They were thought to have a financial interest in or ran protection rackets not only at East End venues but also further afield in places like Earl's Court.

As for their charity work, on 9 November 1961, the Twins had donated a couple of prizes for a boxing tournament run by ex-Mayor Hare. They first dipped their toes in the charitable waters when in the summer of 1961 they had purchased £200 worth of tickets for a Repton Amateur boxing show in aid of the British Empire Cancer Campaign Appeal. Ronnie donated four trophies. Their absence at a later show resulted in much lower takings.

Local shopkeepers had been obliged to buy advertising space in a programme for a show at the Kentucky for the Mile End Hospital. The charity committee was a mixed affair. There was the Reverend John Foster of St James, Bethnal Green; Dr Morris Blasker; Daniel Farson, who, the police noted, was a suspected homosexual and had convictions for drunkenness. The secretary was the disbarred Stanley Crowther and the treasurer Benjamin Lipner, the decorator of the Regency.

Meanwhile Detective Chief Inspector Bob Halliday, of City Road Police Station, ordered that although this was probably nothing more than an attempt to provide a defence in the event of any future arrest. 'renewed attention and closer surveillance will be maintained.'

T.J. James and Wheater, the firm of solicitors who wrote the letter after the Victoria Park incident, were considered suspect by the police. Managing clerk Brian Field and sole partner John D. Wheater were later arrested and imprisoned for their roles in the Great Train Robbery.[95]

And after the unfortunate Wheater, the Twins turned to Sampson & Co, and in particular the clerks Emmanuel 'Manny' Fryde and Ralph Haeems for help.

Manny Fryde's pedigree was never quite clearly established. He probably qualified as a solicitor in South Africa and may or may not have been struck off there. Opinion is more or less equally divided. By the 1950s, however, he was working in England as a managing clerk, and an exceptionally powerful one at that.

A great Zionist who kept a list of known Blackshirts and sympathisers under the carpet in his office, on one occasion Fryde visited the home of a client charged with murder, and when using the lavatory found a swastika painted on the ceiling. He promptly threatened to withdraw from the case, and it took a good deal of persuasion (and no doubt an additional fee) for him to accept that the offending swastika was nothing more sinister than an Aryan symbol of light which had been painted by a previous tenant and had not been cleaned away.

In the early 1960s Fryde took Ralph Haeems, the son of Bombay schoolteachers, under his wing. He offered him a job filing and also used him to collect his winnings from local betting shops. Always a great and entertaining gossip, Haeems recalled:

> 'He [Fryde] never carried less than £5,000 on him. One time he sent me to a small shop opposite the Law Courts and I handed in the winning ticket. The girl went for the manager, who asked who I was from. I said Fryde. He said, "Here's the money and tell the effing bastard not to come in the shop again." It was £12,000.'

This was at a time when a newly qualified solicitor could expect to earn in the region of £20 a week.

CHAPTER 8
THE HIDE-A-WAY

As autumn 1964 became winter, Nipper Read was getting nowhere. The top club owners in the West End such as Edmundo Ros (sic) said they were not paying protection; Danny La Rue, lying through his teeth, said he was not paying protection; Al Burnett, who ran the Pigalle, a nightclub in Swallow Street off Piccadilly, said he was too big to pay protection. That was where Frank Fraser held a homecoming party on his release from slashing Jack Spot; Billy Hill smashed a bottle over a man's head there after a quarrel, and in 1961 'Scotch' Jack Buggy shot Robert Reeder on the pavement outside after an argument in the club.

Nor were the LF men in east and north London turning. From time to time Read thought he had made a breakthrough but at the next meeting the man would bring along a solicitor and say nothing.

There were also noises from the top in the form of Deputy Assistant Commissioner Ernie 'Hooter' Millen, so nicknamed either because of his nose or his foghorn voice or perhaps both. With Fred Gerrard away on leave he took the opportunity to summon Read to the Yard to ask him what progress was being made. The answer with regard to the Krays was very little, because no one dared to say a word against them. The authorities seriously considered winding the investigation up.

The Krays, however, were doing nicely. Along with their other acquisitions was a club in the basement of the Glenrae Hotel in the Seven Sisters Road, Finsbury Park, slightly away from their normal territory.

The owner Phoebe Woods had bought the hotel in 1959 and had renovated it. After a number of incidents the Krays moved in 'to stop further violence'. Billy Exley and Sammy Lederman became the barmen, with the faithful Bobby Ramsey on the door and attempting to keep the books. Exley ordered all the stock and Mrs Woods paid.

That, at least, was the police version of events. It does not wholly coincide with the version offered to me by Micky Fawcett, who said of the club after the Krays had taken it over:

'Within a week or two it was the busiest club in London. Ted [Woods] was highly delighted. The bar had been empty and now everyone was looking at it.'[96]

Just after New Year Read's luck seemed to turn. Or so it seemed at the time. It involved another small West End club, The Hide-A-Way in Gerrard Street, Soho, run by the gay Scots baronet Huw Cargill McCowan.

In its previous incarnations the premises had had a chequered career. At one time in the early 1960s it was the Bon Soir. Gilbert France, the owner of Chez Victor, a nearby fashionable French restaurant in Wardour Street and friend of club owner and Soho hardman Tony Mella, had owned it with Frank Fraser and Albert Dimes. The club did not do well, although Fraser couldn't really understand why:

> 'It was a classy joint… It had a little band, food, everything. That did well for a time but it's the same with everything in Soho, all the clubs, all the restaurants; one day everyone's going there and tomorrow you're yesterday's dinner.'[97]

France had a different view of things, telling *The People* that after he had opened the club in early 1962 it had been successful until, in early 1963, there had been trouble with fights and furniture being smashed and customers frightened, in the traditional way a protection racket operates. He had then gone into partnership with what he described as 'two well-known Soho personalities', presumably referring to Dimes and Fraser, but then once again trouble had broken out, with windows being smashed. The partnership had been dissolved and after bomb threats, France closed the club. Fraser wrote that Dimes had lost heart and Joe Wilkins – the nephew of Bert Wilkins, the old Sabini man – took over his interest but also lost money. A fire was the only solution.

McCowan had already met the Twins through Leslie Payne when they had unsuccessfully tried to get McCowan to invest in the Eastern Nigeria housing project.

McCowan had foolishly mentioned that he was thinking of opening a club and it was arranged he should meet the Twins in the Grave

Maurice. According to McCowan, Reggie had maintained it was essential that he have two of his men installed in the club to prevent trouble. Initially a figure of 25% was suggested, which was to rise to 50%. A table for 10 was reserved for the Twins' party on the opening night but no one appeared. Then at 2.30 a.m. on 18 December 1964 their friend Mad Teddy Smith, the one-time manager of blind pianist Lennie Peters, and who had had a play on television, appeared at the premises drunk, breaking two small neon signs behind the reception desk. The total cost was in the region of £20. Later he returned to apologise, but soon afterwards McCowan settled with the Twins for a flat 20%. He did not, however, let the matter lie and went to John Donald, a Detective Inspector at Marylebone, who in turn contacted Read.

Now McCowan, who had a history of making and withdrawing allegations of theft against boys he had picked up in the Music Box, a club off Piccadilly Circus, convinced Read he would stay the distance. In support was the club's young manager, the 21-year-old Sidney Vaughan, who backed McCowan's story. Read thought:

> '[McCowan is] not a particularly homosexual type in that he does not dress in a flamboyant fashion nor does he adopt exaggerated female gestures. Will make an excellent witness.'

As for Vaughan:

> 'Once he has surmounted the initial shock of the witness box I am sure that he will make a truthful and convincing witness.'

An alternative version of the Hide-A-Way troubles is that on a visit to the Glenrae Hotel McCowan had approached the Twins to go into partnership but changed his mind a couple of weeks later. This was not the sort of behaviour the pair would tolerate, and explains their failure to appear on opening night. As for Teddy Smith, he had not been acting on their instructions. With the gift of hindsight perhaps Read should have made more inquiries into McCowan's background.

In early January 1965 the Glenrae Hotel was raided by the police investigating the disappearance of the safebreaker Tommy 'Ginger' Marks. There is no doubt now that he was shot by Alfie Gerard and Freddie Foreman but, as usual, there are several reasons on offer behind the killing. The generally accepted one is that a Jimmy Evans had shot Freddie Foreman's brother George in a domestic dispute, and Marks was killed in mistake for Evans when they were out on a breaking exercise. Evans' version is that Marks had been badmouthing Foreman to Dukey Osborne in particular and the underworld in general, saying that he was a grass in cahoots with police officers Tommy Butler and Frank Williams. This had been relayed back to Foreman, who took appropriate action. Since the shooting was close to Vallance Road there are also tales that the Twins told Foreman where he might find Marks and Evans that night.

Foreman denied this. He claims his brother George had been having an affair with Evans' wife Pat, and as a result Marks and Evans had gone to George's front door and let off a shotgun in the direction of George's testicles. Both were therefore due at least a major reprisal, but when Foreman and Alf Gerard caught up with them Evans hid behind Marks and escaped. George Foreman survived the shooting and he and Pat Evans remained together until his death in 2017. Ten years later Gerard and Foreman were acquitted of Marks' murder on the direction of the trial judge.[98]

As for that raid on the Glenrae, nothing was found of any interest. However, on the evening of 10 January 1965 the Twins were arrested there to face charges of demanding money with menaces from McCowan.

When Read and other detectives went to arrest them, a distraught Phoebe Woods almost literally threw herself at Read's feet telling him how grateful she was and that he had saved her life. Under the circumstances, perhaps naively, he did not take a statement from her there and then, instead arranging that she should go to a police station the next day.

It was a serious mistake, because overnight things changed dramatically. The next morning Phoebe appeared at Old Street Magistrates' Court offering to stand bail and telling Read that the Krays' management of the club was an arrangement with which she and her husband were perfectly satisfied. 'The difference between this assured, well-turned out woman and the pathetic wretch who had been grovelling at my feet the evening before was remarkable. I just couldn't believe the transformation', wrote Read. He admitted later he should have arrested Charlie Kray rather than leaving him on the outside to work his magic.[99]

Phoebe Woods standing surety or not, there was no way the trio was going to get bail that morning from the stipendiary magistrate Neil 'Mick' McElligott, most of whose career at the Bar had been as a prosecutor. He had a fearsome reputation and kept tight control over the unruly elements of the area. His reputation was such that if he was seen to be sitting that day a defendant would often go home and get a sick note from a tame doctor which his mother would present half an hour later.

After the senior officer Fred Gerrard told McElligott that there were still two people to be arrested, the Twins were remanded in custody. Teddy Smith was one of the two still missing and the fourth man, the Twins' friend Johnny Francis, sensibly absented himself to Torremolinos. Even after Teddy Smith's arrest, repeated bail applications over the following weeks before McElligott, the Divisional Court and the Lord Chancellor, all failed.

At the committal proceedings Sidney Vaughan was called for the prosecution but very soon had to be treated as a hostile witness. He had made a statement to the local vicar John Foster that he was being paid £40 a week by McCowan, who threatened to stop his money if he failed to give the evidence which he now admitted was false. Nevertheless the magistrate committed the Twins and Smith for trial. Leslie Payne would later make a statement saying that it had been Charlie Kray's very sensible idea to involve a local vicar.

In their application to the Divisional Court the Twins' counsel Petre Crowder put it nicely. Bail was necessary because witnesses needed to be found, and these witnesses only surfaced in Soho between two and three in the morning. The only way of finding them was by sight. Their first names were known, but not their surnames. The defendants had competent and experienced solicitors. As for interfering with witnesses, this was far from the case. Even before McCowan had given evidence at the magistrate's court the police knew that Sidney Vaughan had gone sour on them. As Crowder explained it:

'…a curious situation has arisen. Charles Kray, a brother of the defendants, was telephoned by the employee [Vaughan]; it so happened that an inquiry agent and former police officer William Noble was, fortuitously, with Charles Kray and it seemed that the employee asked if he could, and he did, come round to see Charles Kray. The employee said that his conscience had smitten him, that he had been forced by the complainant to give evidence and that his evidence was untrue. Hardly had he said that he had been forced to give evidence than, it so happened quite by chance, the local parish priest appeared on the scene paying a courtesy visit. Solicitors had arranged for the inquiry agent and Charles Kray to make a statement on oath of what the employee had said, and it was also proposed to take a similar statement from the priest.'

As there had been talk of interference Crowder thought that he should expose these matters to the court.[100] He went on to say that the Twins had been arrested on 6 January and were unlikely to have their case heard until March, meaning 'the two young men would be in custody for two months on a charge of which they would very likely be acquitted'. Bail was nevertheless refused.

The next day however, on 11 February, Lord Boothby showed his worth and did what was required of him. While denying he held any brief for the Twins, he asked in the House of Lords whether 'it is the intention of Her Majesty's Government to imprison the Krays indefinitely without trial'. He was soundly rebuked by Myra Hindley's champion, the normally mild and gentle Lord Longford: 'My noble friend will regret this intervention when he reads it afterwards in cold blood'. Which is about as far as Longford ever went in a reprimand of any kind.

Meanwhile, the Krays' pythons Gerrard and Read had died a few days after their owners were arrested.

The police had searched through papers found in the Kray flats but tried, sometimes without success, to match the scrawled names with people. Unsurprisingly they included: William Noble, who, the police noted, had given evidence for the defence in the case against Charlie and Ronnie at Marylebone; the Nash brothers; Danny Shay from the Podro case, whom they still wrongly thought was Frances' brother; Mickey Bloom, who had been with Ronnie Marwood when PC Summers was killed; Billy Gentry, who they did not recognise but who later went down for a robbery with John McVicar; and several men including Micky Fawcett, Peter Wylde and Billy Exley, whom they thought were involved in collecting protection money. There was also a scattering of entertainers: Lita Rosa and Winifred Atwell, described in the notes as a 'Negro pianist'; the artist Francis Bacon; Barbara Windsor; a couple of American gangsters; two journalists from the *Sunday Times*; and Gordon Goodfellow, Boothby's 'manservant'.

Just before the trial the Twins' lawyer, the extremely clever but extremely dubious Manny Fryde, asked for another £1,500 to instruct counsel and Charlie was dispatched to Lord Boothby to request more of the £40,000 he had received in damages. But when he got there the cupboard was bare with Boothby telling him, 'I've spent it all.'

In those days barristers, jurors, witnesses and defendants on bail all mixed happily with each other in the foyer or the basement tea room of the Old Bailey. Criminals are superstitious, and Paul Wrightson, who had prosecuted Reggie in the Podro case, now defended him. When the trial began on 8 March, after lunch on the second day with McCowan still giving evidence, Fryde claimed that he had been told by a man that he had overheard one of the jurors had told a PC Cuff that he knew all about protection rackets and considered it an open and shut case. The man, who had a criminal record and who had been questioned over the sale of the shares in Esmeralda's Barn, picked out the juror and, despite the man's denials, after legal discussion he was discharged. The trial continued with 11 jurors. Read noted that it was clear the jurors had looked too intelligent and Fryde had made the move in the hope of getting a new and less intelligent group.

Much of the ammunition used by the defence to attempt to discredit McCowan came from Vaughan. Neither of the Twins was called to give evidence but Leslie Payne and Gordon Anderson, another who had been involved in the ill-fated Nigerian project, testified McGowan had wanted to meet the Krays, and Anderson had arranged the meeting. Rodney Auerbach of Montague Gardiner, the Shaftesbury Avenue firm of solicitors who had sent the £5,000 to secure Payne's release in Nigeria, gave evidence that he had been at a meeting to discuss the Twins taking an interest in the Hide-A-Way, and had advised them not to do so. Nipper Read rather sourly noted in his report that at the time Montague Gardiner was owed £300 by the Krays, a bill which was settled after Auerbach gave evidence. The Reverend John Foster duly gave his evidence that he had been at Vallance Road when, quite fortuitously, Vaughan had arrived to make his confession. In fact just after 3 p.m. on 20 January that year,

Detective Sergeant Sidney Hall had watched the priest drive up with Billy Exley, Tommy Brown and Bill Ackerman, but for some reason he was never called to give evidence.

The trial ended when the jury failed to agree, and by the time of the second trial, which began on 29 March, McCowan's background had been thoroughly investigated by another private detective, George Devlin. McCowan again gave his evidence well, telling the jury that he had met with Vaughan in the Music Box, where he said Vaughan told him the Krays would pay any money to have him leave the country. McCowan said he decided to go along with Vaughan and asked for £20,000 down and £30,000 when he got to Tangier. 'Sidney said, "If I don't accept I'll be killed",' McGowan told the court. He also said Vaughan was going to arrange a meeting with Lord Boothby and ask for his help.

In cross examination, however, McCowan admitted he had alleged blackmail in three previous cases and in 1953 had been placed on probation for three years on condition he remained in Murray Royal Hospital after he had been convicted at the Edinburgh High Court on four counts of sodomy. He had broken the terms of his probation and had served four months in January 1956 and another 30 days the previous year for having unlawful relations with a male person.

This time Sidney Vaughan was not called to give evidence by either the prosecution or defence. Now, in addition to Auerbach and the Reverend Foster, a Harry Beckett gave evidence he had met McCowan in the Grave Maurice, who told him he was sorry the Krays were no longer interested. Called to discredit McCowan, who said he had put £6,000 into the club, interior decorator Stanley

Peters said he was still owed money. However, he admitted receiving part-payment and that the rest of the bill was being disputed. Stanley Crowther appeared as a witness for the Twins (despite previously telling the police they were blackmailing him over his homosexual activities), and claimed McGowan had expressed regret to him that they weren't taking an interest in his club.[101] This time, before the defence counsel made their closing speeches, the judge told the jury that if they did not believe McCowan, they should acquit. They did so after retiring for only ten minutes. Reg Kray claimed the trial had cost him his flat, a cottage and 600 acres of land near Bantry. He also tacitly admitted that the jury in the first trial had been nobbled.[102]

The Twins returned to Vallance Road in triumph with family, friends and, most importantly, the press, to greet and cheer them. Their grandfather Cannonball Lee and his wife were there, and he threw a few mock punches for the benefit of photographers, who also took the picture of the three brothers in that now-famous cross-hand-shake. The red-haired Frances Shea wore a pair of fluffy mules to welcome Reggie. 'I love you, darling,' Reggie said, before suggesting they might get married the following week.[103]

Ronnie said they wanted 'a bit of peace and quiet'. There were threats to sue the police for malicious prosecution, but nothing came of them. For his part Boothby wrote a letter of congratulation, saying he never doubted the outcome:

'They gave me a pretty rough time in the House of Lords. But they have been proved wrong and I have been proved right. So to some extent I share in your triumph.'

With their acquittal the Krays effectively now had a licence to run Soho and the West End, and within days they 'bought' the Hide-a-Way, renaming it the El Morocco. Now in charge was a consortium of Gilbert France, the three Krays, Teddy Smith and Freddie Foreman. The Twins threw a party on the opening night and among the glitterati attending were Edmund Purdom, Adrienne Corri, Victor Spinetti, Lita Rosa and Roy Kinnear. Also on parade were Dolly, Violet and Frances Shea. Not to be outdone, Charlie, who had by now taken over the Sammy Lederman show-business agency, said he was managing a pop group from Yorkshire, 'The Shots', who would soon be playing there.

Read and his right-hand man Trevor Lloyd-Hughes were watching from telephone boxes opposite the club, marking down those who went to the party. However, George Devlin spotted them and invited them in. Read was reluctant to go but was unwilling to back down, particularly as Gilbert France also said he should come in. He did so, leaving Lloyd-Hughes outside. Once in the club he was confronted by an irate Ronnie Kray, who was calmed down by Reggie. Read had a look round and left within minutes. The next day he found, to his great annoyance, that the *Express* reporter Percy Hoskins wrote that he had looked in, '…stayed half an hour and drank a good luck toast with the Twins'. Although Hoskins immediately apologised for his mistake, it is a story which despite Read's protests has been continually repeated. The photograph said to be taken of him in the club was in fact of the actor Edmund Purdom.[104]

Much to the regret of her parents, on 19 April 1965 Reggie Kray married Frances Shea at St James the Great in Bethnal Green in what was described by the bridegroom as the East End 'marriage of the year'. He'd been courting her since she was 15 and used her brother Frank as a driver.

Father Hetherington had apparently declined an invitation to officiate and appropriately enough John Foster, who had done so much to secure Reggie's availability, officiated instead. Wearing a blue velvet suit, David Bailey, himself an East Ender, took a photograph of the bride and among the two hundred guests were Diana Dors and Joan Littlewood, the dancers the Clark brothers and various East End boxers such as Ted 'Kid' Lewis and Terry Allen. Boothby sent a congratulatory telegram. Cal McCrystal of the *Sunday Times*, there as a guest, recalls that when the congregation did not respond enthusiastically enough to the first hymn, Ronnie as best man, walked down the aisle waving his hands and saying, 'Sing, fuck you, sing.' The bride's mother pointedly wore black, a demonstration of lèse-majesté which the Krays never forgave.

The reception was held at the Glenrae Hotel, to which the happy couple drove in a Rolls Royce. An unhappy honeymoon was spent in Athens, with rumours that the marriage had not been consummated and allegations that Frances had been revolted by suggestions she should accept anal intercourse. The pair then came home to a flat in the Edgware Road and then moved to the ground floor flat in Cedra Court, just underneath Ronnie's flat where he held his homosexual orgies, known as 'Pink Ballets'.

The marriage continued unhappily and the Twins' cousin Ronnie Hart recalled Frances had a fear of blood, and that Reggie, when drunk, which was often, would torment her by deliberately cutting himself and flicking blood on her. He would leave her downstairs when he went up to join his twin at the parties being held there. A member of the Firm always accompanied her when she went out and when she threatened to leave him he said he would kill her father. Within a matter of weeks Frances returned to her family.

Two years later she was dead. She had changed her name back to Shea and commenced a suit for nullity on the grounds that the marriage had never been consummated. Reggie, fearful that his status as a lover would be compromised, asked that he be allowed to bring the petition rather than Frances, but he delayed and dawdled as her mental health deteriorated. Over the months she took more and more pills, helpfully supplied by the good Dr Blasker, and twice tried to commit suicide. On 7 June 1967 she died at her brother's house in Wimbourne Street, Hackney after taking an overdose. By now the Krays were such public figures that her death was reported on the front page of *The Times*.

At the inquest Dr Julian Silverstone said Frances had been admitted twice to hospital after taking drug overdoses. The coroner Ian Milne said, 'She had a two-year history of personality disorder. Her marriage was on the rocks, though there seems to have been recent hopes of a reconciliation'.[105]

Ronnie had always loathed her, insulting her publicly and constantly trying to claim his brother back from her. Her diary and letters were sold in May 2014, and they describe how unhappy she was and how isolated she felt living at their Marble Arch flat, repeatedly being subjected to Reggie's swearing and drunken, abusive behaviour:

'(Reggie) came in late every night drunk. Got up every morning two minutes to dress, left me all day, came back late at night drunk.

Went to his house – his brother walked in bedroom in underwear, swore at me.

Him and his friend took me to the hospital, he was swearing and shouting at me in the car.

Couldn't stand it anymore – left him. When I was packing my suitcases to leave he told me he would bring up fictitious characters against me.'

After her death her brother Frank Shea, as administrator of his sister's estate, sued Reggie for the £1,000 Frances had lent him a month before the wedding. This was a staggering sum, in today's terms rather over £18,000. Reggie was described in the legal paperwork as 'well known in gambling and sporting circles' and his address given as Luke House, Bigland Street, London. Reggie decided to kill Frank but, because he looked so much like Frances, he could not bring himself to do it personally. He offered the job to Tony Lambrianou, who sensibly declined.

According to Ronnie Hart, Reggie went to the mortuary a number of times talking to her and telling her, 'I'll get even with those bastards [her parents] if it takes the whole of my life, because they killed you.' At her funeral Albert Donoghue was ordered to make a list of those who had not sent flowers – for future reference.

After the funeral, for which he had a five-foot-tall wreath made of red roses in the shape of a heart 'broken' by white roses through the middle, Reggie would regularly visit Chingford Mount cemetery. There he would kneel in front of the grave and cry. Before an Italian marble headstone was erected he had bought a three-foot-high plastic windmill. On one occasion he saw a robin perched on it and began talking to it, saying, according to Hart:

> 'I knew you loved me, I knew you'd come back to me. He dug out the windows of the windmill saying, 'There you are darling, now you can get back in. I'll always come and see you Frankie, you know that because you know how much I love you and I know you love me and will come and see me.'[106]

Once when he and Hart visited her grave on her birthday they found the Sheas visiting at the same time. Mrs Shea accused Kray of killing her daughter, saying that it would do him no good even if he spent £1,000 a week on flowers because 'we will never forgive you and neither will she'. The following week on another visit to the grave, Reggie took the Shea flowers from their pots and destroyed them. Over the following months he tormented her parents, ordering children to scratch Mrs Shea's Mini and sending anonymous messages to her saying her husband had met with an accident or had been killed at work.

After their acquittal in the Hide-A-Way case the Twins occasionally showed some sense. They declined an invitation to speak at the Cambridge Union in a debate entitled 'The Law is an

Ass', saying, 'What's the point of talking about the law? You only get yourself worked up and there's nothing you can do about it.'[107]

The Twins soon lost interest in the El Morocco and after a few changes of management, it was eventually run by Barbara Windsor's husband, Ronnie Knight.

CHAPTER 9
THE KILLING OF
GEORGE CORNELL

One large fly in the Kray ointment was the team run by the Richardson brothers from South London. Originally there were three brothers, Charlie, Eddie and Alan, but Alan had been killed in a boating accident on the Thames. The Twins had fallen foul of Charlie during their time in the military prison at Shepton Mallet when he had refused to kow-tow to them, but relations had improved and at one time Richardson was buying goods from the Kray Long Firm being run in Blenheim Gardens, South London.

Now, through his associates such as the fraudster Brian Mottram, Charlie Richardson was himself running a series of Long Firm frauds south of the river. He had also expanded not only into the East End, the Kray stronghold, where another associate, George Cornell, had set up shop, but also an LF with Billy Stayton in Southend, which the Twins considered their territory.

Although the West End, like Las Vegas and Miami, was regarded as neutral gang territory, there were also signs that the Richardsons were moving into Soho – for example, Eddie Richardson and Mad Frank Fraser were minding Charlie Chester's Casino in Archer Street.

In the days when blue films shown in cinemas generally consisted of buxom and naked German and Scandinavian ladies playing volleyball in long shot, the Richardsons, with the approval of certain police officers, had established a circuit in Bloomsbury of rather more explicit private showings. They were also feeding off a car parking fiddle at Heathrow, discovered by Eddie Richardson and Fraser on their return from a trip to Southport. Attendants were adjusting time clocks which marked tickets so it appeared the cars had been parked for a shorter time than they actually had and were pocketing the difference. The scam had been earning the attendants around £1,000 a week but now the Richardsons, after pointing out the undoubted benefits of their involvement and the inevitable danger of their not having a share, took half. The Twins believed they were getting far too powerful for their own good.

One reputed Richardson enforcer was George Cornell, born in 1930 in the East End to an unmarried couple named Myers. His father, who was reputed to carry a Derringer, had been a member of the Watney Streeters and George Cornell grew up with the Krays.

East End underworld folklore has it that in 1955 Cornell's brother Myer 'Johnnie' Myers, then aged 45, killed a prostitute Nancy Wojtasko, throwing her over the balustrade in a block of flats at Norfolk Buildings, Shoreditch. He was indeed charged with her murder in what was a very odd case. The pair, who had been drinking heavily the night before, were found around 7 a.m. on the morning of 9 March at the bottom of the stairs in the block. She was wearing only stockings and a cardigan, while a coat and shirt had been thrown over her. She died in hospital that afternoon. She had been suffering from syphilis and was partially paralysed following a cerebral haemorrhage a few months earlier. Myers, who already had a number of convictions for assault, made various statements, saying they had been out drinking and she had fallen down the stairs around 1.30 a.m. He had not been able to lift her and had stayed with her until they were found. Other tenants claimed they had heard her call out 'Don't hit me!' at around 3.30 a.m. One woman had looked out and seen the pair before going back to bed. She had brought Nancy a cup of tea when she found she was still there in the morning. It was agreed the lighting was bad and the stone staircase with its narrow steps was dangerous. A pathologist agreed she could have sustained the injuries from falling down the stairs a number of times. Myers was acquitted of both murder and manslaughter just over two months later.[108]

George Cornell himself had served a three-year sentence for slashing a woman. Another brother, Jimmy, ran a drinking club, 'Jim's Inn' off Watney Street market. The boys had later moved south of the river and at some time all except George had legally changed their name to Cornell. Nevertheless, by the 1960s he was known by the same name as his brothers.

There was no love lost between the Krays and George. There had been bad blood between him and Ronnie Kray on a personal level. One story, hotly denied by Kray and his supporters, was that in the early 1960s Ronnie had called Cornell out of the Brown Bear public house in Aldgate and Cornell had promptly knocked him out.

The Twins later claimed that they had looked after him on one of the occasions he had been released from prison, and had even given him new clothes and a pension.[109] Despite the fact they had stepped in and taken over one of his LFs, they regarded him as something of a traitor in leaving his East End origins and defecting to the Richardsons when he married a south London girl. Worse, he had also refused to cut them in on the short-term blue film racket he was running in Bloomsbury with Fraser.

At the time of his death in March 1966, in theory Cornell was a partner with Benny Saher in the Sombrero club in Ann Place off Oxford Street. In reality Cornell was minding Saher. He was also trying to persuade several perfume wholesalers in the East End that they needed protection. He was also believed to have been responsible for an arson attack in the area earlier in the month on 6 March. Other stories about him included one that he had killed a man in South Africa. Had he lived, he certainly would have been charged in the Richardson Torture Case along with the fraudster Brian Mottram.

Although he has generally been painted as a ruthless thug, some people spoke well of Cornell. Former Kray associate, the thief Little Lenny Hamilton, remembered him:

> 'When I went back to work in Billingsgate Fish Market at the age of twenty-six, Georgie Cornell looked after me – he was the hardest man I ever saw on the cobbles but he had a heart of gold as well. He gave me five pounds to buy my mother some flowers and said, "Make sure you give her the fucking change!"... He used to line up all the tramps at the market and give them each half a crown and make sure they got a mug of tea and two slices of

dripping toast. Then with the change, he'd say, "Now go down and buy yourselves a pint."[110]

The barmaid Patricia Kelly who witnessed his killing also liked him:

'I know the books that have been written have said George Cornell was a villain, but in the pub he was just so nice to me. He used to laugh at me about the records I used to play in the pub. I've no idea what the quarrel was about. People have always said it was because he called Ronnie "a big fat pouf", but that was just George. If he'd had a few drinks he'd think that was comical and that others should think it was as well. Then again it has been said that Ronnie got upset because George had come on his manor. That can't have been right. George was a regular drinker in the Beggars.'[111]

The Twins' overall fear was that the astute and far better organised Richardsons would muscle in on their enterprises, in particular a fledgling deal concerning stolen bonds they were negotiating with the American Mafia through Leslie Payne.

By 1966 the Twins, in particular Ronnie, were becoming paranoid and members of the Firm were instructed to kill the essentially genial and gigantic Brian Mottram, more of a fraudster with a serious heart condition than a gangster. The difficulty was that apart from any scruples they might have had killing people, the death penalty was still operating and the rank and file were not too keen on putting themselves on offer. Fortunately for Mottram, none of the Firm really knew what he looked like and when a photograph of the Soho Rangers, a football team composed mainly of South London villains, was found, he was not on it.

None of this stopped Frank Fraser from coming onto the Twins' patch to meet one or other of them. Usually he would come on his own but Albert Donoghue recalled that there was often a car outside the meeting place with men in it who would, he believed, have taken action if Fraser had not emerged by a certain time.

The early hours of the morning of 8 March 1966 saw the end of the Richardsons as a force to be reckoned with in South London. Although their demise took much longer, the day after also saw the beginning of the end of the Krays. Quite how it started depends, like all good gangland stories, on who is telling the tale. The most likely version is that it was a dispute over who should protect the Savoy Social Club, known as Mr Smith's Room or Mr Smith and the Witchdoctor's, in Catford. The club was owned by Well Read Ltd with Patrick McKiernan as the managing director. William McLeish was the manager, while the gaming concession was in the hands of the Manchester club owner Owen Ratcliffe, who had once put a bullet in the ceiling of wrestler Jack Pye's Backpool club.

Mr Smith's, with a full licence until 2 a.m., had been opened in the autumn of 1965 and at first was well regarded. There were nearly 1,900 members; food and drink were available at reasonable prices; there was gambling for relatively small stakes and there was a cabaret with the dancers from the Astor in Berkeley Square bussed over to do a midnight stint. And then it went downhill. Two local faces, Billy and 'Flash' Harry

Hayward, indicated they were looking after the place in return for free drinks, and after the influx of local criminals, genuine members began to desert the club. Visitors failed to sign the entrance book and fees went unpaid. The police had already contacted McLeish about possible protection approaches and he had promised to report any.

In February 1966 Eddie Richardson had approached McLeish and promised to keep the club trouble free. As he had promised, McLeish reported the approach to Detective Supt. Cummings. But there were, said a police report, subsequent troubles:

> 'sufficiently harassing the club manager to induce him to clutch at any chance of suppressing by any means the disagreeable troubles then polluting the atmosphere in the club.'[112]

For Eddie Richardson and Fraser – whose 'mere reputation has silenced more witnesses than any other man in the country', thought Detective Superintendent Tommy Butler – one of the benefits of protecting a club was that they could put their own gaming machines, effectively a licence to print money, on the premises. It was an early if less sophisticated version of today's rule of thumb that anyone who controls a club's doors can control who deals what drugs inside.

There are, of course, many versions of exactly what happened that night. For example, sometimes Frank Fraser somewhat disingenuously suggested that it was all a domestic matter because Billy Hayward had been involved with the wife of one of the Richardson firm. Other times he thought that Owen Ratcliffe, whatever experience he had in the north of England, was simply out of his depth in London. What is certain is that on 7 March managing director Patrick McKiernan and Ratcliffe travelled to the club to meet Richardson and Fraser at around 5 p.m. The pair promised to find them security staff to be approved by the manager McLeish, and they would be paid £75 per week for this service. McKiernan does not appear to have thought this to be outrageous. Fraser and Richardson left the club around 8.30 p.m. and returned about 11 p.m. One gambler had already been warned there was likely to be trouble later. Ratcliffe and McKiernan left around 1 a.m. but by then there was a more general feeling among the staff that there would be trouble that night. The doorman Robert Mansfield took his wife and the cloakroom girl home early.

By about 3 a.m. the club had emptied of customers. Billy and Harry Hayward were still there, along with Peter and Mickey Hennessey,[113] their friend Henry Botton, and Dickie Hart, a fringe member of the Firm described by Reggie as 'a nice feller, a good friend. He wasn't a gangster or anything like that'. However, Hart was no shrinking violet, with a conviction for grievous bodily harm when he stabbed a man in the lung, for which he had received five years at the Old Bailey on 7 October 1957. Hart had brought a gun into the club earlier in the evening when an ex-boxer who was on the door at the time, took it from him and hid it in a girl's handbag. On the Richardson side were Fraser, Jimmy Moody, Billy Stayton, Harry Rawlings and George Porritt, who in 1961 had been reprieved after accidentally shooting and killing his stepfather in a quarrel between the Porritts and the Copelands, another south London family.

Around 3:30 a.m. Eddie Richardson said he had been asked to close the club but there would be one more round of drinks which he would pour. It was, said Tommy Butler, 'a classic movement in which one mob will inform another that they are interested in the future of the club and its operation'. Now Dickie Hart told the one remaining croupier to go into the kitchen. Billy Hayward told her to stay but Hart repeated the order. Now, while Eddie Richardson fought Peter Hennessey in a 'straightener', general fighting broke out and the croupier thought that Richardson had been hit from behind with a bottle. In the fracas Hart somehow retrieved his gun. When the fight spilled out of the club and into Farley Street, Hart shot Fraser in the thigh and residents heard cries of 'Shoot him' and 'Kill the bastard' before a wiser man called out, 'Don't, it'll be bloody murder'. Dickie Hart was then shot dead. His coat had been pulled down over his arms so he was effectively powerless. The forensic evidence was that he had been shot in the back, probably by someone on the ground. There was no bullet mark on the jacket, only his shirt, and the police believed it was Fraser, now lying on the ground, who had shot him.[114]

The locals called the police and, it was alleged, Billy Stayton carried Fraser away before dumping him in a front garden, where he was found with the murder weapon under his body. As for Eddie Richardson, he had been shot in the buttocks.

With his death Dickie Hart achieved iconic status.[115] Fraser was later acquitted of his murder, but the police had been quick to round up the Richardsons' team. As of that night, they ceased to be an effective force and were certainly no longer a threat to the Twins. Although there are no other accounts of Cornell being there, over the years the Krays exploited the incident, circulating stories that George Cornell, now given the soubriquet 'The Executioner', had been in the club that night and was actually Hart's killer. It has been used as yet another excuse for his subsequent death.

This should have ended any thought of trouble between the Krays and the Richardsons and according to Micky Fawcett, Reggie was ecstatic when he heard the news, almost literally dancing in the street.[116] He had some reason to celebrate. Charlie Richardson was out of the country; Fraser and Eddie Richardson were in hospital, with Richardson charged with affray and Fraser about to be charged with murder, for which there was no likelihood of bail; and the rest of the team who had been in the club had been charged with affray. Others such as Jimmy Moody were on their toes. It was surely highly unlikely the remainder of the Richardsons would be able to mount any sort of punitive raid, but the Twins put it about that Eddie Richardson and Fraser, the latter with his broken thigh, were planning an attack outside The Lion in Tapp Street on the following Saturday.

On the next evening, Wednesday 9 March, George Cornell died from a bullet in the head while sitting in the saloon bar of the Blind Beggar public house.

The reason for his death is usually given that some months earlier he had publicly insulted Ronnie Kray, sensitive about both his weight and sexuality in either Al Burnett's nightclub The Stork Room or the Astor Club. Worse, this had been both in the presence of other members of the Richardsons and also in front of some visiting American Mafiosi with whom both the Krays and the Richardsons were doing, or hoping to do, business. Now, according to Ronnie

Kray in *Our Story*, Cornell remarked in front of the Americans, 'Take no notice of Kray. He's just a big, fat poof.' He had just about signed his death warrant.

A variation on this theme is told by Billy Frost, the one-time driver of the Twins:

> 'The argument was over a fellow named Nicky [Mickey] Morris. Georgie Cornell told Nicky's mum, May, that Ronnie was after Nicky and "You know he's a fat pouf," and this got back to Ronnie and Ronnie was furious. He had words with Georgie about it, but then Georgie started telling other people, ignoring Ronnie.'

According to Frost, Reggie later stabbed Morris in the arm.[117]

However, in *My Story* Ronnie, rewriting history, gave his version:

> 'I had a pact with some people. Influential people, that if Cornell and the gang he was with − the Richardsons, south of the river − if they started a war, I would do something about it.
>
> Well they did start a war. There was a battle at Mr Smith's Club which was started by the Richardsons and Cornell. A very good friend of ours called Richard Hart got killed in the fight, yet he was just an innocent bystander.
>
> So I kept my word. Even though others didn't, I still kept to the pact. I went and done Cornell. I got a message that he was involved in the business at Mr Smith's. I got

a message asking if I would keep my word. When I give my word, I keep it. I never thought about the police, I just done it. Cornell deserved it. He was a flash, arrogant bastard. He was a bully.'

According to Micky Fawcett, Ron – 'He thought he was Churchill' – wanted the Richardsons eliminated, and to this end he had proposed an alliance between the Firm, Freddie Foreman, the Hennesseys and others from South London. The Nashes were also approached but were simply not interested.[118] The message which came back to the Hennesseys however was that if things went off, the Krays would be backed to the hilt.

The real reasons are more complex. In fact the principal suggestion is that it was because Cornell had been deputed to find out who had knee-capped his friend Jimmy Andrews from Clerkenwell, shot as he walked in Rotherfield Street, Islington on 4 March. Andrews – described by Ronnie Diamond as 'a spiteful little man. Little and deadly. He specialised in cutting people, especially their Achilles tendons' – had refused to split the proceeds of a swindle with the Krays and now Ronnie was the name in the frame. At a south London wedding that weekend Cornell had been asked to go north of the river and kill Kray. Ironically, he had argued that things should be left until they were absolutely sure.

At the wedding reception it was finally decided that Cornell and a younger man, John Daly, should go to see Andrews in hospital to get his version of the shooting. On 9 March after seeing Andrews, Cornell, Daly and Albert 'Albie' Woods, a small-time thief with convictions going back to 1941 when he was fined £5 at the Mansion House for looting, stopped at the Blind Beggar for a drink.[119]

There is yet another version of why Cornell was shot, this time offered by Micky Fawcett, who almost fulfilled the role of the Twins' *consigliere* until the killings started, that is. Fawcett claimed that immediately after the Mr Smith's club fight, a drunken Billy Stayton told an Astor Club hostess he was going to petrol bomb Freddie Foreman's pub the Prince of Wales in Lant Street. In Fawcett's absence the Firm member Nobby Clarke was dispatched to confirm this story and he returned to say it was true. By this time Cornell was in the Blind Beggar and an incensed Ronnie set off to kill him.

Later the Twins, somewhat curiously, decided that Cornell's death was really the fault of Billy Stayton and as a result in turn he should be shot. At a meeting in Walthamstow it was arranged that Stayton would be driven to Hackney Marshes, where Fawcett would shoot him. Eventually sense prevailed. Fawcett declined to take the job and broke off his association with the Twins. 'Ronnie made a couple of attempts to entice me onto the manor but I stayed away,' he recalled.[120]

The most attractive explanation so far as the Krays were concerned was that Cornell was reconnoitering for that rumoured attack on the Lion in Tapp Street the following weekend.

A final explanation, and one dismissed by Tommy Butler, was that the killing had been arranged by Charlie Richardson. The story came from the lorry thief Derek Armstrong. He maintained that Cornell had failed to account to Richardson for the proceeds of one lorry and that he had paid the Krays to have him put away. Asked by Butler why he believed this, Armstrong said that 'firstly Charlie wouldn't have the guts to do it' and that after Richardson had read the newspapers he had told Armstrong, 'I'll have to settle up the cost, the Krays did a nice clean job'.[121]

According to Patricia Kelly (a pseudonym), the barmaid of the Blind Beggar and the single mother of two young children, Cornell used the pub regularly with his wife and brother Jimmy. It was however perhaps reckless to drink on Kray territory the day after Hart's death. It was also rumoured Cornell and been pursued and slashed earlier by the Glasgow hard man Tarzan Wilson, employed by the Krays. Another story, that he had been shot at earlier outside the Blind Beggar, was discounted by the police.

It is certain that Ronnie was drinking in The Lion when he heard that Cornell was in the Blind Beggar about ninety seconds away by car. He ordered Scotch Jack Dickson to drive him and Ian Barrie to Vallance Road, where he collected a Mauser pistol, and then on to the Beggars. Dickson was told to wait outside with the car engine running.

There were about half a dozen people in the bar that evening, including two who knew both Ronnie Kray and George Cornell. At 8.30 p.m. the barmaid put on her favourite record, *The Sun Ain't Gonna Shine Anymore* by the Walker Brothers, and was talking to Cornell when Ronnie Kray and Ian Barrie walked in. They went over to Cornell, who said, 'Look who's here. Let's get a drink.' Kray then shot him at point blank range. The bullet exited the rear of Cornell's head and then hit a wall in the bar. As a distraction Barrie fired shots into the ceiling. The terror-stricken Patricia Kelly ran to hide in the cellar until all she could hear was the needle stuck in the groove of the record and she realised she was safe.[122]

The bar was now empty except for Cornell and an old man still sitting at his table. The barmaid loosened Cornell's tie and was trying to stop the blood from his head with tea towels when ambulance staff arrived. He was taken to the London Hospital and then to the Maida Vale hospital, where he died.

The police had little to go on. Albie Woods, who was later convicted of conspiracy to pervert the course of justice over the Richardson Torture Trial, had very sensibly removed glasses from the bar so there were no fingerprints left.

Dickson first drove Ronnie back to The Lion and then there was a general exodus first to the Stow Club, the spieler in Walthamstow High Street. From there it was on to the nearby Chequers where Reggie bought his brother a clean suit. He also took the two guns and gave them to Charlie Clarke to throw in the canal. The Firm had a contact, a nurse at the London Hospital, and received regular bulletins throughout the evening. When the news of Cornell's death came through, Ronnie gave a cheer and the team, fearing they would be regarded as traitors if they did not, sycophantically joined in. At least Sammy Lederman said, 'Ronnie, you're a cold-blooded murderer'.

Later Ronnie Kray wrote in *Our Story*:

> 'I felt fucking marvellous. I have never felt so good, so bloody alive, before or since. Twenty years on and I can recall every second of the killing of George Cornell. I have replayed it in my mind millions of times.'

Nevertheless, when he was in the lavatory in The Chequers cleaning himself with Vim, he was sick.

Fringe Firm members the Teale brothers were then press-ganged into putting Ronnie up at David Teale's flat in Moresby Road, Hackney. In a statement made to the police, David's wife Christine said she was in bed when 'Ronnie and Reggie, Ian and Jack (Scotsmen) and a few others (including the other Teale brothers) came to the house'. As she got out of bed Ronnie said, 'Isn't she lovely?' and asked if he could stay the night. The Krays said they would sleep on the floor. Barrie and Ronnie Hart slept on camp beds in the lounge.

They seem to have treated the place as their own. Next morning Ronnie woke Christine and asked her to make tea. Alfie wanted to go home, but the Krays wouldn't allow it and for a time insisted on a member of the Firm accompanying the Teales wherever they went.

In the following days there were a number of visitors including some of the Nash brothers, Billy Exley, Pat Connolly, Albert Donoghue, Jack 'The Hat' McVitie, Sammy Lederman, and Nobby Clarke. The kindly Dr Blasker came round to give Ronnie his medication. Exley was sent out to collect two shotguns. Parties were held and there was so much noise that neighbours called the police to complain.[123]

Then all of a sudden Ronnie and Reggie left. The police had visited the previous night on the pretext that a burglar was being sheltered in the flat, and now Reggie took a flat in a block near Manor House.

In the second week of April, along with Bobby Teale, Albert Donoghue and John Dickson, the Twins left for Saffron Walden and stayed under the name of Lee at the Saffron Hotel with various other members of the Firm. They met up with Geoff Allen and the hotelier

Arthur Bray. They took over the bar and wanted to be served after-hours drinks. After a full-scale row, Bray told Geoff Allen they would have to leave and they moved to the University Arms and then on to the Garden House Hotel. At the time it was thought, wrongly, they were planning a raid on a local Westminster Bank, but robbery was never a part of the Kray make-up.

After the shooting, and using the name Davidson, Ian Barrie lived in Kilburn for a while. He later left for Ireland with John Dickson.

Back in the East End it was an open secret who had shot Cornell. Three days after the killing the barmaid Patricia Kelly told the pipe-smoking Detective Inspector Edward Tebbett that she knew the killer was Ronnie Kray. Indeed she had mentioned this to the landlord Patsy Quill, who had told her, 'Well, you might just as well be six foot under'. Reggie claims in *Born Fighter* that he spoke to her and offered her money. She denies this story and is backed up by Albert Donoghue: 'She was contacted and told to meet me in a neutral pub. I was to pump her about what she told the police but thankfully she never came'. In *Our Story* Ron Kray claims she should have been threatened not to identify them, but she was left alone.

Albie Woods was apparently 'spoken to' by a member of the Firm. On 12 March Tebbett had also spoken to Johnny Dale, who had told him Ronnie Kray was the killer but added he would not make a statement and was scared even to leave the police station. It was also claimed Dale had been in the lavatory at the time.

Inspector James Axon was in charge of the investigation, but the barmaid did not get on with him:

'Mr Axon didn't know how to talk to East Enders. You don't have to be an East Ender to do it, but you have to know how.'[124]

Try as the officers might, they could not get her to make a statement implicating Ronnie Kray. Until their deaths, and even after, Patricia Kelly remained terrified of the Twins. Meanwhile Ronnie put it about that Cornell had been killed by Jimmy Evans.

The identity of the man 'Ian' who was with Ronnie (Ian Barrie) was unknown, and for a time Glasgow gang leader Arthur Thompson was in the frame for the murder. At the time Thompson was making regular visits to London, travelling by Jaguar or flying from Renfrew airport, to see the Cantonese-speaking Frankie McGowan who owned the Blue Gardenia club in Soho and who is credited with the introduction of the Chinese into Gerrard Street. Thompson was thought to run several pitch-and-toss schools in Glasgow and one in London.

Just how friendly Thompson was with the London teams once again depends on who is telling the story. Certainly when the robber Robert 'Andy' Anderson got over the Wandsworth wall during the celebrated Ronnie Biggs escape on 8 July 1965 and literally turned up on the doorstep of Eddie Richardson and Frank Fraser's Atlantic Machines in Charlotte Street, the latter was able to turn to Thompson for help. Within forty-eight hours Thompson met Fraser and Anderson in Edinburgh and hid Anderson for months until he developed itchy feet when he was sent to Bobby McDermott, the then king of Manchester.

There is an almost certainly apocryphal story that when Thompson once heard the Krays wished to see him he walked into the Regency, produced a shotgun, made one Twin kiss the backside of the other and then, backing out of the club, said, 'You'll no' forget me now'.[125] Files at the National Archives show that he was regarded as a close friend of the Twins and the police thought he had possibly killed George Cornell on their behalf.

The description of 'Ian' was of a twenty-six or twenty-eight-year-old man, around 6ft in height, light brown hair, spiky, pale complexion and a noticeable scar on the right side of his neck and one on his right hand. The description was nothing like Thompson, and while a man named 'Ian T' was found in the Scottish records, he did not have a scar on the side of his face.

A letter was sent to the police suggesting that 'Ian's' last conviction was in Dublin. This wasn't far from the truth. Barrie and Scotch Jack Dickson had undertaken a spot of work while on holiday in Ireland and as a result had been imprisoned for shop breaking in Enniskillen on 7 April 1965. Dickson had received nine months and Barrie a month less.

Meanwhile the story goes that Cornell's widow Olive, and his brother Eddie, or possibly Jimmy, had visited Vallance Road, where she threw a brick at a window. She was fined £1 by the magistrate at Thames Court the next day but, because she was a woman, the Twins generously left her alone. Other accounts suggest it was Roy Hall who fired shots at the windows and was confronted by an irate Violet Kray who told him to go away and not disturb her boys, who were asleep. And, like all good gangsters who obey their own and other people's mothers, he rather ignominiously obeyed.[126] For a time the Twins ordered Hart, Exley and Connolly to stand guard each evening in Vallance Road. While Hart was on duty Olive came round yelling, 'I know you killed my George. He wasn't frightened of you and neither am I.' Aunt May confronted Olive, who then hit her with her handbag and headed off. Donoghue and other members of the Firm however were issued with small axes, bought by Ronnie, and told to chop up the offending Eddie Cornell. 'All we did was put the word round we were looking for him and he got the message and disappeared', says Donoghue.[127]

In fact, as she told the police, Olive Cornell went to Vallance Road three times. On 14 March she spoke to Charlie, asking him, as he also had two children, how he felt about the killing. His reply goes unrecorded. She went again to try to see the Twins but this time only spoke to their parents. 'They became aggressive with me,' she told the police, 'but I did not accuse the Krays of anything'. She did, however, tell old Charlie and Violet that their sons were 'puffs'. More seriously, her father had died a few months earlier and left her a cottage at Sutton Valence near Maidstone. After she was arrested over the window the cottage was badly damaged in a mysterious fire. No arrests were made. There was also talk of poisoning her, with George Osborne's wife Jeanette to be asked to be the poisoner, but it came to nothing.

As the summer went by, Scotland Yard detectives discussed the case with David Hopkin, from the office of the Director of Public Prosecutions, in particular about holding an identification parade.

One man had said he would definitely be able to recognise the man who had shot Cornell. Another said he saw a man who fitted the description of Kray coming out of the pub but a police report described him as 'a well-known flight of fancy' man. At the end of July a conference was held. Hooter Millen was against an ID parade. He was convinced Albie Woods, who had given a detailed description of the gunman, would deliberately fail to pick out Ronnie, so strengthening his claim that he was not the killer. He also believed that even if one man did make an identification, the witnesses would be got at. By now Tommy Butler was sure Barrie was the second man. However, on 29 July Hopkin advised there was no reason not to try to hold a parade.

So on 4 August Tommy Butler had the Twins arrested and put them with Tommy Cowley on an identification parade. Millen was proved right. The parade itself was something of a farce. After a friend of the Krays had pointed out the danger she was in, Patricia Kelly, the now even more terrified barmaid, point blank refused to attend it and Butler, whom she rather liked, did not force her. As Woods made a wrong identification, a second man who did co-operate was simply not certain that Ronnie was the gunman.

The trio were released and a triumphant Ronnie told reporters he had been well fed, being given sausage, beans, pie and chips. 'Our Mum has been very worried – it's her birthday today – she's 56'.[128]

Immediately after the failed parade, a letter in August 1965 to Tommy Butler read:

'SIR

YOU HAD THE RIGHT ONES FOR THE MURDER OF GEORGE CORNELL THE KRAY TWINS DONE IT. PEOPLE IN THE BLIND BEGGER KNOW YOU CAN EXPECT ANOTHER MURDER IN EAST END SOON THEY WILL BE THE GUILTY ONES WATCH THEM'

Another letter which arrived on 9 August 1965 advised the police:

'Keep plugging at it. Ronnie Kray did the shooting. Try the Cypriot member of their gang. He will crack.'

But there was to be no more 'plugging' for the foreseeable future. Butler returned to Scotland Yard and the Krays became more and more convinced that, if not actually immortal, at the very least they were invincible.

It was time for a holiday and on 13 September 1965 the Twins arrived in Tangier in a six-seater plane from Hastings, refuelling in France. They stayed at the Hotel Resident Bahia, where they met up with Billy Hill and his girlfriend Gipsy, with whom he was now living and running a nightclub. With them were John Barrie and Reggie's then girlfriend Christine Boyce and they all went swimming at the El Minzah, one of the city's best hotels. There were stories circulating in London that Harry Roberts, later convicted of the 1966 murder of three policemen at Shepherds Bush, was also in the city, associating with a homosexual who ran a club under the Hotel Tangier.[129] While there, Ronnie is said to have made a boy kiss his feet and fell in love with another whom he wanted to bring back to England.

At the time Billy Hill might have been a welcome visitor to Morocco but as far as the local police were concerned, the Twins were not. Ordered to leave Tangier, they returned to England on 23 September without Ronnie's boy.

Later, according to Robin McGibbon's *The Kray Tapes*, while in Broadmoor in 1989 Ronnie once more rewrote history by saying that he had heard Cornell was going to kill him and had simply got in there first. 'Best way, innit?' As a further exercise in self-justification Kray would also wrongly claim that Cornell had told him he had killed Ginger Marks: 'I was only killing a killer'.[130]

For some time, it was fashionable to order a 'Luger and lime' in the Beggars.

CHAPTER 10
THE KILLING OF FRANK MITCHELL

Within days of Cornell's killing, the Krays began to organise the escape from Dartmoor prison of the giant Frank Samuel Mitchell, known as 'The Mad Axeman', then serving a life sentence. It was something Ron Kray described as 'The greatest coup, the most brilliant stunt, ever pulled by the Kray Twins.'[131]

As usual, various reasons, some more convincing that others, have been suggested for the Twins' decision to arrange Mitchell's escape, leading ultimately to his murder on 23 December 1966. Ronnie says their decision was totally altruistic, claiming the move was an attempt to force the Home Office's hand in setting a release date for Mitchell. Another suggestion was that Mitchell was needed to help them eliminate Frank Fraser, Billy Stayton, Jimmy Moody and the Richardsons. This simply does not wash; by the time Mitchell escaped, Fraser and the Richardsons had been safely locked up for several months, and Stayton and Jimmy Moody had vanished. A third reason given is that Mitchell had been in prison with Ronnie and had saved him from a beating. A fourth is that he and Reggie had had a homosexual relationship. And finally it seemed the Krays were beginning to lose their popularity in the East End. More sensible associates, such as Fawcett, had distanced or were distancing themselves and some were beginning to refer to them irreverently as Gert and Daisy, after the two East End music hall and radio comediennes Gert and Daisy Waters. The escape would restore their status in the eyes of the community.

Born in 1929 Mitchell, himself an East Ender and one of seven children, had a dreadful criminal record. Two trips to Borstal in his teens were followed by three months' imprisonment for possessing a stolen revolver. His early sentences were for theft and shop breaking and he received 21 months' imprisonment in March 1953 and three years in December 1954. In the first two days of this sentence he attacked a warder and was flogged. In July 1955 he was certified insane and was sent to Rampton, a secure mental hospital in Nottinghamshire. In January 1957 he escaped and while on the run broke into a house and hit the owner over the head with an iron bar. He was sentenced to nine years but within three months he was again certified insane and was sent to Broadmoor.

While he was there he wrote in September 1957 to the Commissioner of Police confessing to the long-unsolved murder of 35-year-old Dorothy Edith Wallis. Known as Daisy, she lived in Wembley with her parents and ran a none-too-successful typing agency in Holborn. On 15 August 1949 she had been stabbed to death in her office. Various suggestions were advanced as a motive: a robbery gone wrong, a jealous lover, a sex attack and even that she had become involved in the post-war black market. None stood up, and of 300 sets of fingerprints taken in her office all the owners except one were eliminated, and the one remaining set belonged to a person without criminal convictions. Mitchell did, however, have convictions for office breaking but when officers were sent to interview him it seems he could have read most of what he knew in the newspapers. Until he had escaped from Rampton he had no convictions for violence and being a blond six-foot giant, he did not resemble the Italianate-looking man seen hurrying down an alleyway around the time of the murder. The general opinion was that Mitchell just wanted to get out of Broadmoor and saw his confession as a means to an end. The case remains open and there are vague suggestions it might have been a lesbian attack. In those days women usually wore gloves outside their homes, something which would account for the lack of fingerprints.[132]

It took Mitchell another twelve months to get out of Broadmoor but in July 1958 he escaped again. He had cut through the bars of his cell with a hacksaw and, leaving a dummy in his bed, climbed over the main wall. On the run, he broke into a private home and held a married couple hostage with an axe, ever after to be dubbed in the press as 'The Mad Axeman'. Apparently insane when he scaled the wall, there was no question of his being insane by the time of his recapture. In October 1958 he received ten years and life imprisonment to run concurrently. Sent to Hull, he beat a warder during an attempted mass escape and in 1962 was birched for slashing another officer. In the September that year he was sent to Dartmoor.

There Mitchell seems to have settled down, and was taken off the escapers' list. In May 1964 it was recommended that he should be allowed to work outside the prison and his behaviour apparently continued to improve. He worked on model cars in his cell, continued a strict exercise routine and bred budgerigars. In September 1966, he was transferred to a loosely supervised 'Honour Party' working in a nearby quarry, but what he wanted above all was a release date, something which had been promised and then denied him. Instead of working on the quarry, he would go off riding the Dartmoor ponies or a motorbike he had bought from a local farmer, drinking in the Elephant's Nest in Horndon, purchasing drink to take back into the prison and having sex with local women, all with money supplied by the Twins. He was not alone in scarpering off for sex. Jackie Bowyer, the model wife of the cat burglar Peter Scott, another long-term prisoner at the time, would bring a van down with a mattress on which they would have sex in an effort to get her pregnant.

In fact, while discipline on the Honour Party was lax, the warders were simply not physically strong enough to handle Mitchell. Since the practice of shooting attempted escapees had been discontinued, there was little they could have done with him. One officer explained to Lord Mountbatten when he was preparing his report into prison escapes:

> 'If Mitchell had escaped at any time of the day, whether he was with me or away from me, there was nothing I could do to prevent him. My duty as an officer working alone would have been to collect the remaining members of the party and walk or run approximately three miles to the telephone kiosk at Peter Tavy... I know of no one who would argue with Mitchell on his own.'[133]

The plan to free Mitchell began as early as 10 March 1966, the day after the murder of Cornell, when Firm member Pat Connelly, mini-cab owner 'Fat' Wally Garelick (calling himself Jacob) and Connelly's 'wife' (in reality Garelick's girlfriend) visited Mitchell at Dartmoor. The visits by various members of the Firm continued sporadically throughout the summer and autumn, including Reggie in disguise accompanied by the boxer Ted 'Kid' Lewis, who was giving a talk to the prisoners.

Visiting arrangements inside this high-security prison were just as lax. Because of the distance visitors had to travel, they would often stay in the area for two or three days and make daily visits. If a prisoner had not used up his monthly visits and someone turned up without a visiting order, the prisoner would be asked if he wanted to see them. If he did, they would be allowed in. No checks were made on possible criminal records. Before and after a visit the prisoner was given a basic rubdown search. Visitors were not.

On 31 May Garelick was back, this time as Mr Connolly, along with his girlfriend whom he had met at the Regency. She was again Mrs Connolly and later gave evidence at the subsequent trial as Miss A.

From September onwards, Mitchell spoke to Ronnie Kray on the telephone and on 13 October Billy Exley and Charlie Kray, using the name Wylie, went to see him. There were two more visits by members of the Firm, on 4 and finally on 11 December, to tidy up the escape details. The next day Mitchell went with a working party to repair fencing on Bagga Tor. The weather closed in and the men stayed in a hut playing cards. At 11.30 a.m. Mitchell asked for permission to go and feed the ponies. He was not back by one o'clock, but no one reported his absence. Nor was he back at 3.45 p.m. when they realised he was missing.

By then Mitchell had made his way to Peter Tor, where he was collected in a black Humber hired by Billy Exley and driven by Teddy Smith along with Albert Donoghue. He was well on his way to London to a flat sourced by Charlie Kray in Ladysmith Avenue near the East London Cemetery.[134] He had been given clothes belonging to Tommy Brown, the only member of the Firm who approximated his size.

The journey back to London was not without incident. First, Mitchell attacked Teddy Smith, who Mitchell believed was about to blow the whistle on him. When Donoghue pointed out Old Ford Road where Mitchell's parents lived, he wanted to stop and see them, but he was denied permission.

It was suggested he could stay with the Krays' parents but for once in his life Charlie Kray put his foot down. Another option was staying at Nobby Clarke's parents' but when they arrived, Clarke sensibly told them his father was ill. Now Mitchell would stay with the wannabee Lennie Dunn, who was to receive £500 for his troubles. Three quarters of an hour after Mitchell was reported missing, he was safely in Dunn's flat at Ladysmith Avenue. The next day his prison clothes and possessions including the sheath knife were found near Widdon Down on the A30.

For the first few days all went well. Letters to *The Times* and *Daily Mirror* were written on Mitchell's behalf by Smith, which he painstakingly copied. Each demanded a release date and had his signature and thumbprint for identification purposes. The letter to the *Daily Mirror* read:

'19/12/66

To the Editor
The DAILY MIRROR

Sir,
The reason for my absence from Dartmoor was to bring to the notice of my unhappy plight. To be truthful I am asking for a possible Date of release. From the age of 9 I have not been completely free, always under some act or other.

Sir, I ask you where is the fairness of this, I am not a murderer or sex maniac nor do I think I am a danger to the Public. I think that I have been more than punished for the wrongs I have done. I am ready to give myself up if I can have something to look forward to. I do not intend to use any violence at any time should I be found, that is why I left a knife behind in my prison things.

Yours sincerely
Frank Mitchell'

The letter next day to *The Times* was in similar vein.

At first Roy Jenkins, the Home Secretary, said he would meet Mitchell but, after an outcry, insisted this would only happen after his surrender.

Within days Mitchell became bored. The Krays did not dare let him out of the flat in case he was recognised and so Mitchell found he had exchanged one prison cell for another. And, after all the years he had spent in jail, Mitchell wanted regular sex.

So a week later, Lisa, a 33-year-old nightclub hostess from Leeds and who worked as a hostess at Joe Wilkins' Winston's nightclub under a Swedish name, was forcibly recruited by the red-haired Tommy Cowley, whom she knew and with whom she had had a few one-night stands. With him were Albert Donoghue and Reggie Kray, who told her she would have the 'respect of the East End'. Although she was paid £100, generously increased to £130, for just under a week she also effectively became a prisoner. When they met years later Nipper Read was impressed with her:

'I liked that woman. She was very, very interesting. She could hold a conversation with anybody. She had a broader knowledge than anyone would give her credit for. She took an interest, as a good hostess should.'[135]

She had left the club wearing a black evening dress, and the next day Billy Exley drove her to her own flat to pick up some clothes. There she left a message for her flatmate, Valerie. 'Half the rent is here, and I will be away for a few days. I'll be back in time for the weekend.'

Lisa was watched the whole time; even when she was in the bathroom the door was left open. She attempted to escape twice. The first time, she told the jury at the Old Bailey in the trial for Mitchell's murder, '…was the first night, the wire was over the door of the bedroom for the electric fire and I fell over it. I didn't see it, and I made a noise.' She received a spanking, hard but not too painful, from Mitchell. The second time when she tried to get out of the bedroom window he merely explained that he was only trying to protect her. She told the jury that Reggie Kray had spoken to her while visiting the flat. 'He said that if I ever told anybody no matter how long or where, they would always find me… well, I would die. They would kill me.'[136]

And now, curiously enough, she began to feel sorry for Mitchell. Both were prisoners. For a while he calmed down, having sex with Lisa and giving demonstrations of his strength by lifting his minders on each arm.

This interlude did not last. The Twins stopped coming to see Mitchell and a proposed visit to his mother never materialised. In turn Mitchell began to issue threats that he would come to find them at Vallance Road or one of the clubs.

Meanwhile the Kray Twins had other troubles of their own making. Ronnie Kray was in hiding to avoid having to give evidence at the trial of police officer Leonard Townshend on a charge of bribery. John Rigbey recalled:

'The Krays liked dreadful two-bar pubs where no one else went. They used The Horns and then they moved to the Baker's Arms, a filthy little pub in Northiam Street off Mare Street. Len Townshend was not frightened of anybody – he'd steam right into them – and the allegation was he told Ronnie he could drink there without anyone troubling him but it was going to cost him 50 quid a week. And Ronnie, forgetting all the rules of the East End, went and had him nicked. I think that was when the East End started to wonder what the Twins were really all about. You didn't do that even to a copper.'[137]

Much has been made of the Krays' obeisance to the East End code of not even grassing up a police officer, but in this case Ronnie had swept that aside and made a complaint to Scotland Yard. This was an ill-considered, but not necessarily unconsidered, move. After the initial alleged approach by Townsend, Ronnie had arranged for the private inquiry agent George Devlin to go to the pub with an assistant and make a tape of the conversation he was having with Townsend. The tapes were then delivered to Manny Fryde's employer, the solicitor Jacob Sampson, who on 12 August made the formal complaint.

It was backed by statements from a collection of Kray acolytes including Teddy Smith and the publican Eric Marshall, who said Townshend told him the Krays could use the pub on his terms.

Scotland Yard believed that provided the voices on the tapes were those of Kray and Townshend, there was a strong case against him.

On 15 August 1966 the trap was sprung and Townshend took a sealed envelope with £50 in it from the licensee of the Baker's Arms. When he was arrested he claimed he thought the envelope contained information and he was being set up. On the latter point he was certainly correct.

Ronnie however, began to have second thoughts, and in turn, his acolytes backed off. On 11 October 1966 Teddy Smith, John Barrie and, curiously, George Devlin all went to Manny Fryde's office where they made statements that while their allegations over Townshend were true they did not wish to go to court to give evidence. Nevertheless the prosecution went ahead.

There were reported sightings of Ronnie Kray but nothing came of them and, with the first jury disagreeing, shortly before the second trial in the summer of 1967, he was said to be living in a caravan in Steeple Bay and waterskiing on the Blackwater River. This turned out to be his brother Charlie.

Despite Ronnie's continuing absence, the case went ahead and after two juries had disagreed, on 18 July 1967 the prosecution offered no evidence on the third go round. Although Townshend admitted he had made false entries in the duty book, no disciplinary proceedings were taken against him. He was moved from G to J division at Leyton and given 'friendly advice'.[138] When he re-emerged, Ronnie justified his conduct, saying, 'I did this because they are always verballing people and now it's our turn.'[139]

As for Mitchell, the Krays quickly realised that they no longer had control of him. He had to go, and it was to Freddie Foreman, the formidable Alf Gerard and his running mate Jerry Callaghan that the Twins turned for help.

Foreman thought Ronnie's request, coming at it did just before Christmas, was something of an imposition. He had plenty of things to do over the holiday without having to kill Mitchell and dispose of the body. Foreman thought of it as something of a mercy killing. Mitchell was never going to come out of prison and it was in effect a form of euthanasia. 'It was the best, most merciful thing for Frank Mitchell.'[140]

Of Gerard, Albert Donoghue said, 'We were none of us nice, but you wouldn't turn your back on him.'[141] 'I thought of him as an original member of Murder Incorporated,' said Mickey Bailey:

'Alfie Gerard was all right. The likes of Gerard wouldn't tolerate things as they do today. They wouldn't tolerate a bully or a car thief. He wasn't very tall but he was a very nasty man. Never pulled his punches. He probably killed dozens of people.'

Another London face thought:

'You'll hear so many versions. He was a man who I would class as a man's man. He was a forthright man. If he had something to say he would say it. He was a very dangerous man. I wouldn't hazard a guess at how many people he'd killed because he and his team had been killing people for years. Callaghan, Foreman and Gerard was Murder Incorporated and they didn't advertise the fact either. They kept a very low profile. Out of villains in London this century he was probably amongst the most dangerous ten.'[142]

In contrast Callaghan was described as 'very much liked, knew everybody, quite clever, never caught on a raid'. Gerry Parker, an old Spot man turned bookmaker, thought well of Callaghan and said in conversation with the author in January 2019, 'You didn't even need to write down his bet. If he lost, the money was there on the nail'.

Francis Wyndham of the *Sunday Times* recalled that when he went to see Ronnie Kray while he was still hiding in west London, Ronnie told him that Mitchell wished to give himself up to him, Wyndham, and the ubiquitous Father Hetherington. Wyndham reported back to the editor and was told to go along with the proposal provided he could have five minutes alone with Mitchell first. However, when he went back to Ronnie he was told Mitchell had changed his mind. Wyndham believed that meant he was now dead.

In fact Mitchell had been offered what was effectively one last chance. Just before Christmas, Scotch Jack Dickson asked Lisa to try to persuade him to give himself up. He would not agree and had to be calmed down. Next, he was told that in a day or so he and Lisa would be taken to France. Then Donoghue told him a new story that he would be moved and taken to Kent – the girl would follow – where he would spend Christmas with Ronnie, who was actually in hiding in Finchley over his botched attempt to bring Townshend down.

Mitchell was told to be ready to leave the flat on the evening of 23 December. He packed his new shirts, a black beret and what Lisa thought was a black mask. He gave Lisa what money he had and Donoghue brought him a large dark overcoat and trilby hat. He wrote down her address and telephone number and said that if he was stopped by the police he would get in touch with her. He was taken to a van waiting in Ladysmith Avenue with Foreman and Gerard sitting in the back. Donoghue later told the court that Ronnie Olliffe, a friend of Gerard, was driving, and he, Donoghue, was told to sit by him and give him directions to the Blackwall Tunnel. As the van pulled away Foreman and Gerard repeatedly shot Mitchell. Donoghue told the jury:

> 'Gerard says, 'The bastard's still alive. Give him another one Fred, because I'm empty.' So Foreman stood up and crouched over Mitchell and held the gun about an inch or

two from his head and fired a shot into his head. That was the last shot fired. I would say it was about 12 shots in all.'[143]

Mitchell's freedom had lasted rather less than a fortnight.

Back in the flat Lisa and the others had heard the shots. When Donoghue returned, Lisa screamed at him that he had killed Mitchell, which he denied. He then telephoned Reggie Kray to say, 'The dog has won', a code used when reporting a success, which Lisa misheard as 'The dog is dead'. For all practical purposes it amounted to the same thing.

Kray told Donoghue to meet him later at a party at Winnie Harwood's flat in Evering Road, and to bring Lisa with him. Meanwhile there were frantic efforts to clean the flat of any traces of Mitchell:

'I [Donoghue] went back and got cleaned up. Then I divided them into teams and made one go over everything with a wet cloth and the second team to go after them with a dry one.'[144]

Magazines were burned and Lisa was told to hand over anything he might have given her but she crucially held back a comb in a grey case, a calendar and a Christmas card.

She was then driven by Donoghue and Connie Whitehead to the party in Evering Road where she was given around £100. On the way she said to Donoghue that when it was time for her to 'go' she wanted him, rather than Whitehead, who had been laughing and whom she regarded as sadistic, to kill her. At the party Donoghue told Reggie Kray of Mitchell's death and Reggie began to cry, saying he had not wanted this to happen. Ronnie questioned her twice and 'she sailed through' although Reggie said Whitehead would 'cut her throat if she spoke out'. When the party finished she spent the night with Donoghue. The next day Kray and Connie Whitehead came back and told her to say nothing. She went back to her flat but she remained in what might be called protective custody. She went to a New Year's Eve party with Donoghue, and attended another in the New Year, when Reggie gave her the further £30. Donoghue was given £1,000 to pay Foreman, and the story was circulated that Mitchell had gone away to France.

In the new year Lisa was allowed to return to work. Later she would tell the jury she was very grateful to Donoghue. 'For what?' asked counsel for the prosecution in re-examination. Her reply was devastating:

> 'Because he saved my life. Really there is no doubt about
> it. Because he convinced Reginald Kray that it was quite
> safe for me to walk around.'[145]

Ironically, on the day Mitchell was killed, the *Daily Mirror* published an open letter to him suggesting he took 'the man-to-man advice' the editor was offering:

> 'Keep your word and surrender at once. By doing so
> you will strengthen your claim that you are entitled to a

fresh consideration of your case. We've given you a fair hearing, Frank Mitchell. Now give yourself up.'

Over the next nine months the police and politicians were sent a regular stream of sightings and suggestions about where Mitchell might be. Home Secretary Roy Jenkins received a Christmas card with a Caernarvon postmark which read 'Happy Hunting, Frank Mitchell'. There were suggestions that he was living with the club owner Joe Wilkins in Coulsdon in Surrey and he was sighted at the Savoy Club off the Strand. Unsurprisingly, police surveillance of the club produced nothing. Another correspondent thought he was living with a man in the north with whom he had been in prison. Then again he had been seen in a pub in Park Side, Romford and in February there was advice that the police should check the London Hospital because he was bound to be suffering from strain. As if no one would have recognised him there!

Or maybe he was in Plymouth, where he visited the Tagada nightclub, or in a basement in Old Market Square, Exeter (4 March). Or maybe he was living with a West End Club owner in Dun Laoghaire. A memorandum from DCI E.G. Harris at East Ham dated 4 March 1967 showed the police still thought the information that Mitchell was in Ireland was accurate. A seeker of 'Justice and Revenge' thought he was in Southampton in April. That month a Hull prison officer overheard two 'serious' criminals say that the Krays had got him over to Ireland to a village he thought was Abbeyfeale. Or what about Tangier, where he was meant to be living with a girl?

Then a story by Norman Lucas in the *Sunday Mirror* of 29 October 1967 to the effect that Mitchell had been killed somewhere in Docklands and his body thrown in the sea near Shoreham, Sussex was deemed inaccurate, and had been put about on the instigation of the Krays by an East End publican.

What actually happened to Mitchell's body? The suggestions have been both numerous and varied, and it is a question of 'take your pick.' On 11 August 1967 a letter in block capitals was sent to the *Daily Mirror*: 'FRANK MITCHEL (sic) WAS MURDERED LAST SATURDAY NIGHT HIS BODY WAS THROWN IN THE THAMES AT WAPPING.' Years later Freddie Foreman, appearing on television, said it had been dropped in the English Channel but, according to Donoghue, Foreman told him they had had to keep the body for some five days before it was burned because the man who owned the furnace had visitors over Christmas. Another member of the Kray team told fraudster and gold smuggler Paul Elvey it had gone into a scrap incinerator where 'all the bones and even the tooth fillings go to ashes'.[146]

It was amazing the conspirators held together for so long. But then again, there was no one from Mitchells' family demanding an inquiry into his disappearance.

CHAPTER 11
THE KILLING OF JACK
'THE HAT' MCVITIE

The 6'2" 16-stone Jack 'The Hat' McVitic is often derisively described as a small-time thief whose one great talent was the ability to walk on his hands, but that does him an injustice. In his day he had been a good robber and, said Freddie Foreman, 'He was a frightening bastard'.[147]

After he received seven years at Cambridgeshire Quarter Sessions for unlawful possession of explosives and possessing a flick knife, in December 1959 he narrowly escaped a flogging after a fight with a prison officer in Exeter prison.

Frank Fraser remembered the fight as a fair one, after McVitie objected to being stopped on the exercise yard and told to keep his distance from the pair walking in front:

> 'The prisoners made a circle so the other prison officers couldn't interfere. It was a fair fight and McVitie knocked him out... McVitie's in real trouble and we asked him what he wanted to happen next. He said he didn't want anyone to be in trouble for him: he would just go in but would we

see they didn't give him a belting, meaning let the authorities know it was a fair fight and he's gone in quietly.'[148]

In fact McVitie was given a beating, and as a result Fraser and the ill-fated Jimmy Andrews attacked Governor Rundle-Harris and another officer in a workshop. The trio were brought up before the visiting magistrates and McVitie was sentenced to 15 strokes of the birch, Andrews to 12 and Fraser to the maximum of 18. It was then Billy Hill's tame MP Mark Hewitson intervened and raised the matter in the House of Commons, describing some prison officers as 'hoodlum warders' with a 'Belsen mentality'.[149] The Home Secretary was required to confirm the birching before it was carried out, and because Fraser had twice been declared insane he declined to do so. It was a question of 'flog all, flog none' and as a result he also refused to confirm the birching for Andrews and McVitie.

This decision not to flog them was not well received by Rolf Dudley-Williams, the kindly MP for Exeter, who in reply to Hewitson said in the House of Commons:

'I very much regret that Fraser was not thrashed, but that was the responsibility of my right Honourable Friend the Home Secretary who, I am sure, weighed the situation very carefully before making his decision.'

It was something of a pyrrhic victory. Fraser lost 400 days remission, Andrews 300 and McVitie 200.

After his release in 1965 McVitie held up the Starlight Rooms, a club off Oxford Street, and forced the punters to drop their trousers. The manager Barry Cayman turned to the Twins for help, who approached Freddie Foreman and Mickey Regan to take over the gaming tables there.

But now, full of booze and pills, McVitie was seriously on the slide and was becoming an embarrassment. One evening in a club he became involved in a shouting match with Dorothy Squires over the sexual prowess of her former husband Roger Moore, dropping his trousers to show the candy-striped underwear he favoured. On another night he shot up the Mildmay Tavern because they would not serve him a drink. To compound his misdemeanours he once appeared at a Kray club drunk, wearing Bermuda shorts and carrying a bayonet. Worse, he caused trouble with Ronnie Olliffe in The Log Cabin, the club in Wardour Street which served as a robbers' employment exchange, in which George Walker, then in between his days as Billy Hill's minder and stock market entrepreneur, had an interest. He had also shot at Tommy Flanagan in the Regency and even more dangerously he had quarrelled with Freddie Foreman in Foreman's ritzy 211 club and spieler in Balham.

More seriously, the Twins had a number of grudges against him. He had told a man he thought they were 'a couple of twits' and the remark had been reported back to headquarters. Then, depending on who is telling the tale, he had been given £100 or £500 or £1,000 to kill their estranged financial adviser Leslie Payne. Half drunk, he had gone to Payne's house with Billy Exley, who would later give evidence against his former friends and employers. They had arrived only to be told by Mrs Payne that the potential victim was out. McVitie had simply turned away and pocketed the advance fee.

Shortly after, George Dixon, one of the brothers who worked both with and independently of the Twins, and had himself been shot at by Ronnie, tried to persuade McVitie to absent himself from the scene at least for a period, but he would not listen.

Not only did McVitie fail to carry out the contract on Payne, he began to boast how he had scored over the Twins, and drunkenly criticised them in public. While the failure to kill Payne might have been accepted, the boasting and criticism could not. And he was dealing in pep pills with the Twins and talking too much about it in the West End. It was also rumoured he may have been enquiring about Frank Mitchell.

The Twins' cousin, Ronald Hart, claims McVitie was targeted after tipping off Bobby Cannon, who Reggie had planned to shoot in revenge for an earlier, accidental shooting incident. Later that night a drunken Reggie had said 'I won't forget McVitie for that'.[150]

There was also another longstanding and seriously important issue. Ronnie had been niggling at his twin, telling him that he had killed a man and it was time for Reggie to do the same. According to Hart, Reggie told him he wouldn't be able to kill someone without a reason. Wally Garelick was one potential target, having sided with Ronnie after he made disparaging remarks about Frances Kray. He had merely suffered minor damage when Reggie, after waiting outside his home one night, shot him in the leg. Now McVitie filled the position of victim admirably.

The evening of Saturday 25 October 1967 started well when members of the Firm went drinking in the Carpenters Arms, then a dingy pub in Cheshire Street near Vallance Road. There are claims that the Krays owned the pub, but it is doubtful whether this is strictly accurate. Certainly they could not have obtained a licence. It is more likely they were leaning on it. Charlie Kray says the Carpenters Arms they owned was paid for by him and was in the Lea Bridge Road. Since Charlie rarely had £2,000 to his name this is also unlikely.

For once wives and girlfriends were there and among the company were Violet and Charlie Kray Snr, Charlie Jnr and Dolly, Ronnie Hart and his wife Vicki, Ronnie Bender and Lily, known as Bubbles (the former girlfriend of Frankie Shea), Ian Barrie and his girlfriend Pat, known as Pifco because she used to give Ronnie a massage with a Pifco, Connie Whitehead and his wife Pat, Scotch Jack Dickson and his girlfriend Stella, Reggie's girlfriend Ginger Carole Thompson as well as Geoff Allen and his girlfriend Annie.

Initially things went well, with Reggie in good humour. Then about 10 p.m. Ronnie telephoned his brother at the pub and, according to Ronnie Hart, Reggie's mood changed and he began drinking one gin after another. People began to drift away but then, on the spur of the moment, Reggie decided to have a party at Blonde Carol Skinner's basement flat at 71 Evering Road, Stoke Newington. Carol was a mother of two who had been a hairdresser's model before meeting the Krays in 1965 and began working at the Starlight. At first they asked permission to use her flat and then just took it over. She would come home and find dozens of empty glasses and overflowing ashtrays.

She and her boyfriend George Plummer, who worked in the Green Dragon club, were ordered out. They and the other wives and girlfriends either went home or across the road to Jenny King (a pseudonym), a friend of Carol, who some years later told me:

> 'The Krays could order her about because she was going with a man Georgie Plummer, he's long dead, who worked in a spieler they either owned or had an interest in. I had worked behind the bar in it and they were always in and out. They just said to Georgie, 'We're going to have a party down your girlfriend's house' and that was it. Georgie was a very nice, timid man; he wasn't going to stand up to them.'[151]

Meanwhile Reggie went to the Regency to see if he could find McVitie. There he told Tony Barry, the owner, that he wanted McVitie fetched in because he was going to do him in. Barry told him he was not in the club and anyway would Kray do him a favour and not kill McVitie on the premises. Kray gave Barry an automatic pistol before going back to Evering Road.

As the night wore on the Twins, Ronnie Bender, Chris and Tony Lambrianou, their friends the Mills brothers from Notting Hill, Connie Whitehead, Ronnie Hart, and Terence and Trevor, two young friends of Ronnie Kray, were in the basement flat idly watching boxing on the television, with the boys dancing to a record player. Reggie then announced he was going to kill McVitie. The Lambrianou brothers were sent to find the erring man – who was by now drinking in the Regency – and bring him to the flat. Hart was told to go and tell Barry to bring the gun left with him. Barry's participation would ensure he kept his mouth shut.

Barry brought the gun and some more drink and left as soon as he possibly could. Reggie told the two youths to begin making a noise, singing and dancing when McVitie arrived. Hart was told to go upstairs and keep watch from the window and let him know when McVitie appeared, so the record player could be turned up. McVitie arrived with the Lambrianous in high good humour. He rushed into the room clapping his hands, shouting, 'Where's all the birds? Where's all the drink?'

According to Hart, almost immediately Reggie pulled the gun to shoot him, but it failed to fire and McVitie managed to trap his arm. Hart told the youths to get out of the room. Reggie then freed his arm and shot at McVitie again, and once more the gun failed to fire. Ronnie then told McVitie to sit down, relax and tell him about the row he had had with Freddie Foreman at the 211 club. Ronnie Bender was fiddling with the gun, and Reggie took it from him and tried to shoot McVitie again. The Hat made a break for the door but Ronnie stopped him, saying, 'Come on, Jack. Be a man.' McVitie replied, 'Yes, I'll be a man, but I don't want to die like one'. He made a dash for the window, smashing the glass with his shoulder. Reggie took a knife from Bender; Ronnie Hart held McVitie in a bear hug and Reggie stabbed him in the face. McVitie began to plead, calling, 'Don't. Stop, please,' while Ronnie urged his brother on, 'Do him Reg. Kill him, Reg.' Reggie then stabbed him half a dozen times in the stomach and McVitie slumped to the floor. Bender put his head on McVitie's chest and said, 'He's dead'. On the stairs outside, Chrissie Lambrianou, who had left the room at the start of the trouble, began to cry.

Later Bender described the killing:

> 'It was terrible. Savagery at its utmost. Reggie was foaming at the mouth like a raging bull. Have you ever seen a bull's eyes before the toreador finishes him off? He was like that. Absolutely gone. Blood was everywhere.'[152]

In his book *Escape from the Kray Madness*, Chris Lambrianou explained he had been upset when Reggie had produced a gun and had left the room. Ronnie then told Connie Whitehead to take him home. He had found two guns there and had returned to the party to protect his younger brother against what he felt would be an aggressive McVitie. When he returned to Evering Road the only person there was Ronnie Bender. Within minutes Tony returned and together they cleaned up the flat. The three of them later wrapped McVitie's body in an eiderdown and Tony drove it to South London in McVitie's car. Even after their years in prison the brothers could not agree about what had happened. Tony claimed he sent Chrissie away to get a gun and when he returned, Jack was dying. The Krays and Hart then left, leaving the Lambrianous, Whitehead and Bender to deal with the housekeeping.

But, according to Hart, it was all hands to the pump and naturally the Twins turned to their ever-helpful brother Charlie for advice. Bender was told to take the body and dump it over the railway line in Cazenove Road, Stoke Newington. Hart took the Twins to Harry Hopwood's home in Hackney Road and the Lambrianous were left behind to clean up. When Bender arrived at Hopwood's, Ronnie was in the bath and Reggie in his underpants. Bender told them he had dumped the body south of the river and now Ronnie called him a 'dozy bastard' and said they would have to get in touch with 'Brown Bread', a reference to Freddie Foreman. Hopwood also rang Charlie Kray with a cryptic message.

At the time there was a tap on Charlie Kray's telephone and a call by a man called Ersh was picked up:

E. Tell the feller who rabbits about Ray Moore. With me?

C. Yes.

E. Tell him to come round right away.

C. Where are you?

E. Where I always am. Got it?

C. I see, what's the time?

E. About three.

C. The fellow there wants to see me?

E. Yes, you know where, don't you?

C. Yes, cheerio.

Then Dolly Kray rang Tommy Cowley:

D. Sorry to wake you. Do you know Tommy Brown's number?

C. No, do you?

D. It's important to the others. Know what I mean the others. Ronnie. Ronnie Bender works behind the bar. Do you know who I mean?

C. Yes.

D. There's been you know. The fellow with the hat.

C. Yes.

D. They want Tommy Brown's number.

C. Charlie's out?

D. Yes.

Meanwhile at they had changed their clothes at Hopwood's. Hopwood had washed their jewellery and Reggie Kray's hair because he had a cut hand. By now it was 3 a.m.

Charlie was told he had to go to see Foreman, and Hart that he must take the mini in which he had driven the Twins and get Foreman to hide it in one of his lock-ups. According to Hart he and Charlie drove over to South London, rousing Foreman from his bed in the early hours.

Arrangements were then made to go to Suffolk where the Twins, Carole Thompson, Hart and a boyfriend of Ronnie would stay at The Swan at Lavenham. On the way Ronnie was in fine form, joking that 'Jack had no heart' and 'He lived and died with his hat on'. They stayed in Lavenham for a week and went to the local Hunt Ball the following Saturday, for which Hart had to go to a local tailor to rent a dinner jacket. He at least showed some finer feelings by never again eating a McVitie's biscuit after Jack's death. As for Reggie, in a later remark which cannot have helped his case for parole, he commented,

'I did not regret it at the time and I don't regret it now. I have never felt a moment's remorse'.

In *Escape from the Kray Madness*, Chris Lambrianou, claiming Charlie Kray and Freddie Foreman were fitted up by the police and Hart over the disposal of McVitie's body, gives a substantially different version of events. He says that his brother Tony drove McVitie's body through the Blackwall Tunnel to south London where the car ran out of petrol. Chris and Ronnie Bender followed so they could take Tony back.

There have been many other accounts of the final disposal of the body and theories as to its whereabouts. Nipper Read rather favoured the theory that it had been returned to East London and put in the furnaces of a local swimming baths. Another version is that McVitie was sent to a friendly undertaker and buried in a double coffin. He may have been buried somewhere in the country, possibly, and rather suitably, in Gravesend. The body may have been taken in a car to South London and ended up as an Oxo cube in a scrap yard.

Freddie Foreman, who of all people should know, has been fairly reticent about the funeral arrangements. In his book *Respect* he says that he was rather aggrieved at being called out in the middle of the night to help clear up this difficult situation. According to him the car which had contained McVitie's body was sent to a wrecker's yard and the body itself was tied up with chicken wire and buried at sea away from the fishing lanes. He also maintains that, at the outset, there had been no intention to kill McVitie, but merely to scare him. Then things had got out of hand.

Jenny King recalls to me:

'Carol and Georgie left my house at about 3.30. Georgie was very drunk but Carol hadn't been drinking because she was on pills for high blood pressure. Georgie was paralytic. I helped her get him downstairs and she said she could manage to get him across the street.

She had the keys to my place and I had hers. A bit before seven I felt her waking me up. She was green, just shaking from head to toes. I asked her what was wrong and she just blurted out, "Something terrible's happened in my house. I think they've killed somebody." I couldn't believe it and I said, "What do you mean, tell me."

What had happened was that when she got back with Georgie they'd been slung into the bedroom by the door. The rest of her flat was in the basement. She'd then heard someone say, "Don't forget his hat." That's when she thought they'd killed Jack McVitie.

I asked her who was there that minute and she said she was on her own so I put some clothes on and went back with her. I've never seen anything so horrific. The walls were covered in blood; the carpet had been set on fire and was smouldering in the fireplace. She'd had it boarded up but the new fascia had been ripped off. There was blood all over the couch, and the window, where Jack had tried to get through, was smashed. The record player just wasn't there.

I said, "Come back to my place and we'll think about it." Then I said, "Let's get the kids and we'll go to the police." She said, "They'll kill us" and I said, "They'll kill us anyway." So we just started to clean up and try and put the place in some semblance.

Georgie simply walked off. I rang her ex and another bloke I knew and said, "We're bang in trouble. Come and give us a hand."

As we came out John Barry, Tony's brother pulled up and asked, "Is everything all right?" We just looked at him and said, "What do you mean?" but he didn't reply and he just drove off. That was the start of things. The next day Carol said, "Don't come over".

The Twins sent Ian round to give Carol £40 to replace the three-piece suite and carpet. Then over the next week they sent more people in to redecorate it. In between times we were making it as decent as we could. By the end of the week the story was that Jack had blown himself up when he'd hit a bollard or something going over Tower Bridge; he'd had a load of dynamite in his car. But I noticed it wasn't in the papers.'

In the days following the killing it was Albert Donoghue who redec-orated and re-papered the Evering Road flat. Second hand furniture was brought in to replace the bloodstained carpet and sofa. A tight rein had to be kept on those outside the Firm who might cause problems, and if Jenny King thought she was out of the woods she was mistaken:

'About four months later Winnie Harwood came over one lunchtime and said the Twins were at her house and they wanted to see me. I was terrified but there was no use in refusing. I had to go. They said I'd been talking out of turn but I stood my ground and said I hadn't. I said I'd heard Jack had been killed when he'd blown himself up on Tower Bridge when he was carrying gelignite. They seemed satisfied but then they just told me that if I said anything I'd be killed. I said, "Can I go now?" and that was the last time I spoke to them.

They sent Winnie over a couple of days later with pens and books and sweets for the kids but I sent them back with her.

As close as Winnie was to the Twins, she was never pulled in to my knowledge, even though Pat Connolly lived at her place and kept a box of guns under the bed. She got Alzheimer's disease and died a few years back.'[153]

For Sylvia McVitie, who had met Jack in November 1965 just after he had come out of Dartmoor, the worst was not knowing what had happened:

'I searched for him in pubs and clubs but all I got were blank stares or lies. They were all too frightened to talk freely.'[154]

CHAPTER 12
NIPPER READ AND THE SECOND INVESTIGATION

In the latter half of 1967 Nipper Read received both good and bad news almost simultaneously. Since the abortive Kray inquiry of 1964 and the fiasco of the Hide-A-Way trial, Fred Gerrard had retired. Read's career had been onward and upward, including a spell back in the West End breaking up gangs of pickpockets from Europe, Australia and South America who had arrived for the 1964 World Cup. Now it was time for another step up the ranks. The good news was that he was promoted to Superintendent. This normally meant four years on a Division and then, with luck, a transfer to C1, the elite Murder Squad. Read recalled, 'I was promoted on the Friday and Hooter Millen said I would be told on the Monday by the Assistant Commissioner Peter Brodie where I was going'.

And on the Monday, there was more good news from Brodie who told Read he was going straight to the Squad. Read was delighted. He had pulled off a hat-trick: the first post-war Superintendent to be posted to the Murder Squad, the first ever to be promoted from Chief Inspector and the first to reach the Squad without serving a period of grace on a Division. The bad news was that it was to be on special assignment to bring down the Krays. Read recalled Brodie telling him:

> 'The Krays have been a thorn in our sides for long enough. Now you can do it any way you like but I'm looking to you to get the right result. I know you will wish to run this thing entirely properly and fairly – I don't even need to say that. It is important to nail these bastards.'[155]

Brodie added, 'Always remember we are here to help in any way we can'. Later Read would think 'hinder' was a more appropriate verb. The likelihood of a leak was high, but for the time being the cover story was that he was conducting an inquiry into a major corruption allegation. This was by no means farfetched. In the days before the creation of A10, the squad investigating police corruption, Murder Squad officers often dealt with serious corruption allegations and there was certainly enough corruption around at the time to justify a major investigation.

What had been happening at Scotland Yard in the three years since the fiasco of the identification parades in the Cornell shooting? Not very much is the answer. In overall charge of the Kray investigation was the Munster lookalike, Assistant Commissioner John Du Rose, given the soubriquet 'Four Day Johnny' because he supposedly solved his cases in record time. In fact, a look through the cases in his anodyne autobiography rather belies the nickname, but he was involved in both the Jack the Stripper and the Haigh murder cases which, as far as Scotland Yard was concerned, reached successful conclusions. Although much more was due to Gerald MacArthur, Du Rose was also given a great deal of credit for bringing down the Richardsons.[156]

Du Rose's version of events was:

'Having formed the basic plan for a major investigation into the Kray "Firm", I selected an officer to take charge of the affair. He was Ferguson Walker, a detective superintendent at Central Office whose knowledge of the underworld from Soho to the East End could prove decisive for the work in hand. He had had Flying Squad experience and at the time was a successful member of the Murder Squad.'[157]

Walker chose Detective Sergeant Algernon Hemingway as his assistant and, said Du Rose, 'to their credit they never gave up trying and after several months they got a line on the Krays which indicated "the investigation was off the ground".'

Although John Du Rose wrote in his memoirs that Ferguson Walker had been doing a good job keeping tabs on the Krays after the Cornell murder and the disappearance of first Frank Mitchell and then Jack McVitie, Read believed it was very far from the reality.

The truth, believed Read, was that somehow information was being leaked to the Krays' great friend, the club owner Bernie Silver, head of what was called 'The Syndicate', which ran clubs and porn in Soho during the 1960s and who had many of the Obscene Publications Squad under his control.

Throughout his career Read continually ran up against Walker, rarely with satisfactory results. I remember him telling me that when he was at Paddington as a Sergeant, one day Walker called in on Read who asked:

'What are you doing here?'

'I'm sent by the Yard. I'm special intelligence gatherer.'

'What are you gathering?'

'I'm the best-informed officer in the Met Police'.

An irritated Read replied, 'Why don't you go and fucking nick someone then?'

At the time Scotland Yard was in one of its worst periods and Read wanted certain precautions to be put in place. First he wanted to move the Kray inquiry away from the Yard itself, where he feared there could be serious and compromising leaks. He wanted to base it at Tintagel House on Westminster Bridge. Secondly, he wanted to pick his own team who he knew were clean, trustworthy and who would be loyal to him. This was all agreed, but for the first three months, Read's team comprised only himself and two sergeants. Read was appalled by the lack of anything on the files which indicated any action had been taken:

> 'There was not one single item added to the wealth of stuff I had put in during my Commercial Street days. We had put in a ton of stuff and I believed it was important we did so. Now I found to my dismay that there wasn't another single fact in there.'[158]

Among reports which were missing was the contact Bobby Teale had made with the detective Tommy Butler after the Cornell shooting. It was something which would cause Read some problems at the trial.

What is certain is that in the best traditions of Scotland Yard of the time, Read was not dealt a full hand of cards. Du Rose, who was running a parallel investigation into the Krays, kept a great deal back from him and also suborned at least one of the men working for him.

There had certainly been some activity under Butler. Some weeks after the Krays had arrived locust-like at David Teale's flat, his brother Bobby contacted New Scotland Yard and according to his account was put through to Tommy Butler. A meeting was arranged in Fleet Street and it was decided that Teale was to be 'run' by Detective Sergeant Joe Pogue. In his book Teale recalls a number of meetings but seemingly there were no records kept of Teale's involvement and when it came to the trial, Ronnie's QC, John Platts-Mills, was able to put a number of names of which he had no records to an embarrassed Read. Quite how the Krays' solicitors came to know of these is another matter.

DS Ferguson Walker had actually been fairly active. The former Flying Squad officer John Rigbey recalled that Walker had overheard him talking with his informer Charlie Clarke on a telephone intercept and Walker wanted to know all about it. It would seem, however, that Walker made no use of the information, except possibly to pass it on to Silver for onward transmission. Rigbey recalled:

'Charlie Clarke was a cat burglar who lived in a bungalow behind the Walthamstow dog track. Someone tipped me off that he had stolen goods but when I turned him over there was nothing. What he did have, however, was a rail of clothes like you see in shops which had a row of Ronnie Kray's suits. He was staying there on and off. I managed to turn Charlie and he gave me good if selective information. It's rare you find a thief who won't turn grass. They all do it. Charlie wouldn't grass up his friends but he didn't mind doing it to other people. Once you have a grass, do it once then he's yours. You can always put the black on him, saying you'll leak it that he gave you such and such a person. I never went to see him. It was all done on the blower. One day I'm called in by my boss Frank Nicholl who tells me that Fergie Walker of C1 wants to see me. In those days C1 was serious crimes and also discipline so I wondered what went wrong. When I went to see him he's like one of those Scots actors in Whisky Galore. What he wanted to know was if Charlie had said anything to me about the Twins or the others. He hadn't but I realise that there must have been a bell on him.'[159]

Was Du Rose himself corrupt or simply an autocratic man who craved results? Read, who prefers the latter theory, recalled being told:

'I shall want to see you at Morning Prayers. This was when he saw the head of the Murder Squad and the Head of the Flying Squad. I was the boy. All the others were pre-war men. I said to Tommy Butler, who was also waiting to see him, "I can't afford to do this. I've other things to do." Butler said, "Tell him." So I said to Du Rose, "If you want to see me, call in at Tintagel on the way home." He called occasionally but he had to ring first to make sure I was there.'[160]

This did not endear Read to Du Rose or make the latter any keener on sharing his information.

By now Read's tactics had improved and he made a positive decision not to attempt to investigate the rumoured murders, but again to look at the Long Firm frauds the Twins had been running through Leslie Payne. There was no point in simply picking off one or two people. While the Twins and other senior members of the Firm were at large he would never get people to talk about the murders. It had to be a clean sweep.

He began his inquiries by making a numbered list of people whom he should interview. Some such as Frank Shea (No. 3) and Sylvia McVitie (26) were known to be bitter enemies of the Twins. Others were the ex-boxer Johnny Cardew (20) whom he knew had been attacked by Ronnie Kray; some, such as Bill Ackerman (7), Bobby Ramsey (9), and Bill Exley (24), had worked for the Firm. Yet more were people whose businesses had been appropriated, including Freddy Gore (4), Leslie Payne (12) and Johnny Hutton (8). Despite their subsequent claims that it was they who had brought down the Krays, possibly because Read had not been given the full information about them, the Teale brothers were not in the top 30. First on the list was Lanni, the former owner of the Cambridge Rooms.

Read decided simply to talk to men he knew from the first investigation; peripheral members of the Firm who for one reason or another might have drifted away. He met with many rejections, but eventually in December a meeting was arranged with Payne, whom he had known for years, at the Lyons Corner House next to Charing Cross Station. The Krays' use of gratuitous violence had begun to upset Payne, not least the botched attempt on his own life by Jack McVitie. He was a swindler, not a killer. Read promised that if Payne helped him, so far as he was able he would ensure the fraudster was not prosecuted. Payne began to talk on the proviso that no one at the Yard was told.

Over a three-week period in a hotel in Paddington, Read took a 146-page statement from Payne covering the sale of drugs, blackmail, stolen bonds, Long Firm frauds and forged currency. Payne also began to name names including his one-time partner Freddy Gore, who had been involved in the Krays' LFs, and the attempt to establish a housing project in Nigeria. Payne and Gore told Read the Twins had been dealing in bonds stolen from deposit boxes in America and Canada and sold by the thieves to the Mafia, who in turn were using the Firm to cash them in Europe.

One by one, fringe members of the Firm and their victims began to talk to Read, who would often take the smooth-talking Payne with him to establish his credentials. One early convert was Lennie Hamilton, who had lost his hair at Esmeralda's Barn. Another was the old boxer Billy Exley, who would tell him of the Mitchell escape.

Exley had fallen foul of the Twins when they used him as the dupe in a plan to swindle two businessmen. According to a report he forgot his lines and leaned over to Reggie, asking, 'What do I say?' The

TOP (R-L) Reggie, Ronnie, Charlie Kray and Billy Hill. Photo believed to be taken at Billy Hill's bar inside his own home.

RIGHT Daily Mirror front page, March 1969. GUILTY OF MURDER.

TOP Ronnie, Reggie and Johnny Squibb
photographed outside their apartment in
Cedra Court, London in 1966.
RIGHT Dancing at Esmeralda's Barn, one of
the clubs owned by the Krays.

e

LEFT Ronnie and Reggie with Billy Hill at his house in Tangiers in 1966.

LEFT Reggie and Ian Barrie at Billy Hill's place in Tangiers, same holiday 1966.

Ian Barrie went to the Blind Beggar pub with Ronnie where he shot George Cornell.

ABOVE Enugu, Nigeria. Leslie Payne and MP Ernest Shinwell. BELOW Reggie with Ernest Shinwell.

ABOVE Reggie, Johnny Squibb and a friend on the boat heading to Morocco on holiday. BELOW Reggie, Christine Boyce (his girlfriend after the death of Frances) and 'Big' Albert Donoghue (known as Reggie's right hand man).

TOP Reggie and Frances Shea, Reggie's first
wife, at the Latin Quarter Night Club in Wardour
Street, London.
ABOVE Reggie and Frances on holiday in Morocco.
RIGHT Reggie and Frances wedding day. Reggie has
his hand on Frances' father's shoulder.

OP Reggie, Charlie and Ronnie in 1965.
GHT A rare photo of Frances Shea.
ELOW Violet Kray, Limehouse Willy and his wife,
hristine Boyce, Reggie and Albert Donoghuc.

ABOVE The Kray women: Christine Boyce, Violet Kray, and Dolly Kray. BELOW Brooks cottage in Bildeston, Suffolk. Mr Kray Sr. is pictured far left. The house is attached to Brooks Mansion that the Krays owned. Violet Kray would often stay at the Brooks cottage.

businessmen promptly shut down the discussion. He was summoned to Vallance Road and told that he would forfeit his 'pension' of £10 a week for two months. He annoyed the Twins again by then joining a Turkish Cypriot gang. He never returned to the fold. When Read first went to see him in early December 1967 he found him with a loaded shotgun. 'If they come looking for me I've a shotgun behind the door and that's what they'll get. Don't worry, it's licensed,' he told Read.[161]

In the middle of his inquiries Read was sent to investigate the murder of Peggy Flynn, a middle-aged prostitute found dead in February 1966 on a beach in Dublin. She had been strangled with one of her stockings.[162] No progress was made in the case until a British army officer suddenly confessed in December 1967. In a way this was convenient because it enabled Read to keep his cover that he was simply on the Murder Squad. It was time-consuming, however, and meant he had to attend the ensuing trial in Dublin the following March. In the end the jury rejected his confession and the officer was acquitted. When Read returned he found the hierarchy at the Yard had leaked news of his inquiry to the press. The *Sunday Mirror* featured the headline, 'Gangbusters Move in on the Top Mob' followed by the news that Read was investigating the murders of Cornell, McVitie and Mitchell. And, with the Richardsons safely serving sentences, it could only refer to the Firm. It was yet another example of inopportune leakage, if not sabotage, by Scotland Yard.

As for the murders, Read faced considerable problems. In Cornell's case, no one was prepared to make an identification. There were no bodies in the other two. For centuries, after the Camden Wonder case in 1661 when a victim had turned up alive and well a few weeks after his 'killers' had been hanged, the law had been taken to be 'no body – no murder'. In 1948, however, when a Polish farmer had killed his business partner over a land ownership dispute, it became clear that given sufficient circumstantial evidence – in this case blood splattering – it was possible to convict without a body.[163] But there was still the problem for Read that without hard evidence a jury might not believe that either McVitie or Mitchell was dead.

Then in the spring of 1968 came a substantial breakthrough. On 8 March Read received a call that a female informant wanted to see him urgently. A meeting was arranged for the next day at the Sir Christopher Wren, a pub near St Paul's Cathedral. There Read learned some details of the McVitie murder. The woman knew it had taken place in Evering Road in a basement flat owned by a blonde woman with two children. With Sergeant Pat Allen, whom Read later married, and another woman officer, posing as door-to-door detergent market researchers, he was able within two days to provide Read with the house number and the name, Carol Skinner. Frank Cater, now seconded to Read's squad, already knew Carol from a drugs case in 1964 when her then husband Colin had received three years. Her maiden name had been on the label of one of the suitcases used to carry the drugs. But from past experience Read knew all too well that seemingly staunch witnesses could be turned, and for the moment the information was put in cold storage.

After the Twins' arrest, Carol Skinner was brought to Tintagel House, where she flatly denied any knowledge of McVitie's death and was sent away. The Krays might have been locked up but they still held a tight grip on the minds of East Enders.

It is curious that neither the Twins nor any other Firm member (with the exception of the Lambrianous) made any attempt to leave London, let alone the country, at this stage. They seemed like rabbits trapped in headlights. It was almost as if a pall of inevitability was hanging over them. 'They didn't think,' said Micky Fawcett dismissively. 'Their idea of escape was to move from Bethnal Green all the way to Finsbury Park.'

According to Albert Donoghue there was idle talk that the troubles of the rank and file would be over if the Twins were killed. Years later Freddie Foreman confirmed that members were planning to kill the brothers just before their arrests:

> 'The Twins were a nuisance and causing grief for every-one else. Some people felt they had to go. If they hadn't been nicked then they would have gone missing very soon afterwards – forever.'[164]

However, the Twins did have vague plans to deal with Dukey Osborne, whom they believed was talking to the police. Donoghue recalled:

> 'It was how Dukey Osborne fell out with the Krays. They wanted a fellow silenced. They thought he was talking to Nipper Read. Osborne was in Pentonville with him at the time. I went to see him and suggested he put something in the man's tea or his food, but he refused and they were not pleased.'[165]

Then matters became urgent. It was through Leslie Payne that Read learned the details of the Twins' involvement with the American Mafia and their dealing in stolen bonds. Through him he learned the name Alan Bruce Cooper and it opened up a whole new line of inquiry.

As with many others, the English-born Alan Bruce Cooper, small and with a pronounced stammer, little hair and a penchant for large cigars, came to the Krays in a roundabout way. A man of whom it was said that he would shop anyone to ensure his own survival, he had once grassed up his father-in-law Harry Nathan. Read had, in fact, seen him at Bow Street court watching the unfortunate Nathan's committal proceedings, which ended in a seven-year sentence for conspiring to manufacture LSD.

Even now, nearly half a century later, it is still not clear in just whose pocket Alan Bruce Cooper could be found or for whom he was working; certainly for Scotland Yard in the shape of Du Rose and for the Bureau of Narcotics and Dangerous Drugs (BNDD), who had also turned him.

Cooper had originally met Charlie Kray through the dog doper and fraudster Charlie Mitchell. Cooper had then been introduced to the well-connected American Joseph Kaufman by Charlie Kray at the Colony in August 1966. At the time Mitchell was in possession of stolen Canadian bearer bonds and was trying to sell them for 50 per cent of their face value. Cooper, who had offices in Albemarle Street off Piccadilly, told him they were worthless.

According to Cooper everyone was swindling everyone else. The Krays claimed they had bought stolen bonds at 35% of face value, when in fact they paid 25%. They now wanted 60% and Cooper's associate, Heinz Pollman, said he could get the 60% but should tell the Krays he could only get 50% – Pollman and Cooper would then receive an extra 10% plus commission from the Krays. Pollman actually sold the bonds for 95%!

After a delay in the money filtering through, Reggie, Charlie and others were regular visitors to Cooper's Albemarle Street offices, demanding to know where it was.

It was Cooper who thought up the 1966 takeover of the stock market-quoted company New Brighton Tower Ltd, which owned the Victoria Sporting Club off the Edgware Road and was run by the crooked solicitor Judah Binstock, who had at one time acted for the remnants of the Messina brothers empire. There had been troubles in the club and the Krays were brought in to sort out the problems. However, once in they stayed, and the straight clientele began to drift away as they had done from Esmeralda's. It was after an associate Jack Dawson-Ellis was badly beaten that Binstock brought in members of the Corsican mafia who had interests in casinos on the south coast to explain to the Krays why they should withdraw.

The Krays wanted more, and on a bond-collecting trip to Montreal, Charlie Kray, Leslie Payne and others travelled on a plane which by chance carried a number of Playboy Bunnies. Unfortunately the mood turned sour when most were refused entry and kept in custody overnight. Rather than contest the matter, they took the option of being refused entry and were returned in rather less style.

In November 1965 Charlie Kray, Cooper, Payne and new boy to bond-smuggling Freddy Gore went to Paris to meet American

Mafiosi and collect forged bearer bonds. According to Charlie Kray, Gore lost his nerve and said he couldn't carry the bonds; Leslie Payne said it wasn't part of the deal that he should do so and Charlie was left to bring them through Heathrow himself. It is probable that this was the final straw for the Krays as far as Payne was concerned. It was time for him to go, and McVitie was instructed to kill him.[166]

Shortly before the roof fell in, Ronnie, Cooper and the Twins' old friend Dickie Morgan went to New York in early April 1968. There were to be negotiations over final approval of the book John Pearson was writing about the twins for which McGraw Hill had paid a $25,000 advance. And Ronnie wanted to meet a number of old-time boxers. Quite how they managed to overcome the fact that four years earlier Ronnie had been denied entry is a matter of speculation. Almost certainly it was stage managed by John Du Rose in an attempt to incriminate New York's Gallo brothers. Under Du Rose's direction Cooper took Ronnie Kray and Morgan to Paris, where they stayed the night at the Hotel Chateau Frontenac off the Champs Elysees. The next day they were given visas at a purported branch of the American Embassy there.

They already knew Joseph Kaufman who had been bringing over 700 punters a month on gambling junkets to the Colony and the Victoria Sporting Club. The players were charged $280 for their fares and hotels and Kaufman added another $280 to be split between himself and the Krays. Now Kaufman met Ronnie and the others at the airport.[167] They stayed at the Hotel Warwick and he took them to Gallagher's Steakhouse off Broadway, where they met some of Kray's boxing heroes, including Rocky Graziano. Also there was the former boxer turned mobster Frank 'Punchy' Illiano, a capo of 'Crazy' Joey Gallo's crew who owned what Kaufman described as a 'pouf' club, The Mousetrap, on Broadway where he took Ronnie.[168]

In *Villains We Have Known* Reggie Kray has a more romantic version of Ronnie's meeting with Punchy Illiano. He claims Ronnie and Kaufman went to a small café in New York's Little Italy and there Ronnie introduced himself to Edmondo, a dwarf mascot to the Gallo Family, who was outside. Ronnie was taken into the café and was introduced to Illiano, who checked him out. In a matter of moments Ronnie was surrounded by Gallo Family members including Al, one of the brothers, who apologised that his brother Joe was away on business while a third, Larry, was dying of cancer in hospital. Otherwise they would both have come to greet him. It is likely most of the men there were not the genuine article, but actors hired by Cooper to play the part.[169]

It was now Cooper arranged for Kaufman to deal in $160,000 worth of bonds. According to Kaufman, Cooper said that the bonds were straight but, in fact, they had been stolen from the New York office of a firm of lawyers in January that year. Later Kaufman arranged for them to be sent to the Mayfair Hotel in London where he was staying.

In late April 1968 Cooper was summoned to The Horns and told by the Krays that two of their enemies were to be killed the next weekend. One was the Maltese club owner George Caruana, who had offended the Kray's friend, the pornographer and club owner Bernie Silver. Silver had merely wanted Caruana to be given a beating, but the Krays believed it would be better for everyone if Caruana was dead. His continued existence and their apparent inability to do anything about it was showing them up. The other enemy was Jimmy Evans, who, in a domestic dispute, had had the temerity to shoot Freddie Foreman's brother George in the groin. Caruana was to be blown up when he started his car and Jimmy Evans was to be stabbed with a poisoned syringe, symbolically at the Old Bailey. There were certain problems with both initiatives. First, gelignite had to be obtained and secondly, even in the days when security was effectively non-existent, how was a syringe to be smuggled into the Old Bailey in such a way that the user could escape? How could Cooper help?

The answer to both problems was Eugene Paul Elvey, a one-time hairdresser, whose real name was Levy. In his early days he had worked with the smuggler Michael Kendrick taking gold to India and Cairo. He was already deeply involved with the Krays. Around the time of the death of Frances Kray he had agreed to hurt the wife of a West London smuggler as a punishment for informing on her husband. He then told Tommy Cowley he would give the Krays the money to have it done for him. Reggie turned down the offer.[170]

Cooper took the opportunity to tell Elvey about the plot to kill Caruana and that Charlie and the Twins were putting pressure on him. He asked Elvey to fly to Glasgow to collect some dynamite. So on 30 April 1968, unaware he was in Nipper Read's sights, Elvey took the Cunard Eagle flight to Glasgow, bought the gelignite and was waiting in the passenger lounge for the return flight when he was arrested by a senior customs officer.

Nipper Read was notified and immediately flew with Frank Cater to Glasgow, where Elvey initially denied any knowledge of the gelignite but then began to tell what was an almost unbelievable story.

Originally, said Elvey, it had been decided that Jimmy Evans should be shot with a crossbow and he had been commissioned to buy the weapon along with bolts and a telescopic sight for which he paid £51.2.3d. at Lillywhites, the sports outfitters in Piccadilly. When he found he was unable to shoot with the bow, the alternatives of a harpoon gun or a telescopic rifle were rejected and the syringe plot was devised. Cooper then contacted another friend, the gold and people smuggler and former ace speedway rider Francis Squire 'Split' Waterman, to make a suitcase which would go unnoticed at the Old Bailey. It would have a retractable syringe built into the leather.

According to Elvey's statement to the police, he went to the White House hotel in Central London where Waterman showed him the case he had made, and they then took it to Charlie Kray at Grace Mansions. The pair, along with Waterman, went to the Old Bailey where Evans was watching a case but, according to Elvey, initially he was unsure they had the right man and then on the second occasion at the crucial moment his arm froze when about to use the syringe.

In the end Elvey's reward for his cooperation was a fine for currency offences at Ealing Magistrates' Court and the opportunity to atone for his sins in the witness box.

The next step was to arrest Cooper, but when Read did so he had a serious shock. When he was told he was to be charged with conspiracy to murder, Cooper nonchalantly asked to see Du Rose for whom, he said, he had been working as an informant and spy for two years. When Read confronted his superior:

'I really let go at Du Rose and his reply was simply, "He never gave me anything substantial. I'd have let you know." Du Rose must have had someone on my squad he was talking to.'[171]

In a matter of moments Cooper was transformed from an accused to a witness. Read later came to believe it was another member of the Squad, Henry Mooney, who had been running Cooper for Du Rose but from then on, Du Rose was rigorously excluded from any meeting in which confidential decisions were taken.

If Cooper simply disappeared off the streets, Read feared that the Krays would know he had been arrested and probably turned. His plan was therefore to put Cooper in a clinic in Weymouth Street to which Ronnie could be lured and where Read would be in the next room recording the conversation. The plan did not work. Ronnie rang to say he had been away and was tired. Instead of coming himself he would send over Tommy Cowley with some eggs – not quite what Read had hoped for. The one benefit was that while the tapes were running, Kaufman turned up to confirm he had arranged for the bonds to be sent to the Mayfair Hotel.[172]

On 6 May, the last night of liberty for the Twins, it really was a question of the 'Gang's All Here'. The party at the Astor showed that a slashing between friends could be forgiven because, according to Joseph Kaufman, some of the Cardew brothers were there along with the three Lambrianou brothers, Checker Berry, Scotch Ian Dickson, Dickie Morgan, Leslie Berman and Albert Donoghue. Members of the Firm thought there was an increased police presence in and around the club and took to going to the lavatory in pairs to avoid any possible fit ups. Orders were given that no photographs should be taken.[173]

The arrests were scheduled to happen simultaneously on the morning of 7 May. Read had been afraid that there might be a shoot-out with the police or that, pre-warned, the Krays might try to flee or to dispose of witnesses against them. This time there would be no opportunity for a leak.

Read telephoned the Detective Inspectors in each of the 10 branches of the Regional Crime Squads in the London area and asked them to have men available at short notice. The DIs had to telephone Read at midnight and, when they did, he told them to call back at 3.30 a.m. This time the men were told to report to Tintagel House in an hour's time. Once the men arrived they were kept together until they were sent on the raids. Read reserved the arrests of the Twins for himself.

At 6 a.m. Algie Hemingway jemmied the front door of the flat at Bunhill Row. Two minders were in the front room and Reggie was in bed with a former girlfriend of Chris Lambrianou. Ronnie, in bed with a young boy, was amazingly sanguine. 'Yes, all right, Mr Read, but I've got to have my pills, you know that,' was his reply when he was read his rights. Back at West End Central, told he would be charged with conspiracy to murder an unnamed man, he asked, 'Did you remember my pills, Mr Read? I shall have to have them.' Charlie Kray was arrested at his home. Kaufman was arrested that morning in the Mayfair Hotel, where some $190,000 worth of stolen bonds arrived a couple of days later.

After the Krays' arrests the Commissioner held a celebratory drinks party at Scotland Yard, and who should be there but Ferguson Walker. Read was not pleased:

'I went over to him and said, "What the fuck are you doing here?" He wouldn't answer; he just looked away.'

CHAPTER 13
THE COMMITTAL

On 9 May 1968 *The Times*, reporting the arrests, was guarded:

'The Kray Twins are well known in sporting circles in the
East End where they have both distinguished themselves
as amateur and professional boxers. With their brother
they raised money for old people's charities in the area.'

For the moment all Read had was two charges of conspiracy to
murder an unnamed man, two of blackmail – demanding money
from Payne and Gore – four of Long Firm frauds and one of grievous
bodily harm. Holding charges only. Attack is often the best defence,
and when Read charged Reggie with demanding with menaces
and conspiracy to defraud he replied, 'Yes, Mr Read. We've been
expecting another frame-up for a long time. But this time we've got
witnesses. There's plenty of people will want to help us.' Charlie Kray
said, 'I've never asked anybody for anything in my life, Mr Read.'[174]

In all, 18 appeared at Bow Street court that morning. In addition
to the Krays, stalwarts Tommy Cowley, Charlie Mitchell, Tommy

Brown, Charlie Clarke, Alf Willey, Billy Exley and Sammy Lederman were in the dock along with a number of others charged with fraud. There were no immediate applications for bail for the Twins and Charlie. Their biographer John Pearson had approached Read volunteering to stand as surety for the Twins, but Read told him he should wait until he heard some of the evidence, which might make him change his mind. Most of the fraudsters were released to appear in due course. Joseph Kaufman, however, was remanded in custody.

There were still major players at large. Donoghue had been staying with a girl and so avoided the police when they called at his home the morning of the swoop. Later that morning he went round to the Krays at Bunhill Row and found the police there. He told them his name was Barry, that he had a minicab firm and had come to have the Twins settle their account. The police let him go.

Ronnie Hart was another who had avoided arrest. On the morning of the police raids on the Krays he had gone to Bunhill Road to discuss the potential killing of a bookmaker. He had seen the door off its hinges and left. Later he and Albert Donoghue went to stay in a caravan in Poole. After two weeks they split up and Hart and his girlfriend Vicki James went to live in Ashford, Kent, where he was sent a message that he was to stay until he heard from Freddie Foreman. Donoghue's version was that they stayed in London collecting protection money, before heading to Sussex rather than Kent. He returned to Bethnal Green and stayed in a flat with Dickie Morgan where they were both arrested. According to Mickey Bailey, Donoghue had approached him to see whether the receiver Tony 'The Magpie' Maffia could smuggle him out of the country by boat but nothing came of the plan, possibly because Maffia was shot and killed within the month.[175]

Until 1967 all committal proceedings could be reported in detail. A change in the law then meant that proceedings could only be reported on the application of the defence. However, if one wanted the ban lifted, everybody suffered. On 17 May Paul Wrightson (defending Reggie) asked for the ban to be lifted at this early stage. Quite what induced him to do so is unclear. At that time no actual murder charges had been laid and, presumably against all advice, Reggie had insisted. The other thought is that with a rather nebulous conspiracy to murder and some uninteresting fraud charges, he wanted to expose the police case as weak and garner some sympathy for oppressed defendants everywhere. Whatever the reason, it backfired spectacularly.

At first, the remand hearings leading up to the committal proceedings seemed to go well for the Krays and they received some favourable copy in the newspapers. The police were holding back on the so far unnamed man whom the Krays had allegedly conspired to murder. They were balancing the protection of vulnerable witnesses on the one hand with the right to confront one's accuser on the other. It was, in fact, all a game acted out to obtain favourable press coverage. And with every refusal to disclose the name of the potential victims, sympathy for the Twins mounted.

The defence wished to know who the victims were, and Ivan Lawrence (defending Ronnie) quipped that if one of them was Santa Claus, bail would have to be allowed. Five weeks later on 14 June he was still trying: 'For the sixth time I rise to my feet to allow the officer in the case to answer the question, "What are the names of the two persons in the conspiracy to murder charges?"' And for the sixth time the sitting magistrate replied it was an inappropriate question for a remand hearing. Eventually an application was made to the Divisional Court to order the Director of Public Prosecutions to release the names, which he did the day before the next hearing. As expected, one of the two names was George Caruana, the Soho Maltese club owner. The other was Jimmy Evans, the alleged attacker of Freddie Foreman's brother George.

But well before then, things had improved for Read in the Frank Mitchell case. On 13 May, the *Daily Express* had run a headline, 'Krays – New Moves Today'. As a result Frank Mitchell's minder, Lennie 'Books' Dunn, believing that it referred to him, walked into West Ham police station, Read was informed of this immediately, but by the time he arrived, Dunn had already made a suicide attempt, convinced the Krays were out to get him. His fears were probably justified. There had been a plan to throw him from the 14th floor of the block of flats where he lived.[176]

Now a terrified Dunn gave details of the time when Frank Mitchell had stayed at his flat. Dunn had always wanted to be a friend of the Krays but after a dose of the limelight with the arrival of the 'Mad Axeman', he realised he preferred anonymity.

At first Read did not believe his tale of watching Mitchell copy out the letters written for him, of the arrival of Lisa the nightclub hostess, of the final moments of Mitchell's life and the frantic clearance of the flat, but as Dunn provided more and more detail he became convinced it was true. Read's next problem was that Dunn was at best an accomplice. Read and his team had to find corroborating witnesses. Billy Exley provided some help, but he too was an accomplice and by the time of the trial was himself serving a sentence for attempted murder. The best option would be to try to find Lisa before the Krays got to her.

In the end it was Frank Cater who traced her through good old-fashioned police work. Exley knew he had taken her to Bayswater when she went to pick up some clothes and he pointed out the house. Cater spoke with the then tenant and she confirmed Lisa came from 'up north' and had stayed with her for 18 months, but around Christmas one year she had gone away for a week and refused to say where she had been. Cater asked if she knew Lisa's doctor, but all she knew was that she had once had been taken ill at the West London Air Terminal on the Cromwell Road. Cater traced the hospital to which she had been taken and they provided details of her mother in Leeds. A photograph of her taken at Winstons was sent by train. Her mother identified her and told the police that Lisa was living in Battersea, but was planning to travel to Australia in a motor caravan with her boyfriend. When Cater went to the flat, he was told she had left, but the motor caravan was being repaired in Paddington before they took it abroad. Cater traced it, and the garage owner told him the Australian owner was staying somewhere in Earl's Court and had hired a Ford Transit van with a Stuyvesant cigarette advertisement on a door. Cater found the van parked outside a small bed and breakfast hotel, went in and woke Lisa up, telling her he was from Scotland Yard and his visit was about Frank Mitchell.

She was driven to Scotland Yard with Cater and Sergeant Bert Trevette. It was a smooth journey until, on Lambeth Bridge on the way to Tintagel House, Lisa panicked and tried to get out of the car.

She had realised she was not going to Scotland Yard and thought Cater and Trevette were Kray men flashing her a fake warrant card. Pulled back in, she then asked to see Cater's hands. When she examined them she was convinced they were not workman's hands and calmed down. Although technically she could have been said to be an accomplice in the escape, she was now the witness who provided sufficient evidence for charges to be brought. By 31 May Read was in a position to lay specific murder charges, the first of which was the murder of Frank Mitchell. The committal proceedings began on 26 June.

Defections among the ranks were to be expected, but Read never thought the first one would be the dog doper and fraudster Charlie Mitchell, whom he had thought to be 'a real hard nose'. Nevertheless his wife telephoned Read, who went to see him on the afternoon of 5 June. Apart from giving details of stolen bond transactions he also said there was a contract out on both Read himself and Leslie Payne. He, Mitchell, had been approached in the exercise yard at Brixton by Tommy Cowley, to find the money, said to be £5,000, to pay for the black New York hitman 'Junior' who had a panther tattooed on his arm. Killing Read and Payne was a step too far for an extortionist and dog doper.

Read checked the story and independently received a call from a colleague saying he had been to see one of his snouts in Brighton and the word was that Mitchell's story should be taken seriously. There was also corroboration because when one of the defendant's cells was searched, a series of messages were found instructing someone called 'Junior' to 'do the business'. Read next contacted Alden McCray, head of the FBI in Europe, who told him such a man did exist in the States. Read, who drove to Tintagel House every day, began to change his route and to look under his car before he started it. Eventually 'Junior' was stopped at Shannon airport and sent back home. Charlie Mitchell went on to make a complete statement and on 25 June when Kenneth Jones, appearing for the Director of Public Prosecutions, told the magistrate, 'It has been decided he should be used as a prosecution witness'. It came as a body blow to the Twins.

Read recalled:

> 'Mitchell walked from the back row [of the dock] as though he was going to collect a prize at a Sunday School. Even then the Twins could not believe what was going on. It was only later that they realised the full implication of the betrayal, and, by then it was too late for them to show their displeasure in a tangible way.'[177]

After Charlie Mitchell's disappearance into the witness protection scheme, Ronnie sent for the diminutive receiver Stan Davis:

> 'What Ronnie wanted to know was where Charlie [Mitchell] was, and I was to find out. I was living in Clapham at the time and I went to Brixton. I'd given a false name at the gate but the next day I had a visit from the police. "Why had I given a moody name?" I told them I didn't want to give my own and they left it at that, but it put me off and I didn't do anything about finding Charlie. I never saw Ronnie again.'[178]

From then on there was a steady trickle of defendants who wanted to see Read or Henry Mooney. Scotch Jack Dickson had been picked up in an East End pub a few weeks after the sweep and was charged with harbouring Frank Mitchell. He soon said he would plead guilty and made a statement to Mooney. Unfortunately many of the others were either unable to make substantial contributions or were still sitting on the fence. They included Connie Whitehead, who said he would make a statement if Read could guarantee to protect his wife and son. Read said he could arrange protection whether he made a statement or not. No statement was ever made but Whitehead told him that Ronnie had said, 'Me and Reggie done McVitie. He tried to make us look silly and he was getting too flash anyway.' At the time Ronnie had a flick knife and he told Whitehead to 'keep your mouth shut or I will stick this in your head'. Whitehead also told Read that McVitie had been given £100 in the Grave Maurice to kill Payne and there was the promise of a further £400 on completion.

On 31 May Reggie and Donoghue had been charged with the murder of Frank Mitchell. Ronnie, Charlie Kray, Connie Whitehead, Tommy Cowley, Wally Garelick, Scotch Jack Dickson and Pat Connolly were all charged with harbouring Mitchell or helping in his escape.

On 5 July Charlie Kray and Connie Whitehead were found to have no case to answer on the charge that they murdered Frank Mitchell. That left the Twins and Donoghue on the murder charge and the others on harbouring and helping him escape charges.

31 May had also been the day when Robin Simpson, applying for bail for Joseph Kaufman, pressed Read as to why the police were objecting. There was a certain amount of ducking and diving

between them as Read tried to avoid answering the question, but as Simpson pressed on, the worse it became for him. 'Well what is it? Let us have it out. Let us be honest, let us have the truth,' said Simpson.

In bail applications there was no such thing as the hearsay rule. The police could rely on fact, gossip and speculation in equal parts. The answer, said Read, was:

> 'The suggestion made by my colleagues in America is that he is a member of an organisation known as the Mafia and that he is already suspected of offences in America, and if he is granted bail he will be arrested when he arrives in America.'[179]

End of bail application.

The next week Kaufman told the magistrate, Kenneth Barraclough, that he had been a spy for the FBI. 'I have pretended to be a communist and have attended meetings and reported back to the FBI in New York.' He still went back to Brixton.

As for the fraudsters, one of the first to be arrested had been the disbarred barrister Stanley Crowther who complained that he had been left holding the baby. 'A singularly unattractive baby,' said the committing magistrate Geraint Rees, wittily. At the end of June Crowther received 15 months for fraudulent trading. He claimed he had only been a clerk earning £15 a week in a company which was running up losses of over £24,000. Who was behind it, then? 'It is more than my life is worth to tell you.' Nevertheless he had made a very long and detailed, if often self-serving statement to the police.

As for the Cornell murder, John Alexander 'Ian' Barrie was not arrested until 29 June at the British Oak Public House in the Lea Bridge Road. At the time he told Henry Mooney:

> 'I feel sick. I have been like an animal for some days. I knew you would come for me, and such a lovely day too. I did not shoot Cornell. I wish I could tell you what happened but I would get shot.'

Five days later, on 4 July, he was put on an identification parade over the Cornell murder. Police officers Henry Mooney and Pat Allen had been nursing the barmaid and her family for the past weeks, taking her and the children to Heathrow. While Allen took the children to watch the planes landing and taking off, Mooney, exercising all his Irish charm, coaxed the barmaid into believing the police could, in fact, protect her from the Firm. Finally, just about the only one of the civilian witnesses without a prior conviction, she agreed to co-operate.

Barrie had originally had Bernie Perkoff as his solicitor, but the Krays had made him change to Sampson & Co. Now it was Ralph Haeems who attended to watch the parade on his behalf. The barmaid was sat down at a table and each of the men on the line-up – with lint and sticking plaster by their right ears because Barrie had a scar – had to stop in front of the table and turn before walking back to the line. After they had all completed the exercise the officer in charge of the parade asked if she wanted to see anyone again and she said, 'Number Five,' before she realised she had miscounted, and said, 'No. Number Six [Barrie].' Haeems then claimed the barmaid had said she was not certain Barrie was the man with Ronnie, so statements were taken from all the other men on the parade who confirmed her identification of Barrie.

Ronnie and Ian Barrie were committed for trial on the Cornell murder charge on 17 July.

By that time the committal proceedings on other charges were in full swing, with Alan Bruce Cooper telling magistrate Kenneth Barraclough how he, Elvey and Split Waterman had devised the suitcase plot. He, Cooper, was to receive £1,000 for the contract. By now Caruana had sensibly left the country and, the court was told, was not likely to return. When Kenneth Jones, opening the case for the prosecution, gave an outline of Elvey's likely evidence, Reggie leaped to his feet to ask, 'Excuse me, sir, is James Bond going to give evidence in this case?... this is ridiculous'. The magistrate, Kenneth Barraclough, told him to sit down. Eventually he decided the Caruana and Evans cases were too fanciful for a jury, and in turn the prosecution decided not to proceed on these charges.

Back in Brixton things did not go well for Kaufman, where on 13 September he was given a belting by Reggie Kray in the D Wing recreation room. He had been telling Reggie that as a defensive measure he should take a summons out against Cooper. Reggie had said, 'Leave me alone. I don't want to know.' Kaufman had replied, 'You Limey bums, you got no balls.' Other prisoners at the scene told the police they thought Kaufman so angry he was going to attack Reggie, and very sensibly Kray had hit him first. Kaufman suffered a fractured nose and left cheekbone. After a trip to hospital, he was transferred to another prison. No charges followed.

Nor were things going well on the domestic front for Reggie. 'Ginger Carole' Thompson, to whom he had given tickets for the trial, had abandoned ship. He had, he claimed, given her £1,750 out of £5,000 he had received from a newspaper, but when he found another man's clothes mixed in with the clean laundry she sent him, he decided she had been unfaithful. This was little harsh considering the fact he had been found in bed with another woman at the time of his arrest.[180]

There was, however, one shaft of light. Reggie and Charlie applied for permission to take evening classes in French, presumably so that if they ever escaped or were given bail they would be able to ask, 'Où est le train for Paris?' It was granted, subject to there being no more than three men in the class.

Overall, prison security was not that tight. Chris Lambrianou claimed that in early August he also turned up, signed the visitor's book as Mickey Mouse, Disneyland, and was allowed in to see the pair.

With all the negative publicity, Paul Wrightson, representing Ronnie, tried to have the reporting ban restored, but was turned down by the Bow Street Magistrates and the Divisional Court. Unable to believe their good fortune, the papers lovingly continued to report on the Mitchell killing.

But the biggest catch for Read was Albert Donoghue and that was wholly the fault of the Twins and Manny Fryde. In July Donoghue had been making notes to give to Fryde who was representing him, and one day he was called to the solicitors' visiting room and there he found the Twins, Charlie and Fryde. According to Donoghue he produced the notes, which Reggie took from him and ripped up. Fryde excused himself, saying he would go and get another chair despite the fact they already had one each. While he was out of the room Ronnie told Donoghue that Scotch Jack Dickson was going to hold his hands up for the Cornell murder; Ronnie Hart would wear the McVitie murder and he [Donoghue] was to accept that he had shot Mitchell. What the Twins did not know was that Hart and Dickson had already turned.

Donoghue was horrified. He thought he might be killed if he did not go along with the scenario and he now wanted to see Read. His main worry, however, was that prison officers would tell the Twins that he'd asked to see the police. Therefore, when his mother came to visit him the next day, he passed her a screwed-up piece of paper saying he wished to see Read but not in the solicitors' rooms. Read was given the note on 16 July and immediately telephoned Donoghue's mother, who told him it was a matter of life and death. That evening he and Frank Cater went to see Donoghue in the prison hospital. There Donoghue told him that he had been set up to take the Mitchell murder and that if he did, 'my wife and kids will be all right'. Afraid of being poisoned, he was now having his meals sent in. Over three days from 16 July Donoghue made what Read described as a 'cold, clinical statement' about Mitchell's escape, harbouring and death at the hands of Alf Gerard. He was also able to bolster the case against them for the killing of McVitie, telling Read of the redecoration of Carol Skinner's flat.

Read then introduced him to the solicitor Victor Lissack, a dead ringer for the actor Robert Morley. At a conference on 19 July between Read, David Hopkin of the DPP's office and counsel

Kenneth Jones, it was decided that for the time being Donoghue should still be charged with Mitchell's murder. Later a decision could be taken whether to use him as a witness. In the meantime, he was moved first to Chelmsford, then to Maidstone and finally to Winson Green in Birmingham with a cover story that he had been sent there as a punishment for his non-cooperation with the police. The Krays obviously accepted this story at face value, because Reggie arranged a daily £5 payment to Donoghue's mother, and provided transport whenever she wished to visit him.

Over the summer, one by one, the remaining members of the Firm were brought in or surrendered. Some, like the Lambrianous, dithered about on which side of the fence they would sit. On 7 August Chris, Tony Lambrianou and their brother Nicky had been found by West Midlands Police in Hart's Hotel, Walsall where they were staying under false names, and Chris was brought to London.

Questioned by Read, he denied he had been at the Evering Road party and was released after Read had given him his card and said he should ring if he wanted to talk to him in the future. Ever the good soldier, Chris Lambrianou trotted round to the Twins' parents in Bunhill Row, who persuaded him to go and see their sons in Brixton. He then went to see Manny Fryde at Sampsons and made a statement that he knew nothing about the McVitie murder and wanted to be left alone. After that he went back to Birmingham and was arrested a fortnight later on his way to the Elbow Room in Aston.

Then on 8 August, when Carol Skinner was taken to see Read again, she asked for protection. She broke down in tears and this time told him what had happened.

Her friend Jenny King told me:

> 'Carol and I knew the police would come one day and we
> worked out how we would know if the other was helping
> them. So we agreed that we'd have a code. 'It was the day
> they took the stereo back.' That was the words Nipper
> Read used to me when he had me in to Tintagel after the
> Twins had been arrested. Up until then I'd said nothing
> but it was then I knew Carole had talked.'

Some, like Harry Hopwood, who had been the best man at Charlie Snr
and Violet's wedding, co-operated and were marked down as potential
prosecution witnesses. Then at the end of August, Ronnie Hart's
cousin, Terence, went to Read to say he had been paying protection
money to the Twins ever since Ronnie had escaped from prison. To
find the money Terence Hart had embezzled around £4,500 from his
employers, a car dealership in Ashford, and paid the money over to
Ronnie Kray either in a pub near Vallance Road or in the lavatories
at Charing Cross railway station. Read explained it was vital for him
to see his cousin and on 2 September at 4.45 a.m. he had a call to say
Ronnie Hart would come to Tintagel House in an hour's time.

Once Hart began to tell his story of the McVitie killing, from
the moment he was sent to tell Barrie to bring the gun in person to
Evering Road, to the visit to Freddie Foreman to dispose of the body,
Read knew he wanted him as a witness. John Dickson could not say
what actually went on in the Blind Beggar; Donoghue could not say
what had actually gone on at Evering Road; but Ronnie Hart could

– never mind the fact he was also heavily incriminated in the McVitie murder. He was needed, and the ends were certainly going to justify the means. In turn Hart justified his defection on two grounds. First, there was his own self-preservation and that of his family. Secondly, and more righteously, was his discovery that Ronnie Kray had been leaning on his car salesman cousin Terence.[181]

During the week Read also saw the good Dr Blasker, who admitted treating various members of the Firm for gunshot wounds. He had not felt obliged to report the injuries to the police because his first loyalty was to the Kray family. They were private clients and, according to Donoghue, paid Blasker with a tenner and a bottle of spirits.

With Hart's statement in the bag and the authority of the DPP to use him as a witness, on 11 September, Henry Mooney conducted another sweep. Chris Lambrianou was taken to London again where he continued to say he was not at Evering Road when McVitie was murdered.

Chris Lambrianou also denied he had set up McVitie and refused to answer questions about cleaning up 97 Evering Road. His brother Tony denied all knowledge of McVitie's killing and said he had seen him around Christmas in the Balls Pond Road in North London, well after the time of the murder. Ronnie Bender denied being at the Evering Road party. All were charged with McVitie's murder and sent to Brixton and elsewhere to join the other Firm members in prison.

Once he was in prison Chris Lambrianou was seen by Ralph Haeems, still choreographing the Krays' defences. And he was horrified to hear Haeems tell him they wished him to say there had been no party at Carol Skinner's on the night McVitie was killed. It was clear that Haeems was acting in the Krays' best interests and not those of his other clients. When Lambrianou later discussed it with the Twins he was told, 'It was a party that never happened. Don't even *think* it did.' And foolishly he agreed to go along with the story.[182] Later he would write to the Court of Appeal saying that with his brother Tony in Brixton with the Twins, he had been afraid to do anything which might harm him.

Charged on 19 September with the murder of McVitie, Ronnie Kray replied, 'Your sarcastic insinuations are far too obnoxious to be appreciated.' Reggie merely said 'Not guilty'. On 10 October Sammy Lederman and Micky Fawcett were discharged on the fraud charges. And five days later Lissack, acting for Donoghue, put the boot in by having the reporting restrictions lifted in the McVitie case. A week later on 22 October, the Twins were committed to stand trial at the Old Bailey on the McVitie charge. By now Freddie Foreman had been arrested and he also was committed for trial.

CHAPTER 14
THE FIRST KRAY TRIAL

In the late autumn of 1968, with the Twins and cohorts finally committed for trial, the prosecution was tidying up its case. Junior counsel John Leonard was advising what evidence needed bolstering, what further statements should be taken and what witnesses should be called. Despite Bobby Teale's later claims that he and his brothers brought down the Krays, by October, Leonard did not think there was any point in calling him at that stage.[183]

As for the defence, after the committal proceedings it was time to give notice of alibi witnesses. Until the Criminal Justice Act 1967 the prosecution had no idea whether a defendant was going to call an alibi and if so, who DPP the witnesses might be. If, for example, the defendant said he had been at Walthamstow dogs on the night of the robbery or whatever, the Act now gave the police the chance to check that at least the animals had actually run that evening.

Things had changed with the introduction of the Act and, if an alibi was to be called, details of witnesses had to be given to the prosecution within seven days of the committal proceedings, and the police were to be allowed to interview them to test their stories. There were fears among lawyers that this would frighten off the witnesses and no half-way decent lawyer would allow his alibi witnesses to be seen without a senior member of his firm being present. Even then the interviews could often be described as 'heavy'. There were also fears that the police would see the witnesses a second time without a defence lawyer being present, and so have two bites at the cherry.

In fact it was the first bite which caused problems for Fryde and Haeems. The latter wrote to the DPP telling him that Ronnie Kray's defence would be that at the time of the Cornell shooting he was in The Lion in Tapp Street with, among others, John Dickson, Sammy Lederman and Robert Buckley. Unfortunately John Dickson had already seen Henry Mooney on 17 August in Wandsworth prison and had told him he had driven Kray to the Blind Beggar.

When Lederman was interviewed with Haeems present, he said he had been at home with his father and not in The Lion, 'much to the dismay of Haeems', noted Mooney delightedly. Nor was Buckley, who by this time was serving his four-year sentence for robbery, any great help. He had already told Mooney he had been in The Lion and said that he would not be giving evidence. He was, he said, terrified of the Twins. If called as a witness, he said he would tell the truth.

On 9 September 1968 Henry Mooney telephoned Haeems to make an appointment to see the alibi witnesses Lederman and Bobby Buckley. Initially Haeems refused but after taking counsel's advice eventually agreed to the meeting. When Buckley said he would only tell the truth and was saying nothing more, Haeems told Mooney this indeed confirmed he was sticking to the alibi he was providing for Ronnie. It was a serious miscalculation.

In the 1960s, murder trials were presided over by what were called 'red judges' from the High Court, so called because of the colour of their robes. None of the lawyers acting for the defendants can have been that pleased to learn that the red judge in this case would be the acerbic and autocratic Mr Justice Melford Stevenson. A man who cut a Nietzschean figure as he posed when he came into court, barristers almost knocked their heads on the bench in front of them as they tried to bow lower than their colleagues. Generally hated by defendants for the lengthy sentences he handed out and the comments he made, he once sentenced a 19-year-old to Borstal training on his first offence, saying he hoped 'no soft-hearted official will recommend your early release'.

He was, wrote the Appeal Court judge Sir Robin Dunne in his memoirs *Sword and Wig*, 'the worst judge since the war' – and Stevenson had faced stiff opposition to achieve that particular accolade. Very pro-police, he lived near Winchester in a house named 'Truncheons'.[184] It was to be a trial in which the defence could expect little in the way of discretion exercised in their favour.

Kenneth Jones would lead for the prosecution. By no means the roughest of prosecutors of his generation, Jones, the overweight Recorder of Wolverhampton, had the reputation for meticulous preparation along with the ability both to cross-examine and to appeal to juries. He would lead ex-Guards officer John Leonard and the vastly overweight Caesar James Crespi, a man said to be able to eat eighteen Wimpeys at a sitting.

Meanwhile it was time to instruct barristers to appear for the various defendants. Generally the burden of the defence case falls on the shoulders of the barrister appearing for the defendant first named in the indictment. That defendant was Ronnie Kray. There was logic in this from the point of view of the prosecution. Cornell's was the first murder chronologically, and was said to have been committed by Ronnie. It would, however, have been far better from the defence point of view if Reggie had been named first. Then it would have been the incisive Paul Wrightson QC, who had prosecuted Reggie in the 1969 Podro blackmail case, who would have had first crack at the witnesses and would have borne the brunt of the inevitable quarrels with Melford Stevenson. As it was defendants often believe in luck and Wrightson, albeit with considerable unrequested help from Manny Fryde, had achieved an acquittal for Reggie in the Hide-A-Way case. Reggie now regarded him as a talisman and wanted to keep him for himself. Curiously, Petre Crowder, who had appeared for Ronnie in that case, was shuffled down the pack.

Quite why Fryde chose the New Zealander John Platts-Mills QC for Ronnie remains something of a mystery. For a start, Platts-Mills' politics fell into Stevenson's category of major dislikes. This 63-year-old tall, distinguished-looking man of infinite kindness was a former socialist MP who had been a conscientious objector during the War, working as a Bevin Boy. He was still a committed left-winger. It was not something likely to appeal to Stevenson, who said of him maliciously, 'he helps solicitors on with their coats like Father D'Arcy elevating the host.'

One barrister who was with Platts-Mills in another case told me:

'He was a Stalinist, humourless and dull, but he had moral courage in spades and was utterly fearless in advancing his clients' defences, quite regardless of how unpopular they might have been, and he was utterly unmoved by judicial hostility. Exactly what a barrister should be. But not everybody was so fastidious about the duty to the client.'[185]

But, fatally for the defence, Platts-Mills, who had appeared for Charlie Richardson two years earlier, was not a man who could ask a straight question. Instead he had an alarming tendency to go off on tangents. In his opening speech in the Cornell trial he took time out to give the jury the definition of the word 'juggernaut':

'I am not sure that I remember exactly what a juggernaut was. I think it was a great chariot in an ancient, barbaric, pagan religious festival, where Bacchanalia of a sort, drunken old men roared in stupor on a chariot and drunken young women danced with them, and as it dragged forward in ecstasy or hysteria people were thrown under the wheels or threw themselves under the wheels in religious fervour.'

Another good, if shorter, example of this came in his questioning of Alfie Teale, a prosecution witness in the later Mitchell trial, over the name of a public house in the East End:

Q. 'The Grave Maurice, the Graf meaning Prince Maurice, the brother of Prince Rupert?'
A. 'The Grave Maurice, I know it as.'

He led the rising star Ivan Lawrence, who would go on to be a Conservative MP. Charlie was represented by the rough and tough Desmond Vowden QC; Tom Williams QC and Ivor Richards appeared for Freddie Foreman. Chris Lambrianou was represented by Petre Crowder QC, along with Patrick Pakenham, the son of Lord Longford. Pakenham was one of the more flamboyant of the juniors and on one occasion was asked why he was wearing Union Jack socks. 'To give the middle classes something to talk about,' was the reply. Donoghue was represented by another Conservative MP Edward Gardiner QC, along with Evan Stone.

The dissolute and gold-bedecked Sir Lionel Tennyson Thompson appeared for both Tommy Cowley and Connie Whitehead. The last in the line to inherit the baronetcy created for the poet Alfred Lord Tennyson, stories of the louche barrister abounded. One was that a barrister chanced upon him drinking champagne alone in a wine bar in Westminster. 'Sit down, Smith. Have a drink,' he said, 'I'm celebrating. Mother's dead'.

In long trials judges often pick on one particular counsel as their butt, usually a junior counsel if all the others are QCs, and Thompson served that purpose for Melford Stevenson, who called him 'Mr Thomas' and, when corrected, 'Sir Thompson' before Platts-Mills intervened and said the proper address was 'Sir Lionel'. Stevenson was quite capable of this sort of mockery. He once referred to another barrister, Michael Beckman, as Mr Bechstein. Beckman retorted, 'I may be Jewish, my Lord, but I am not a grand piano.'

Also on parade for the defence were the austere William Howard QC, who once criticised a junior barrister for wearing a purple shirt in court. The Recorder of Leeds, Rudolph Lyons QC, appeared for Ronnie Bender.

The fly in the defence ointment, however, would be the very talented, garrulous, gossipy Barry Hudson QC who had been a top-class athlete in the 1930s and had narrowly missed selection for the Berlin Olympics. Known as the 'GIs' QC' after he had represented American servicemen in eleven courts martial over an 18-month period, he appeared for Anthony Barry, instructed by Bernie Perkoff.

On 3 December, Paul Wrightson suggested to the DPP that the Twins might plead guilty to certain charges – but not to the murders – if Charlie was allowed to go free. At a meeting between Treasury Counsel, DPP's man David Hopkin and Read, it was decided that it would be a question of all or nothing.

Read recalled:

> 'There's an entry note in my notebook, "Let's fight it all the way." If we had accepted a plea it would have seemed to undermine the enormity of the charges. I wanted Charlie to be convicted. My mistake was to have left him out of the Hide-A-Way. It might have prejudiced my thinking. I would have had an input but the end decision was up to Jones and Leonard.'[186]

In a murder trial there is always a medical report as to whether the defendant is fit to stand trial. In the Kray trial both Twins were seen in a series of five hour-long interviews in December 1968 for pre-trial reports. On remand both had been making cuddly toys. Reggie was good at bears and the doctor noted his 'extremely good workmanship'. 'Mentally he was alert, friendly, and pleasant and indeed one might say charming.' Ronnie's speciality was rabbits. They presented themselves as being 'highbrow cultured men'. Reggie admitted to being a heavy drinker – up to a bottle of gin a day.

Reggie told the doctor that he liked reading, particularly books on sayings and proverbs. Ronnie had battled against schizophrenia for some 16 years. It had been under control for the last ten years and he was taking 25 mg of Stemetil three times daily. He had told the doctor he was fond of listening to the opera singers Maria Callas and Gigli and reading biographies, including those of Gordon of Khartoum, Genghis Khan and Lawrence of Arabia. 'He says he is a friendly man, not bad-tempered normally, a believer in God but not a churchgoer'.[187] They were naturally both deemed fit to plead.

The press and others began applying for tickets for the trial in December. Each defendant was allowed two tickets which were sent to their solicitors. Reg's were forwarded to Uncle Alf and Carole Thompson. Ronald's went to Violet and Charlie Snr. Lissack returned the tickets sent to him as Mrs Donoghue was under police protection and no one else wanted them.[188]

But when the trial began on 8 January, black market tickets for the public gallery were on sale at £5 each per day. As a result all tickets to relatives were temporarily withdrawn.

Arguments that the Cornell and McVitie murders should be dealt with separately were rejected by Stevenson; the first trial would be in relation to those murders. The charges relating to Frank Mitchell would be heard later. The fraud and lesser charges would be heard after the murder trials were finished.

And if the Krays did not know before the trial what a hard time they would have with Melford Stevenson then they found out very quickly. On 9 January he decided they should wear placards around their necks with numbers so that witnesses could identify them better in the dock. It was not something which appealed to Ronnie in particular. The best thing for a defendant in a criminal trial is to try to get along with the judge, but Ronnie made no effort to do so. He was not going to wear a placard around his neck. For the moment there was anarchy in the dock. 'I have known of many a factory on strike for far less than that,' commented Platts-Mills. Stevenson was implacable. If they did not wish to wear placards, then they could go down to the cells until they co-operated. And down to the cells they duly went.

But already there was a split in the ranks. Barry Hudson for Anthony Barry, who had brought the gun to the party at which McVitie was killed, said that his client would be quite happy to wear a placard. Could he remain in the dock? 'Certainly,' said Stevenson. This was a shrewd move by Hudson. His client was going to run a defence of duress and here he was in front of the jury – a man who would do what the court asked – as opposed to the rebellious and dangerous rabble. At the time of his arrest Barry had made a statement to the police:

> 'Whatever I did that night, I did because it was beyond my power to refuse to do what I was asked to do in the circumstances. It was more than my life was worth to refuse.'[189]

There is little a prosecutor likes more than when defendants start squabbling among themselves in what is known as a 'cut-throat' defence, and here things were working out nicely. If a grown man such as Barry was going to tell the court how much in fear he was of the Krays and the rest of the Firm, it would be easy to see just how terrified the barmaid, the hostess Lisa and Carol Skinner would have been. There had been talk before the trial of offering no evidence against Barry but Read wanted him in the dock and, as harsh a decision as it might seem, he prevailed.

During the day a compromise was worked out. The defendants would not have to wear placards but there would be numbers placed in front of them on the dock and a plan drawn up showing who was where. Peace was temporarily restored.

All the defendants pleaded not guilty except Donoghue and Dickson, who pleaded guilty to harbouring Frank Mitchell. Dickson was sentenced to nine months imprisonment which, since he had been in custody for over four months, meant his almost immediate release. He was to be called as a prosecution witness in the Cornell case.

What the defence also feared was that the Cornell and McVitie counts on the indictment would be tried together. If they were, there would undoubtedly be considerable prejudice for some of the defendants, such as Charlie Kray and Freddie Foreman, who were not concerned in any way with the Cornell murder. Applications to divide the indictment were made repeatedly throughout the trial but Stevenson was adamant in refusing them.

In a way the 36-day trial ended on day one when the first of the key witnesses in the Cornell murder was the barmaid Mrs X, who had seen Ronnie Kray shoot Cornell at point-blank range. She stepped into the witness box wearing a camel-coloured suit over a green jumper. What she needed was firm handling from the defence counsel to exploit any inconsistencies in her story and particularly why, after so many years, she had changed her evidence and could now identify Ron and Ian Barrie. And firm handling from Platts-Mills was exactly what she did not get. His first 18 questions were about her taking off her hat and coat when she arrived at the Beggars and talking to the publican's wife. By the time he came to cross-examine her over her lies and evasions, she was settled in. The best Platts-Mills could suggest was that she had been bribed by the police with the promise of a new council house if she provided false evidence. 'You should have my nightmares, then you would know whether I was inventing it or not,' she replied, explaining she was terrified of the Twins and particularly of Ron. Identification evidence of strangers is always dangerous, but so far as Kray was concerned she was identifying a person she knew. A woman of completely good character, all Platts-Mills and William Howard for Barrie could do was to try and discredit her, and they failed lamentably. Why, asked Howard, was she now giving evidence and had lied at the inquest? 'Ronnie was about outside then. He was not inside then.' Once she had completed her evidence, the Krays' case was lost and everyone knew it.

As Chris Lambrianou later wrote, 'That softly spoken barmaid was genuine. She was word perfect. And she was credible'. And a few paragraphs later:

'It was credible, damning stuff. And we all knew it. I glanced at the others in the dock. They were all visibly shaken. You did not have to be a fortune-teller to know that our futures, like Ronnie's, were being destroyed in front of our eyes.'[190]

The Twins certainly knew the gig was up. Ron wrote:

'The moment the blonde barmaid began to give evidence against us a smile appeared on Nipper Read's face, a gleam of triumph. He knew he'd got us bang to rights.'[191]

To Stevenson's annoyance, Platts-Mills recalled the barmaid two days later. Earlier she had said she had been ill and now Platts-Mills saw a ray of light if he could show she had been suffering from mental illness. In fact, it turned out she had been ill with fibroids.

Although Stevenson later told the jury to disregard his evidence, backing her up was John Dickson. During his evidence Reg called out, 'If the story is true why isn't he on a murder charge?' To which Dickson replied, 'It's because of them that I'm doing nine months.'

And if there was any lingering doubt about the barmaid's apparent failure to pick out Barrie at the identification parade, Stevenson settled that. Why had Haeems not been called to give evidence about it?

'Do you not think if there was anything really to be raised as to the validity or the apparent irregularity of Mrs X's identification that man would have been put into the witness box. You were told, if you remember, that he was only an articled clerk who had not passed his examination. Gentlemen, you don't have to pass any examination as solicitors to qualify yourself for telling the truth if there is something useful he can say and he has not been called. That is a matter which you may think it is worth giving some attention when you are generally assessing the weight of the barmaid's evidence.'[192]

The evidence of the Twins' cousin Ronnie Hart was crucial to the McVitie case. Even though it was backed up by others such as Harry Hopwood, they could all be accused of being co-conspirators motivated only by self-preservation. Indeed, the prosecution was forced to admit that Hart was as much a murderer as Ronnie Bender and the Lambrianou brothers. If he could be roughed up sufficiently in cross-examination there might be some hope. Reg did his bit to help by calling out, 'If there was any stabbing it must have been done by you.' But although there were inconsistencies, which in time Melford Stevenson glossed over, Hart and the other co-conspirators stood up well. However, Billy Exley was forced to admit he was serving two years for attempting to kill a Greek Cypriot.

Carol Skinner provided some support for Hart's story, saying how she had returned to her flat in the early hours, to find Whitehead there along with Bender with her son's socks over his hands cleaning up, as well as seeing Chris Lambrianou pour a bowl of blood down her lavatory pan. Cross-examined, she denied she was lying because she disliked Tony Lambrianou, who had rowed in prison with her husband. Harry Hopwood told the jury of the arrival of the brothers and the summoning of the unfortunate Charlie Kray in the middle of the night. Donoghue was there to tell of the re-papering of Carol Skinner's flat and a visit to Freddie Foreman to get him to dispose of McVitie's body.

Before that, Stevenson had again rebuked Platts-Mills, who was trying to show that Cornell had a number of enemies and so any of them, not just the Krays, could have killed him.

> Stevenson: 'That had been established about four witnesses ago, wasn't it?'
> PM: 'I didn't realise it was so sustained and so well charted.'
> S: 'The last few minutes were a complete waste of time.'

And again:

> P-M to witness: 'You were suggesting to this jury that you never went back there [to his flat] for some such reason as the ghastly experience you had with the Krays or something of that sort.'
> Jones: (for the prosecution) 'With respect, witnesses don't suggest things. They answer questions put to them.'
> S: 'It is one of the examples of putting words into the witnesses' mouth which he has not used. I hope it won't happen again.'
> P-M: 'My Lord, I am responsible for it. I am sorry.'

S: 'You were. I hope you will stop it.'

P-M: 'I venture to justify my question on this basis…'

S: 'You cannot justify putting words into a witness's mouth that he has not used.'

P-M: 'Your Lordship will not permit me to explain. I am always in the wrong in the eyes of your Lordship.'

And he was right in that observation at least.

Overall Hart and the other witnesses stood up well to their cross-examinations. Their line was that they were terrified of the Krays and wanted to protect their families. Unfortunately for Whitehead and others, Read told the court about the partial admissions that Firm members had made when he visited them in prison. Whitehead had told Read about the time Ronnie had threatened him with a flick knife and went on to say 'he tried to make us look silly. He was getting too flash anyway.' Technically this was inadmissible evidence against Ronnie, but may well have influenced the way the jurors were thinking.

There were, however, some hiccups for the prosecution along the way. When Bobby Teale was giving evidence about the Cornell murder, his approach to the detective Tommy Butler and a meeting with him and DS Joe Pogue at the Hackney greyhound track, Platts-Mills put it to him that he was lying. Later Read admitted there were no notes of any such meeting in the files, and as a result Pogue had to be called to confirm Teale's story. It was correct, he said – he and Butler had indeed had the meeting. Almost unbelievably, he had made no notes suggesting Teale was prepared to give evidence against the

Krays. This was often the case with potential informers, said Pogue. There was, he said, a note in his diary that there had been a meeting, but it was not produced. Butler was not called.

By the end of the prosecution case Melford Stevenson was clearly getting irritable, but not only with Platts-Mills. When Paul Wrightson for Reggie Kray asked whether the jury should be present during a submission he was about to make, the judge replied, 'I don't see any reason why the jury shouldn't be here, but mercifully they haven't got to be.' All submissions that there was no case for the defendants to answer were firmly rejected.[193]

There is a maxim in a criminal trial that the high watermark for the defence is the close of the prosecution's case. And it would prove to be so in this trial. Immediately there were more troubles for Platts-Mills, who in his opening address could not resist giving the jury a synopsis of Henry IV Part 2, Scene 4. Much worse was to come. Ronnie was now proving almost impossible to handle. At that time he could either give evidence, make a statement from the dock which meant he could not be cross-examined, or remain silent. Although the second option, which is no longer available, in theory did not carry as much weight as giving evidence, in practice juries did tend to listen to these speeches. Well before the end of the prosecution case a decision should have been taken as to which course Ronnie would adopt, but this had not happened. Now Platts-Mills tried to hide his intentions and to bat until the close of play for the day when a long conference could be held with Ronnie:

'What I say is this – that we treat the giving of evidence on oath in this court as a precious coin, and these witnesses have debased that coin and dishonoured it so that Ronnie Kray will say, 'I am not going in that box where they stood.' He might well say his words spoken from the dock here unsworn were just as good as the coin that they have so gravely tarnished with their stories. So you may well hear Ronnie Kray give his evidence from the dock where he sits.'

But Melford Stevenson was well up to this. Was Ronnie Kray going to give evidence or simply make a statement? Well, he might not give evidence, he might just make a statement. In that case Platts-Mills should not have used the words 'he will tell the jury'. But this time Platts-Mills was able to counter that he could 'tell the jury' from the dock. Which was it to be? asked Stevenson, and Platts-Mills was about to obtain a ten-minute adjournment to take further instructions when Ronnie stood up and announced he would give evidence.

It was not a good decision, although he managed his examination by Platts-Mills reasonably well. Ronnie claimed Cornell had been a friend. Indeed, the week before his death he had sent a basket of fruit to his young son who was in hospital. There had never been any trouble with the Richardsons. He hadn't been in the Beggars that night. They'd all been in The Lion until they'd heard of a shooting and then they'd gone to Walthamstow.

He first started showing signs of wear when Barry Hudson began cross-examining him on behalf of Anthony Barry, denying that after the McVitie murder he had agreed the Regency should pay a reduced sum of protection money each week.

And then things went rapidly downhill. Very soon he was engaged in a slanging match with Kenneth Jones for the prosecution, who wanted to know why since the age of 17 he had been called The Colonel:

> Ron Kray: 'You are known as Taffy Jones by all the prison officers; that ought to make us both equal, don't it? Taffy Jones, they said you ought to have been a miner instead of a prosecutor, you might have done more good. Taffy Jones – we have both got nicknames. Taffy Jones and The Colonel. Mine sounds better than yours.'
> Stevenson: 'Kray, listen. You won't do yourself any good with anybody by being impertinent.'

As for the McVitie murder, he had not been at Evering Road that night. Indeed, there had not been a party at all.

One of the more extraordinary decisions of the defence was to call the old Kray enemy Frank Fraser to give evidence on Ronnie's behalf. If a defendant wishes to do something, there is not a lot his advisers can do about it. They can tell him firmly that something is not advisable but if he insists, all they can do is have him sign papers to say that the pros and cons have been explained to him and that he has chosen such and such a course. It really was a last throw of the dice. Fraser had by now been convicted in the Richardson Torture Trial and was serving sentences totalling 15 years. Platts-Mills had tried to dissuade Ronnie, but in the end had little option. 'I was persuaded… it would not make the slightest difference to the outcome of the trial', he justified in his memoirs. Which meant he had already effectively thrown in the towel.[194]

Fraser was able to tell the court that any suggestion of a disagreement between Ronnie and Cornell was so much rubbish. Indeed shortly before Cornell's untimely death Ronnie and he had met to discuss the man's drink problem. Ronnie had asked him to have a word with Cornell and to get him a job, possibly in Billingsgate. His other contribution was to say that apart from Ronnie being a fine fellow it was common knowledge throughout the criminal fraternity that it was the mild-mannered fraudster Jack Duval who had murdered Cornell. His convictions were lovingly put to him by the prosecution, as was the incontrovertible fact that he had been certified insane twice. 'That does not stop me telling the truth,' he complained. As he was taken down to the cells through the dock, he shook hands with the Twins, calling out, 'Good luck.'

Things did not improve for Ronnie when Platts-Mills next called John Shea, who had only made a statement to Haeems an hour before giving evidence and who was serving ten years for manslaughter. At least the next witness Sammy Lederman had only a conviction for being in a common gaming house back in the 1940s. Lederman had been turned again and now said he was in The Lion from shortly before 8.30, where he had seen Kray and Barrie. He accepted that he had driven with the others to Walthamstow but had heard nothing about Cornell's death. Unfortunately the prosecution put to him the interview he had with Henry Mooney at which he said he had been home with his father, but he was unable to explain the discrepancy satisfactorily. Nor did Joey Cannon, then serving four years for robbery, help much either. The next witness, an optician, said Ron Kray had such defective eyesight that he could not have recognised Cornell at a distance of more than eight to ten feet.

After the mauling Ronnie and his witnesses had received, his brothers had learned their lessons. Reggie Kray made a statement from the dock denying he had killed McVitie or that Connie Whitehead was in fear of him.

> 'I would like to say the evidence against me is a pack of lies and I accuse Mr Read of being a liar in two instances and I would wish to show the jury the scar which has been indicated in evidence [Read had said he had two scars when Reggie only had one].'

Now he told the jury that young Connie had been at Violet Kray's place over the weekends. Kray also read out a long sub-Pam-Ayres-style poem he had written and sent to Whitehead's little boy.

> 'Connie is bright and bonnie
> with mischief in his eyes,
> a saucy smile,
> he stood and pondered for a while
> I mustn't tell lies
> yet I must go out to play
> thought little Connie:
> "wonder what I can say".'

And so on ad nauseam.

Kray also read out two letters, one he had written to his parents and a second from Mrs Whitehead written on 15 August the previous year when he was in custody. He then called on his boyhood mentor, the faithful Father Hetherington. The pastor had only come to court because he had read reports in the papers. Little Connie and Mrs Whitehead were not frightened of Reggie, and indeed Connie was fond of him. Reggie Kray made no mention of McVitie's murder nor of being an accessory to the murder of Cornell.

Charlie Kray said nothing, advised, he said later, by Desmond Vowden not to give evidence. Memory both fades and is enhanced. In his book *Me and My Brothers* he complained about how unfairly and rudely Judge Stevenson had treated his Auntie May Filler: 'abominably with a total lack of respect'. However, the transcript of the trial shows Stevenson made no comment to her during her evidence.

Charlie's big point was that John Dickson had said he had been with him in one of the Pellicci cafés on a Sunday morning but when Pellicci was called, he said he had not opened either café on a Sunday for the past 17 years. There was, however, at least one other café in the area which did open on a Sunday. Charlie believed this was evidence Dickson had lied on oath. According to Kray, 'Dickson's jaw dropped'. In fact he was not even in court. It was during the summing-up that Stevenson put things right so far as the prosecution was concerned, saying if it could not have been the Sunday it must have been the Monday.

Ian Barrie made a statement from the dock denying he had killed Cornell.

Now the trial was moving more speedily. On 5 February, taking Petre Crowder by surprise, Chris Lambrianou suddenly decided to give evidence.[195]

That day both the Lambrianous and Ronnie Bender were in the witness box. So far as the brothers were concerned their defence was a complete denial that they had been at the flat when McVitie was killed. Chris Lambrianou had been with a girl he had met at Euston Station. He had not met McVitie that night. The reason Carol Skinner was telling lies about him was that Skinner blamed him for the break-up of her marriage. Lambrianou claimed she had never seen him carrying a bowl of blood and pouring it down the lavatory. 'She has been watching too many Dracula films… It is a wonder she did not say I drank it as well.' He was never used as bait to get McVitie to the Evering Road flat. Read had fabricated the case against him.

Tony Lambrianou claimed, 'I don't believe he is dead for one minute.' Indeed he had seen McVitie in Sainsbury's in the Balls Pond Road around the Christmas after the murder was meant to have taken place. He had not been to the flat that night. He also was being framed.

Nor had Ronnie Bender been there that night. In fact he had been with his girlfriend 'Mrs S', Bubbles Shea, Frankie Shea's former girlfriend, at the Greyhounds before moving on to the Regency, which he left around 2.30 a.m. He had seen Hart there who had invited him to go to a party, but he had refused. Indeed, Hart was probably the actual killer. He had rowed with Hart, which was why the man was giving evidence against him.

Freddie Foreman denied Hart and Charlie Kray had come to the Prince of Wales to get him to dispose of McVitie's body and the Mini. He had once ordered Hart to leave his 211 Club in front of two girls and this was the reason he was giving evidence against him. He called witnesses who said they were in the public bar of the Prince of Wales courting until around 4 a.m. and had not heard Hart and Kray outside. In his evidence he told the jury that he had known the Krays, whom he described as 'nice people', for about ten years, but he had not known McVitie. How he could reconcile this with having once ordered him out of his club is difficult to understand.

However, just as the prosecution intended, things were spoiled by the Regency's Anthony Barry, who gave evidence of the pressure he had been under from the Krays and how he had not dared to disobey their order to bring the gun to Evering Road. Worse, Hart, when cross-examined by Hudson, had told the jury that Barry had been forced to pay £50 protection money to the Firm after Albert Donoghue broke down doors in the club and beat up the barman. Platts-Mills tried to intervene but was told by Stevenson the questioning was proper. If Hart was to be believed about the killings, then he would also be believed about the pressure the Krays put on Barry. John Dickson supported this:

> 'You have got the three Krays in the dock, and that is the only reason why I have come forward. If you had one of them out, you would not get me to give evidence, you would get no witnesses, for if you had one of them out, you would find he would terrorise the life out of them.'[196]

Platts-Mills did what he could in the closing speech he made for Ronnie Kray, so much so that according to Eric Crowther, the stipendiary magistrate, a note was passed to junior counsel for onward transmission, reading, 'Well done, my boy. Keep it up. If you carry on like this you'll get promotion,' signed The Colonel.[197]

In those days there was no question of juries deliberating for weeks on end. It was reckoned that a verdict in the first two hours would be for the prosecution; in the second two hours it would be for the defence; and after that it would more likely be in favour of the prosecution. The jury retired at a quarter past 12 and returned shortly after seven in the evening with guilty verdicts for all except Anthony Barry, who was acquitted.

The next day, the barmaid and the jury returned to listen to the sentencing from Stevenson which was, as might have been expected, swingeing. Life for Ronnie and Reggie with a recommended minimum of 30 years and the famous words, 'Society has earned a rest from you'. Life with a recommended minimum of 20 for Ian Barrie, the Lambrianou brothers and Ronnie Bender. Ten apiece for Charlie Kray – who had been expecting, if not an acquittal, then three or four years – and for Freddie Foreman for assisting in the disposal of McVitie's body; and seven for Connie Whitehead for helping clear up. Not that it mattered, but Reggie received ten for assisting Ronnie after he had killed Cornell. That would be concurrent.

Donoghue was then brought up for sentencing and was duly rewarded for his co-operation. He received two years, which meant he also had only a few weeks left to serve.

Would things have been any better if Platts-Mills had run the defence he wanted, and argued that a mentally-ill Ronnie was the dominant brother, with Reggie acting under duress? It would certainly not have been a defence which appealed to Melford Stevenson. In any event, to run a defence of duress as Anthony Barry did, Paul Wrightson would have had to show that the danger to him and his family was imminent and that he had no opportunity to seek the help of the police. The first part that Ronnie was mentally sick had possibilities, but duress for Reggie was never a runner, even if he had agreed to go along with it. Curiously, the gentle, if sometimes naïve Platts-Mills, who thought the Twins would have been acquitted if Stevenson had split the Cornell and McVitie trials, later wrote, 'I genuinely believed they were not guilty,' always a dangerous thing for a legal representative to believe.[198]

And so the long road to the canonisation and, in time, the beatification of the Krays began. But again there were many more difficulties along that road.

CHAPTER 15
THE MITCHELL TRIAL AND THE SPLIT IN THE FIRM

As soon as the sentences had been passed on the Firm, the prosecution counsel Kenneth Jones called a conference to decide what was to be done about the Frank Mitchell case. It was decided to recharge Charlie Kray and to charge Freddie Foreman with the murder. A week later Manny Fryde made an offer of pleas from his clients to harbouring and conspiracy if the murder charge against Charlie could be dropped. Charlie would also make a statement. The offer was declined.

The second trial began on 15 April 1969 before Mr Justice Lawton. Before it, perhaps inadvisedly, and certainly to the annoyance of prosecuting counsel Kenneth Jones and John Leonard, Nipper Read threw a party on Saturday 23 March 1969 at the Mount Pleasant Hotel in Calthorpe Street for the jurors in the first trial to meet their bodyguards. The hosts were nominally the officers (paying 25 shillings a head). Eleven jurors were present. The twelfth had had a heart attack a week before the party. There were complaints by the civil liberties lawyer Benedict Birnberg suggesting this might even be contempt of court. If the police could throw a party for the jury, why not a successful defendant?[199]

Mr Justice Lawton's father had been a deeply disliked prison governor whom Frank Fraser claimed in *Mad Frank*, and with some evidence to back his story, to have tried to hang as he walked his dog on Wandsworth Common. Early in his own career Lawton had been a member of the British Fascist Party. That had been forgiven if not forgotten, and Lawton was a much more jovial judge than Stevenson. Summing up he described the defendants as 'not angels, not even perhaps demoted saints' and, questioning Read about Albert Donoghue, he asked if he was in the First Division of informers (there was then no Premier Division):

> Read: 'I would put him in the bottom half of the First Division.'
>
> Lawton: 'He will have to keep his eye on relegation.'

Despite this apparent amiability, once again the defendants could expect no sympathy. Lawton was neither a notably lenient nor a tolerant judge. However, the immediate problem was, given the amount of publicity following their convictions and sentences in the first trial, could the Krays get a fair hearing?

John Platts-Mills, again appearing for Ronnie, asked the judge to invite the prosecution to drop the entire proceedings. Naturally that met with little sympathy and so he applied for leave to challenge the jury for cause, in this case bias. His argument was that every single juror among the 250 who had been assembled should be disqualified because of what they had read and heard. His problem was that in English law a challenge for cause cannot be made unless there is some basis for the challenge before questioning the juror on his or her views.

Lawton believed:

> 'The reporting of trials which take place in open court is an important part of the functions of a newspaper and it would not be in the public interest, in my judgement, if newspapers desisted from reporting trials, and from reporting verdicts and sentences in those trials merely because there was some indictment still to be dealt with.'[200]

Now he found a half-way house. He accepted that some of the newspapers had gone into such background detail that if a potential juror had read them then he might be prejudiced. Platts-Mills could examine the jurors on that basis. He did and a number of them were rejected.

When the trial finally began, Reggie, Ronnie and Charlie Kray along with Frederick Foreman were in the dock charged with Mitchell's murder. With them were Wallace Garelick, Patrick Connolly, Thomas Cowley and Connie Whitehead, variously charged with conspiracy and harbouring. Absent were Teddy Smith and Ronald Olliffe, who had both disappeared. Others who perhaps might have been in the dock were the fearsome Alfie Gerard and his close friend Jeremiah Callaghan. They had very sensibly left for Australia after being involved in an attack on a Salvation Army worker Gwyneth Redhead in January 1968 and were not retrieved until after the end of this current trial.[201] Now, Cowley, Whitehead and Garelick wanted to change their pleas and Whitehead and Cowley pleaded guilty to harbouring and a plea of not guilty to accessory after the fact to the murder charge, and the Crown agreed. Whitehead had seven convictions, including, of course, the seven years he received for being an accessory after the death of McVitie. Tommy Cowley had convictions for receiving stolen coins and for housebreaking. Lawton said that he would have taken a much less lenient view of John Dickson, who had only been sentenced to nine months in the first trial, but he felt he was morally bound by Stevenson's sentencing. They also would each receive nine months. Could it, asked Sir Lionel Thompson, be made concurrent with Whitehead's seven years? No, it could not and nor, when Garelick, a man with no previous convictions, pleaded guilty to helping in the escape, could he have bail until he was sentenced.

The principal witness for the prosecution was now Albert Donoghue, a taciturn and, many thought, uncharismatic man. He nevertheless stood up well to cross-examination, denying Ronnie Kray's version that he had accidentally shot Mitchell while the Axeman was being handed over to some Cypriots who had arranged to take him out of the country.[202] He denied Foreman's allegations that he had been taking protection money from him. Quite the reverse. 'He was part of the Firm and I used to go to him regularly to give him his whack of the protection money.' Donoghue said that Jerry Callaghan opened the back door of the van, and he and Mitchell got in. Foreman had told him to sit with Ronnie Olliffe, who was driving, and tell him the best way to get to the Blackwall Tunnel. Gerard and Foreman then opened fire.

The defences were complicated. First, there was still the possibility Mitchell was alive and Platts-Mills suggested that he might have been the man who had pulled a woman's car out of the mud in County Clare the summer after he was alleged to have been shot. Billy Exley denied that in 1968 he had told the armed robber, Panayiotis Georgiades, that Mitchell was in Hamburg making his way to Cannes. What he did damagingly tell the jury was that the day after the party held after Mitchell's disappearance, when Teddy Smith organised a further clean up, he (Exley) took Mitchell's wireless and broke it up. Worse, telling Exley they were all in it together, Reggie wanted him to kill Lisa. He had replied, 'Fuck off. I ain't in anything.' Even as late as 1990 Reg Kray was insisting that Exley and three Greeks had killed Mitchell.[203]

At the end of the prosecution case, with no evidence that they had been involved, the charges of murder against Ronnie and Charlie Kray were dismissed.

Foreman called an alibi that on 23 December he had been at a London nursing home visiting his wife, Maureen, who had had an appendectomy that week and was due for discharge the next day. While there he had particularly noticed a nurses' party... A Dr Barry gave evidence that he had taken out Maureen Foreman's stitches and given her an injection of morphine but he had no notes on times or dates. A crucial question was the nurses' party attended by surgeons and one of the only two days a year they were allowed to have alcoholic drink in the hospital. This, said the matron, was on the 22nd. The question was whether there had been an informal and unauthorised party on the 23rd. The matron said this was impossible.

The prosecution then called rebutting evidence to show the nurses' party had been the night before. Maureen Foreman told the court she had flown to Australia to try to trace the nurse who had looked after her but had been unsuccessful.

There was also the question of the driver of the van in which it was alleged Mitchell had been shot. Ronnie Olliffe had completely disappeared and an oblique alibi was called in his case. If it could be shown he was not the driver on 23 December when Mitchell was taken away, then Donoghue's story could not be relied on. As a result Foreman must be innocent. Witnesses, including the former boxer Terry Spinks, came forward to say they had been with Olliffe that night at the Log Cabin, the drinking club in Wardour Street frequented mainly by criminals.

When he began summing up on 14 May after lengthy speeches by counsel, Lawton, who could not understand how Mitchell had effectively had the run of Dartmoor, was clearly getting testy:

> 'Now, my task at this stage of the case is to direct you as to the law – and that won't take me more than a very few minutes because the law applicable to this case is very simple – to analyse the issues in the case and to comment on the evidence. I can analyse the issue in this case in one sentence. "Do you believe Donoghue?" Because if you don't there is no case against Reginald Kray or Frederick Foreman on the charge of murder. That's all this case is about. But it has taken six and a half days of oratory to get to that very simple issue.'[204]

During the remainder of the summing up he did what he could to blow holes in the defence cases but, when on 16 May after a six-hour retirement the jury finally returned, everyone was acquitted except Reggie Kray, who was convicted of aiding Mitchell's escape. He received a concurrent five-year sentence. 'God bless you, members of the jury,' he said as he left the dock. The unfortunate Garelick, who had pleaded guilty to conspiracy at the beginning of the case, received 18 months. Much later Read thought that the prosecution would have been better to have considered Manny Fryde's plea-bargain offer more carefully and dropped the charges against Charlie Kray.

Enough was now enough. There was no real point in prosecuting the Krays yet again on the fraud and other charges. Sufficient time and money had already been spent. Even if they were found guilty, the sentences on the Twins would have been meaningless. On 25 May 1969 the remaining Long Firm fraud charges were dropped and many of the fringe defendants who had been in custody were released or given short sentences. Among them was Joseph Kaufman who was sentenced to 15 months for his part in the stolen bonds case, meaning he would be released in six weeks' time.

The defence cost of the trials had been £152,771, which in today's terms roughly equates to £2,370,000.

After the sentences came the splits in the ranks. Realisation set in among the lower orders that they had been induced into throwing away what were possibly good defences through misguided loyalty and, in some cases, fear. On 7 March 1969 Haeems and Fryde filed the initial notices of appeal and were told the perfected grounds of appeal had to be filed by 2 June. Principally the grounds were that Stevenson should have split the indictment so that the Cornell and

McVitie murders were tried separately. The Twins also argued that the defence run by Tony Barry had unfairly prejudiced them.

But soon there were applications to change solicitors. The first signs of trouble came on 28 April when a handwritten notice came from Chris Lambrianou saying he wanted to change his solicitor to the highly talented and thoroughly dishonest Bryan J.C. Gammon, writing:

> 'I have no faith or trust in Sampsons and I feel they will not let me put my case properly to the appeal court as they stopped me doing so at the trial.'[205]

His application was followed the next day by one from his brother, and on 5 May the legal aid orders were amended. Now it was a question of 'Your Lordships, please let me into another lifeboat', a far cry from Tony Lambrianou's later autobiography in which he styled himself the 'former Kray Boss' and enjoyed a successful media career on the back of the Twins.

On 12 May Whitehead wrote asking to be allowed to change solicitors and the same day John 'Ian' Barrie joined the defectors and asked to have his case transferred to Claude Hornby & Cox. Bender's sister then wrote to the court saying she had been to see Rudolph Lyons, who had advised her to stick with Sampsons. She had no quarrel with him but had no confidence in Fryde. The family had also received threats about what might happen if they strayed from the fold and in turn Whitehead repeated his pre-trial claim that he and his family were at risk.

The Lambrianous' new defence was that like Anthony Barry, they had been terrified of the Krays and had been pressured into tailoring their defence to fit that of the brothers.

Tony Lambrianou set the tone. Ground 2 of his Appeal read:

'That his defence was not presented by his solicitors as a result of pressure being exercised upon their clerk Ralph Hyams [sic] by Charles Kray, Reginald Kray and Ronald Kray.'

Now he wanted to call Detective Inspector Frank Cater and the two boys, Terence and Trevor, who had been at the party when McVitie was killed, to give evidence on his behalf. He also wanted to give new evidence in line with an attached statement.

In it he dealt with what he now said his relationship with the Twins had been. And a very different one it was:

'I have never belonged to the Kray Firm. I met them at the same time as my brother Christopher and only really started to see much of them about eight weeks prior to the murder of McVitie; this was primarily because I was also a member of the Regency Club and also drank in the same Public House. I personally was never asked to do anything by them but I knew only too well of their reputation.'

Chris Lambrianou more or less followed his brother's statement. He had met the Kray brothers casually in 1963 but it was not until August 1967 that he had had a drink with them. Hart had taken him to the Carpenters Arms and they had told him that if he took gamblers to their club at the Grand Hotel, Leicester, they would give him a commission. 'I was aware of who they were and the power they held; I was at no time a member of their Firm'.

Whitehead claimed that Carol Skinner, whose evidence was crucial against him, should have been treated as an accomplice. Bender, who had called an alibi in the trial, now amended it, saying that while the first part of his evidence had been true and he had been at the greyhounds with Bubbles Shea, he had in fact been to the party where he had been shocked to see the killing but powerless to prevent it.

It was never going to be a change of tactics which was likely to find favour with the Court of Appeal. The judgment on the application for leave to appeal was given on 22 July 1969.[206]

The Lord Chief Justice quickly dismissed the indictment and prejudice arguments. Another ground for appeal was that Melford Stevenson had not put the defence side of the case properly. This too received short shrift:

> 'When the defence call evidence, a failure to put the case
> derived from that defence will almost always be fatal to
> the conviction but it is well established that the judge
> need not repeat all the argument of counsel and, when
> no evidence is called, the defence necessarily consists of
> argument.'

Then Lord Justice Fenton Atkinson poured scorn on the Lambrianou brothers' *volte face,* as he dismissed their appeals:

'We perjured ourselves at the trial again and again. Those witnesses whom our counsel attacked so vigorously told the truth. We did take McVitie to the party. We were there when he was murdered. We did clear up afterwards, indeed we took the body away in McVitie's car and disposed of it south of the river. No doubt we were accessories after the fact but we were not charged with that offence. We had no idea in advance what was going to happen. We wished to tell the truth about this matter at our trial but such threats were made against us and such strong pressure was brought to bear upon us by the Kray twins that we realised if we wished to remain alive we had to toe the Kray line.'

There were also appeals against their sentences and these met with no more success. Mr Justice James, giving the decision of the court, had this to say:

'Above all, this case tells a deplorable story of the activities of a gang in which the accessories sought to cover up the vicious and brutal conduct of the gang leaders. When such cases are brought to justice it is not sufficient to pass exemplary sentences on the leaders alone. It is equally necessary for the Court to show that a grave view will be taken of the activities of the lesser fry, and the more responsible the part played by an accessory the heavier the sentence he can expect.'

Fat Wally Garelick, who had helped in the Mitchell escape, thought his fifteen-month sentence too long when compared with that of Donoghue. He was not a hardened criminal and had no previous convictions, whereas Donoghue had several. That argument was soon disposed of. There might have been special considerations in Donoghue's case and he might have been lucky to have received only two years, but 18 months was not a day too long for those helping prisoners to escape.

The Court then certified a point of law of general public importance in the cases of Ronald Kray and Bender, but refused leave to appeal to the House of Lords. In turn their Lordships declined to hear the case.

CHAPTER 16
CHARLIE KRAY – INSIDE AND OUT

In the autumn of 1969, following an article published the previous year in *Vogue*, Charlie Kray saw damages for libel winking at him and was tempted to sue. As a first step he wrote to the Home Office asking for permission to issue writs.

The offending words in *Vogue* had come from the unflattering remarks:

> 'I've been to Vallance Road to Mother Kray's house once. All the doors have lace done up in pink bows like a gypsy caravan which makes me think they have gypsy blood. Nightclub wallpaper, velvet stripes and stars on the ceiling. Everything's spotless. Mother Kray spends her time polishing keyholes. The Krays, like a lot of cruel people, have a streak of sentimentality.'

Kray was most upset about his mother being described as 'cruel'.

The Home Office was wary. The European Commission, it noted, had been taking 'great interest in our control over prisoners' access to solicitors and the courts'. The Commission wanted a statement of criteria by which applications were dealt with. If the Home Office refused Kray permission to sue, that would no doubt cause adverse publicity. Since the time limit to bring proceedings over the *Vogue* article was running out, they were hoping the problem would just go away. A first step, however, would be to allow Kray to obtain counsel's opinion on the merits of the case.

On hand to help him was solicitor Alan Lorenz, and he instructed the charming and extremely dubious barrister Ronald Shulman to give written advice on the prospects of success of the action. Shulman and Lorenz turned up more or less unannounced at Chelmsford prison where they were admitted on a 'sight and sound' visit, meaning it had to be in the presence and hearing of a prison officer. Afterwards Shulman wrote an opinion in Kray's favour. Perhaps the kindest thing which could be said of it was that it was not the strongest of opinions and seemed to ignore the decision that a convicted person was stuck with his conviction and could not use a libel action to reopen his case. The Home Office thought it could refuse Kray's petition on its merits and indeed, as they had hoped, the matter lapsed.

Shortly after, Charlie Kray instructed the struck-off solicitor Ellis Lincoln, then working as a managing clerk, to see if there was any evidence available that would discredit Ronnie Hart and his story which had convicted him. In turn Lincoln instructed an inquiry agent, Derek Higgins, to investigate and at first it seemed that some progress had been made.

Higgins telephoned Hart on 16 September 1970 and asked to meet him at the Golden Arrow Bar at Victoria Station. They met around 4 p.m. and Higgins said Lincoln wanted to meet Hart at his offices and drove him there in a Rover. Higgins asked Hart if McVitie was dead, because there was a rumour that he was still alive. Lincoln told him, 'If you could find someone respectable who will alibi Charlie, it would be guaranteed safety from the Firm.' The next day Hart duly reported this to Inspector George Clarkeson at Scotland Yard.

When Lincoln submitted the petition to the Home Office, there was the alibi, already given before the trial but never called, that Charlie and Dolly Kray were at a caravan site at Steeple in Essex on the night of the murder. He was sure that Rose Clara Clark, who ran the site, would remember him being there. She did not. She agreed the party would have been on 28 October but as she had not attended it she could not say whether he had been there.

Charlie's son Gary was now roped in to say he would have known if there had been a call to his father on the night of the McVitie murder. The police were not impressed. Why, they wondered, had Gary not been called at the Old Bailey in his father's defence, and why had Charlie not called his alibi some years earlier?

When he was next seen by the police, Hart was soon returned to the fold. On 3 March 1971 Ronnie Hart, terrified of the Krays and believing himself to be a marked man, told Det. Ch. Supt. Terry O'Connell:

'If I make a statement to Lincoln, Quirke or Higgins it is only because I have got to pretend that I am helping them, otherwise I am a dead man. In this statement of 16

September 1969 I told a lot of lies because I know Lincoln
is close to the Firm. He is well known as a bent brief, and
I was frightened to upset him because I knew he is close to
the Firm and I know what the Firm would do to me.'

The Home Office took no further action and the file was duly closed,
only to be brought out of storage when Henry Botton, who had been
in Mr Smith's Club the night Dickie Hart was killed, was himself
murdered.

However the enquiry agent Derek Higgins, along with 60-year-old
clerk Alexander Thompson and journalist Kenneth Prater, paid a
price for his investigations when they were charged with conspiracy
to defeat the course of public justice between 2 and 12 December
1969 in attempting to persuade Ronnie Hart by threats and induce-
ments to change his statements over the McVitie murder. They were
committed for trial in January 1970 but the charges were dropped
the following May. If, said John Leonard for the Crown, they had
merely been trying to discover whether Hart had lied at the Kray
trial, there would have been no offence and given that they were of
good character it would have been extremely difficult for the Crown
to prove otherwise. The Crown would have had to show that they
had believed Hart's evidence at the Kray trial and were now trying
to persuade him to make a false statement. However, the Common
Sergeant said he thought that Higgins and Thompson had brought
things on themselves and ordered Thompson to contribute up to
£2,000 towards his legal aid costs and Higgins, who thought the
adverse publicity had cost him £5,000 of business, £500.

At the time of Thompson's arrest his employer Brendan Quirke wrote to the President of the Law Society:

> 'It is a sorry day when the managing clerk of a responsible firm of solicitors who was acting properly, regularly and in consultation with counsel can be arrested and thrown into prison and detained for fourteen hours.'[207]

In February 1970 Ellis Lincoln was discharged from bankruptcy but in May the next year failed in his application to be restored to the Rolls of Solicitors. His request to the Home Office for permission to visit Charlie was granted, but the prison governor was advised Lincoln was well known to the authorities and not to be trusted. The meeting was to be 'within sight and sound'. It must have been difficult for the authorities to work out who Charlie's solicitor actually was, because meanwhile Ralph Haccms had visited him in Chelmsford to talk about the article in the *Daily Mirror*, 'New Evidence in the McVitie Case', and Hart's statement and retraction. Their meeting was again within sight and sound of Prison Officer R.W. Horne, who duly reported back to the Governor, who in turn sent his notes to the Home Office. Haeems was now confident that there would have to be a Commission of Inquiry. Charlie's wife Dolly (now Grey) had contacted Tom Sargent of Justice, the organisation involved generally in penal reform but specifically in cases of potential wrongful conviction. Haeems told Charlie, 'He'll [the Home Secretary] have to do something about it now. This thing will cause a hell of a stink'.[208] But he and it never did.

In 1973, this time through little fault of his own, Charlie Kray became involved in one of the more sensational murder trials of the decade when George Ince, later convicted of a major bullion robbery, was accused of the murder of Muriel Patience in a bungled robbery known as The Barn Murder in November 1972. Again the judge was Melford Stevenson, whose acidity had not sweetened over the years. The evidence against him rested solely on identification by Muriel's daughter Beverley, and Stevenson seemed set on obtaining a conviction.

Ince had first met Charlie's wife Dolly towards the end of the 1950s either in the Double R or at one of the many parties thrown by the Kray Twins. By the mid-1960s Ince had fallen in love with Dolly and was a regular visitor to her flat in Poplar from 1968 once the three Kray brothers were in custody. While arguing with Charlie, Dolly would tell him that Nancy, their daughter, was in fact Ince's and although she later denied it, it was something that Charlie appears to have accepted as true.[209] Charlie Kray in his book *Me and my Brothers* says, 'Deep down I knew Nancy was not my child', 'Even though I knew Nancy was not my child I still wanted to see her' and '...I'd thought the world of her. Even though she was another man's child.' Charlie was indeed enormously proud of her, producing photographs of her at every possible opportunity.

When an informer implicated him in the Barn murder, George Ince believed he could prove his innocence and went to see Ralph Haeems, who took him to the police. Dolly Kray gave Haeems a statement providing an alibi for the night of the murder, but Ince never expected he would need to produce it.

The trial opened at Chelmsford Crown Court on 2 May 1973 and it did not go well for Ince. On the fifth day, with Ince convinced he was going to be convicted by Stevenson without need of the jury, he said he wanted a different judge. Stevenson told him he was not going to get one and Ince said he wanted to go down to the cells. Stevenson refused him permission and Ince yelled that he was 'biased, rude, everything'. Stevenson told the warders to 'keep him there'.

Over the weekend Ince's family sent a telegram to the Lord Chancellor asking for Stevenson to be replaced. The request was refused. Ince sacked his counsel and refused to take any further part in the trial, sitting with his back to the judge. The jury disagreed and a retrial was ordered.

Ince's second trial began four days later and this time the judge was the far more approachable Mr Justice Eveleigh, the antithesis of Stevenson, who actually believed Ince was not guilty. During the second trial the question of the killer's accent, described as a Yorkshire one, was brought up but Beverley Patience remained certain that she had correctly identified Ince.

On 18 May, the fifth day of the second trial, Ince's defence began. On the evening of the murder he had been with a Mrs Grey at an address which he was allowed to write down. If correct, this put Ince more than 60 miles from the Barn only 90 minutes before the murder.

Mrs Grey was in fact still Charlie Kray's wife, and it was to protect her from her husband and his family that Ince had not called her during the first trial. When Charlie was told she was coming on a visit to tell him she was going to give evidence, extra security was arranged. Kray wanted to know if Ince had some sort of hold over her but she told him her story true and he had been with her the night of the murder.

The prosecution wanted Mrs Grey's true identity known to the court, but they were only allowed to be told that she had changed her name.

After a three-hour retirement the jury found Ince not guilty. In August 1973 the northerner John Brook and Nicholas Johnson were charged with the murder and in February 1974 Brook was convicted of the murder and sentenced to life imprisonment and Johnson was convicted of manslaughter and sentenced to ten years.

Poor Dolly. After the hearing, Violet Kray told reporters, 'I never liked Charlie's wife but now I hate her. The family has cut her off completely.' Dolly Kray received £20,000 from a newspaper for the story of her involvement with Ince. She told Charlie her relation-ship with Ince was over, but in turn he told her their marriage was finished. Ince had a hard time in prison and while he was serving his sentence in Long Lartin over a bullion robbery he was slashed by Harry 'Hate-em-all' Johnston, then serving 18 years. True to the Samurai's code, when Ince was asked at Evesham Magistrates' Court to identify Johnston, he replied, 'I wouldn't like to take a chance on identifying anyone. You know what I think of Identification Parades.' Johnston still received five years. He was said to have been given a Rolex gold watch by the Twins as a reward for the cutting.[210]

Dolly may no longer have been in love with her husband but she was still supportive, lobbying for more visits and pleading for him to be moved from the Special Security wing in Chelmsford to the general prison population. In its turn the Home Office told her he was getting more privileges than most.

Charlie had two sets of home leave, during the latter of which, together with his parents, he went to see his brothers in Parkhurst. That evening Violet threw a welcome home party at the Blue Coat Boy pub in Bishopsgate where she now worked. He was denied parole in July 1974.[211]

On 5 January 1975 Charlie Kray was released and left Maidstone prison under a cloud of death threats. The big question is just what did Kray do after that? Perhaps he would return to his career as a theatrical agent? It seemed not: in March 1975 Kray said he was opening a restaurant in the country where he would be a meeter and greeter.

He was certainly used as a meeter and greeter in the Gallipolli restaurant in Bishopsgate, and there were plans for him to be the front man in Kray's Casino, a restaurant-cum-club in Benidorm, which was to be financed partly by Colombian interests. It fell through when the local authorities kept upping their demands for licence fees. He managed a pop group and sold cutlery at the Ideal Home Exhibition. For a time he was a consultant for J. Levisky & Associates, 'Registered bailiffs to the County Courts, Debt Investigation for DTI, Customs and Excise etc.' In time the theatrical agencies he ran were wound up, as was a clothing and makeup factory which owed £5,671.

He borrowed money from all and sundry, including £2,000 from the landlord of the Blue Coat Boy. It was never repaid.

He had interests in clubs throughout England and the police believed he was also dealing in counterfeit videos and amphetamines. Some old officers still believe, despite all evidence to the contrary, that he was the brains behind the Firm.

There were rumours he derived some of his income from inform-ing. One Eastender recalled in a conversation with me:

> 'Billy Rees stole an articulated lorry and his usual receiver, saying he could not handle such a big vehicle, recom-mended him to Charlie Kray. Kray told him to drive the vehicle to a lock-up behind the billiard hall in the Mile End Road where the police were waiting.'

Apologists for him take the view that he was a good-looking wastrel who lived off handouts from former friends and such small deals as he could put together. The wife of one East Ender recalls that after his release:

> 'Charlie was a sponger. That's what he did all his life. He'd borrow and never repay. Then he'd borrow say £100 and use the money to buy all the ladies in a club a flower each.'[212]

Others discount the brains theory. Nipper Read, giving some weight to the sponger theory, believed, 'All he had to say was that he was Charlie Kray. People looked over his shoulder and wondered where the Twins were.'

Other police officers believed there was more to Charlie than his public image. Six months after his release, a DCI Price wrote in an internal memorandum dated 3 July 1975 that he thought Charlie was associating with professional criminals and 'is believed to be organ-ising criminal activities of a serious nature'. He asked for copies of mail and visitor details for the Twins.

By 1986 Charlie was running Krayleigh Enterprises, a bodyguard service, advertised as 'Personal Aides to the Hollywood Stars and Arab Noblemen'. In October that year his book *Me and My Brothers* was published.

Charlie was never long out of the news. In October 1976 he was out with his fiancée Diane Buffini, when his North London flat was burgled and cash and jewellery worth about £2,000 was stolen. In April 1978 she was refused permission to visit the Twins.

One of the 'criminal activities of a serious nature' was the contract killing of Barbara Gaul, the estranged wife of the Maltese-born property millionaire John Gaul, shot and killed outside the Black Lion Hotel, Patcham, in Sussex on 12 January 1977. She had been visiting her daughter Samantha.

Since the shotgun used to kill her had been dropped from a car window, it was not difficult to track the actual murderers down. They were brothers Roy and Keith Edgeler from Norfolk, who were jailed on 24 June 1976.

In a contract killing it is desirable if not essential to place several layers between the hirer and the killer, and the firm belief in the underworld was that it was Charlie Kray who had approached the Edgelers.[213]

By the mid 1980s the Krays were almost certainly making more money than they had done on the outside, with up to £3,000 a week coming from the sale of authentic Kray T-shirts and other memorabilia, and fees, said to be £1,000 a time, payable to Charlie for the privilege of an audience with one of the captive Twins.

In 1970 *Performance* was released, starring James Fox and Mick Jagger. The following year saw Richard Burton appearing in *Villain*, both films very loosely based on the Kray story. In 1981 Robert Duval, fresh from critical acclaim as the detective in *True Confessions*, had said he would like to play Ronnie Kray and hoped Bob Hoskins would play Reggie. If need be he would be prepared to live in the East End for six months to acquire the accent.[214]

Nothing came of it, but what really projected the Krays onto the public screen and sealed their oxymoronic temporary immortality was the casting of Spandau Ballet brothers Gary and Martin Kemp in *The Krays*. Gary was Ronnie and Martin played Reggie. Billie Whitelaw and Alfred Lynch played their parents. Stephen Berkoff was George Cornell, but there was criticism that Tom Bell was too fragile and sympathetic as McVitie. Charlie was written out of the script. Despite these criticisms it was an enormous success.

The fee paid to Charlie was £250,000, to be divided equally between the three of them. Additionally Charlie organised a £10,000 sweetener for himself by signing away all his and the Twins' future profits from the movie. It was not an astute move. First, it alienated him from his brothers and secondly, given the movie and other rights grossed £10 million, Charlie had signed away literally hundreds of thousands of pounds in exchange for a quick buck. Even worse, the Twins were very protective of their mother's image. She did not swear and they were furious that Charlie had allowed 'bollocks' to be the first word spoken by Billie Whitelaw. His brothers did not speak to him for the better part of a year.

However, there were other earners to come. A computer game called The Firm was marketed, and Charlie's company Krayleigh Security began to provide doormen for clubs countrywide.

When Frank Sinatra Junior visitied England after his 1983 kidnapping, Krayleigh looked after him, as well as providing an 18-strong bodyguard for his father at Wimbledon in June 1985.

In 1984 there was more unwelcome publicity for Charlie, when Dolly's brother, Ray Moore, was shot and killed outside his house in south London during a domestic incident.

Seven years later in October 1991 Kray was in the news again when his driver and bodyguard Bruce Bryan was stabbed to death in Stocks Nightclub on the King's Road, Chelsea. How the now unemployed and seemingly unemployable Charlie could afford a chauffeur and bodyguard was never satisfactorily explained. Ronnie O'Sullivan senior, father of the world snooker champion, was said to have serviced Charlie Kray's car. O'Sullivan Snr was jailed for life for Bryan's killing. Bryan had been in the club with Charlie's one-time girlfriend Angela Mills and according to the prosecution evidence, O'Sullivan and a certain Edward O'Brien had been shouting racist taunts and singing football songs. A fight broke out and O'Sullivan stabbed Bryan with a hunting knife after being hit with a champagne bottle. O'Sullivan claimed mistaken identity but was convicted nevertheless. Charlie declined to give evidence on his behalf.

Kray's name surfaced yet again in 1994 when millionaire businessman Donald Urquhart was gunned down after drinking with his girlfriend at the Queen's Head in Marylebone High Street on 2 January. A man, said to have been red or fair-haired, had ridden up on a 250cc Yamaha motorbike and shot him.

It was clearly another contract killing and Charlie came under suspicion as the potential broker. He was arrested and questioned with tapes being played to him which allegedly implicated him. He refused, as was his right, to answer any questions. The death of Urquhart, a money launderer suspected of handling some of the proceeds of the Brink's Mat robbery, was only partly solved. An unemployed roofer Graeme West was convicted of killing him for a fee of £20,000, but his employer was never disclosed. Charlie claimed that it was simply the Kray name which again was causing him trouble, and, with the help of his publisher Robin McGibbon, he appeared on a couple of television shows in an effort to prove it.

By now he had separated from his girlfriend, the long-suffering Diane Buffini. He had been involved in a relationship with her during his marriage to Dolly, and after his release from prison, a friend traced her for him. By then she had married Daniel Buffini, but this marriage was in difficulties and now they set up light house-keeping together in what he says was an open relationship. The split with Dolly had been acrimonious and his son Gary had at one time gone to live with his grandfather before moving to Blackpool to help out at a hotel. Their daughter Nancy had remained with her mother. Now Diane was not prepared to tolerate another long-term affair, this time with middle-aged Judy Stanley, the daughter of a head teacher. Stanley had met Charlie in a restaurant run by Diane when her 14-year-old marriage was breaking up. 'He has a powerful presence – I suppose some would say an aura of danger – which I find sexy,' she told reporter Sheron (sic) Boyle. Charlie thought he 'could not bear not having Judy in my life… I was even more in love with Judy and knew I wanted to spend the rest of my life with her and her children.'[215]

In January 1996 Gary was diagnosed with lung cancer. He spent some time in a hospice and was taken to Maidstone to see Uncle Reg in a farewell visit. Charlie contacted Dolly, and after a long absence Nancy came to see her brother in the hospice. She was welcomed but Kray's relations with Dolly had not improved and he claimed that some years earlier she had evicted Gary so that George Ince could move in with her.

Gary's funeral at St Matthews Church, Chingford, conducted by the Reverend Kenneth Rimini, was paid for by Reggie, who sent a tape to be played, and the cortege of seven limousines included an empty one, directly behind the hearse, symbolising his absence. The congregation filed out to Whitney Houston's 'I will always love you'. Gary was buried in the same grave as Frances Kray. Dolly did not attend.

Then on 31 July 1996 came a bolt from the blue: Charlie was arrested over a £39 million drug deal and was charged with conspiracy to sell cocaine to undercover officers. Kray watchers could not believe it and the charge was greeted with ridicule among the underworld, who regarded him as a pathetic old man trading off the names of his younger brothers for handouts for old times' sake. He had been, they pointed out, unable to pay for his son's funeral. There were confident predictions of an acquittal.

Despite efforts by his friends to wean him from Ralph Haeems with suggestions of other solicitors, the umbilical cord was too strong to cut and Charlie went again to him for his defence.

The evidence was that Charlie Kray's name had been heard on police intercept tapes, and when Scotland Yard set up a police undercover operation, senior officers were worried that the supposedly ultra-cautious

Kray and his friends would be wary of anyone with a London accent. Detectives from the North were therefore brought in to act as 'buyers'.

The police believed Charlie was still deeply involved in the underworld who had been investigated on at least three occasions. There were unproven allegations linking him to amphetamines, counterfeit videos and fake coins. He had neither a bank account nor a credit card. He never claimed benefit. This, said the police, showed that he was still an operator to be reckoned with. Charlie countered by saying he sponged off people, including his new love Judy Stanley.

In *Me and My Brothers*, Kray's version of what had happened was that, financially bust to the wide, and devastated by his son's death, shortly after Gary's funeral he had accepted an invitation from Big Albert, a friend in Birmingham, for him and Judy to go, all expenses paid, to stay a couple of days in the city. On 9 May there was another call, this time from Patsy Manning, saying that there was another party for his (Patsy's) 60th birthday being thrown by Big Albert. This time he went to Birmingham without Judy and stayed at the Wake Green Lodge hotel in Moseley, comped by the owner. At the bar that evening along with Manning were George, whom he had met at Gary's funeral, another man Deano, and a third man Jack from Newcastle, who joined them later. According to the writer Bernard O'Mahoney, Charlie had been out of his skull that evening, snorting cocaine with a £50 note and urging his friends to share a line with him. Charlie took the opportunity to touch Deano for a loan and over the next fortnight Jack kept in touch with him.[216] The police sting had begun.

In May Kray invited Jack to a benefit in a friend's pub in Kent to raise money for the hospice where Gary had been cared for at the end of his life. Jack produced a football signed by the Newcastle United players to be raffled.

At another benefit night in memory of Gary on 2 July at the Mermaid Theatre, Kray introduced Jack to his associates Ronnie Field, a builder from Raynes Park, south-west London, and Robert Gould, an electrician from Wimbledon.

Eight days later Jack arranged for Field and Kray to fly to Newcastle to discuss business. There, Kray met Brian, another friend of Jack. And on 11 July there was another party, this time for Charlie's 70th birthday. Now, again pleading poverty, he touched Jack for £500. This time he took Judy with him. Again they were comped at the Wake Green Hotel and Jack and Brian gave Charlie a gold cigarette lighter. The next he heard was when Jack telephoned him to ask Ronnie Field to call him. And, said Charlie, the next he knew about anything was that he had been arrested after he returned home from working on a new edition of *Me and My Brothers.*

This was not a totally frank account by Charlie. The police had 20 tapes of him discussing drugs with his new friends. Jack, who was never identified and gave his evidence from behind a screen, had explained to Kray on the tapes that his supplier in Amsterdam had been 'topped' and that he was short of drugs. Could Kray assist? Charlie fell for the bait.

Kray told him he had people who were 'sat on a ton' and he could 'put Jack's name on it'. Jack said, 'That's a lot of puff [cannabis].' Kray then said, 'I know it's not the place, we will talk in the morning'. Jack said okay and they shook on it.

Charlie had told him, 'I put people together but I won't go there when they do these things, because I have too many eyes on me.' In subsequent conversations Kray offered to supply five kilos of 92% pure cocaine every fortnight for up to two years. The price was to be £31,500 a kilo. If the deal had gone ahead Kray and his associates would have grossed £8 million.

According to Jack, finally a deal was arranged, with Kray shaking his hand with the words 'Done, mate.' But nothing happened immediately. Despite the pressure to complete, Kray kept delaying, claiming at one stage to have just lost £1 million on a deal.

Finally drugs were handed over by Field and Gould at the Swallow Hotel, Waltham Abbey, in exchange for £63,000. The pair were followed and arrested near the Dartford Tunnel. Charlie was arrested later at his home in Sanderstead. Next day he was remanded in custody and sent to the high-security Belmarsh Prison, from where he wrote to his friends in the hope they would stand surety for him if he was granted bail. He was not.

Kray's defence was one of entrapment and that he was simply stringing the purchasers along in the hope of conning money from them. Two things militated against this. First, there was no doubt that one delivery of drugs had taken place and secondly, it was highly unlikely that the 70-year-old Kray would dare to try to pull off a multi-million-pound scam on top-class drug dealers. Death would have been almost instantaneous. His trouble was that, as with much of his career, he took chances, thinking the pot of gold was simply there for him to pick up. As Frank Fraser pointed out:

'There is no problem in saying, "This is Tom, this is Dick, this is Harry" and having a chat, but once Charlie'd started talking serious what he should have said is, "What's your surname?" "Can't tell you." "Who do you know?" Any bona fide villain would ask. Then if the man can't put up names of people he's worked with or he won't tell you his name, you know the score – and it's "On your bike. Get back to your local police station."'[217]

There was some help for Kray during the trial. Sadly the bright lights of the Midlands and London had proved an unhelpful distraction for some of the police on the operation. An undercover officer, using the name 'Brian', plunged somewhat too deeply into his role and became very close to a barmaid at a Birmingham party thrown for a Kray friend. In court, hostess Michelle Hamdouchi described a night of passion with Brian, followed by a massive drinking session with another northern undercover officer and a member of a pop group whom they had met at a hotel bar.

Brian admitted going to bed with Hamdouchi, but denied having a sexual relationship. Kray's counsel Jonathan Goldberg QC seized on this to hammer home to the jury that the police evidence was unreliable and tainted. In fact as more reports of the conduct of undercover officers in other cases have come to light, it seems to have been pretty standard behaviour.

Nevertheless at the time, heads were in hands. One exasperated London detective was reported to have sighed and said, 'You know the film on now about FBI agent Donny Brasco infiltrating the Mob?

Well, we had Johnny Fiasco for our job. What we had in mind was infiltration – he went in for penetration.'[218]

One of the standard tactics is for a defence barrister to denigrate his own client in an effort to show what a fool he is and so obtain sympathy from a jury. Goldberg shredded Kray, depicting him as a semi-derelict who was trying to make a few pounds out of a small-time scam. His problem, however, was the massive amounts of money at stake.

Unfortunately Charlie was caught lying, or at the very best prevaricating, never a good thing to happen to a defendant. He told the jury that Ronnie Field was not a close friend but someone he had seen three or four times in the past two years. It was then John Kelsey-Fry for the Crown produced the BT bills for Judy Stanley's number. In six months there had been over 50 calls to and from Field.

Those who fail to learn from history are condemned to repeat it, and so incredibly, and once more highlighting the triumph of hope over experience, Frank Fraser was again wheeled out to give evidence on behalf of a Kray. This time Fraser's function was to explain that he believed that the financially unsophisticated Charlie could never have negotiated himself into such a deal. 'He is a lovely, lovely man. He is as innocent as you are, my Lord.' 'You are probably more into drugs than he is,' he told John Kelsey-Fry.

In all, 18 character witnesses were called for Charlie, including a former Miss UK, who trod the party line when she described how England was a 'much nicer, safer place' when the Kray Twins were around. Efforts were made to persuade Reggie Kray to give evidence on his brother's behalf but he declined. Goldberg told the jury, 'He is a very decent loveable and thoroughly charitable man who has brought joy into the lives of many'.

Those who had confidently predicted an acquittal were wrong. Despite a plea that he would be subject to bullying in prison and be the target for every up-and-coming criminal who wanted to make a name for himself, on 23 June 1997 Judge Carroll sentenced Charlie to 12 years' imprisonment, saying:

> 'There was never a real question of entrapment by those officers but, when caught, you cried foul. I am pleased to say this jury saw through that hollow cry.'

Judy Stanley, who always believed in his innocence, said, 'He wasn't a drug baron. I kept him. He couldn't even afford a mobile phone. His Cartier watch was a fake.' She was certain that he would survive incarceration.

After Charlie was jailed, a £100 a ticket benefit night was held at Mr Big's nightclub in Maidstone to raise money for an appeal. On 26 January 1999 his appeal against both conviction and sentence was dismissed. Kray had hoped that his sentence might have been halved on the grounds of his age. After the verdict Les Martin, liaison officer for the Charlie Kray Appreciation Society, told the press, 'He will be gutted. I am very disappointed. Charlie is innocent in all of this and was targeted by police just because he was a Kray. If he wasn't, he would have his sentence cut. Everyone has just got it in for him.'

Kray did surprisingly well in prison. He was liked by staff and the other prisoners. He was co-operative, cheerful and a calming influence.

In October 1997 he tipped off the prison staff that a female officer was at risk from an unstable prisoner. Nevertheless it was not until after his appeal was refused in 1999, and following a letter to the Home Office from Goldberg, that he was downgraded to a Category B prisoner. He was now able to speak with Judy Stanley on a daily basis.

On 4 October 1999 he wrote to his friend Mickey Bailey, 'I wish I had taken your advice [to change his solicitor] when all this started. I would have been better off.' He now had a new solicitor in the form of Michael Holmes of Andrew Keenan.

But when it came to it, Judy Stanley had been wrong. An increasingly frail Charlie was not strong enough to see the end of his sentence.

CHAPTER 17
THE TWINS IN PRISON

Back in 1968, the first problem for the Home Office had been what to do with the Twins, then aged 34. There were four categories of prisoner, all based on the risk factor if they escaped. Category A was for those who would be extremely dangerous if they escaped, and the aim was to make escape impossible; Category B was those for whom escape had to be made extremely difficult; Category C for those who could not be trusted in open conditions and Category D those who were a low risk to security. Those on Category D would be tested in the community by being given work release and day and home release.

It was for a Home Office committee to determine whether a prisoner was downgraded from Category A to B. Downgrading Category B to C would be an internal matter for the prison governor, and C to D would again be determined by the Home Office.

For the Twins it had to be Category A status, and naturally their mother Violet was an early campaigner for them to be kept together, writing to the Home Office in May 1969:

'I am already broken hearted over the terrible sentence they have been given which I think was very unfair. If they are separated it will do more harm than good to them.'[219]

She received a neutral reply. There could be no undertakings, but consideration would be given to her letter. The Home Office did not want to keep the Krays together and, despite the apparent reconciliation with the Richardsons after Frank Fraser's appearance on the Krays' behalf, it was thought that there would be trouble if they were in the same prison. So Ronnie was sent to Durham, Reggie to Parkhurst, and Charlie, the most stable of the three, to Chelmsford. Foreman went to Leicester, and Whitehead, who was said now to be 'in considerable fear' of the Krays, to Hull. The Home Office thought he would be the tenth Category A prisoner there.[220] Of the others, for the moment the Lambrianou brothers were in separate wings in Wandsworth.

But for every major decision there seemed to have to be a couple of more minor ones which had to be dealt with. In June 1969 a Suffolk shoe repairer wrote to the Home Office saying the Krays had left two pairs of shoes to be repaired. The cost of soles and tips on the heels was 35 shillings and with postage this would come to £2 and 5 shillings. If they did not want them, he would sell them and send any surplus to them. The Home Office officials were worried it might be a hoax. It wasn't. Letters were sent to all the brothers, and Ron Kray said they were his and advised the repairers to get in touch with his father.

Copies of some of their early correspondence were kept and in late July Ron wrote to Charlie commiserating with him on the loss of his appeal, adding, 'Bender and the Lambrianous went against us on the appeal but it did not do them much good, did it'.

Some letters were withheld from them. On 7 May a letter had been sent to Ron, then still in Brixton, beginning, 'My darling Ronnie' and promising not to go with any other man but to wait for him. The writer wanted permission to visit. 'The letter looks like the work of a homosexual', noted a Home Office official, perceptively.

Long or short, a prison sentence can be done the easy way or the hard way. The former involves cooperation with the authorities to ensure that the inmate is released at the first available opportunity. Any sensible criminal will choose it. Some will have their families lobbying on their behalf even before the sentence is passed. The hard way involves fights with the prison staff, a total lack of cooperation and a breach of prison rules whenever possible. Frank Fraser is an example of doing time the hard way and the Krays, possibly because of their notoriety and certainly because of their mental health and temperament, at first chose to follow in his footsteps. In a way it was not wholly their fault. Every up-and-comer might fancy making a reputation by fighting with one of them.

Unsurprisingly Ron did not settle easily and shortly after his arrival in Durham he was in a fight with a fellow lifer Mick Copeland, who had been reprieved after being convicted of what were known as the Bubble Car murders.[221] The pair had taken an instant dislike to each other. Kray was fined £3 from his canteen money and Copeland transferred. Another fight took place, this time with another inmate John Richard Jones over a comment he made about Frances Kray. And then Ronnie seems to have settled down.

The Twins were not quite as destitute as Nipper Read had believed at the time of their trial. A broker wrote to Reg Kray advising him he had shares in Southern Rhodesian Copper Ltd, which in 1968 had restored its dividend. There were also shares in Ultramar, Brit/Borneo and AMPOL. The broker thought Reg should make a will.

The month after Reg Kray began his life sentence, Frances Shea's mother Elsie petitioned the Home Office to permit the reburial of her daughter under her maiden name away from what she called the 'showcase' Kray family plot in Chingford Mount cemetery.[222]

Elsie Shea said that she did not want her daughter's grave to be linked to that of a notorious murderer. Frances had changed her name and when she died was in the process of getting the marriage annulled. Elsie also complained that flowers placed on the grave by her family were immediately removed.

Since he owned the grave, it could only be done with Reggie Kray's approval, and Elsie Shea was his bitter enemy. Broaching the subject with Reggie was not something the Home Office officials wanted to do. Separated from his twin, he was already 'causing control problems' without this additional aggravation making him worse.

Reggie Kray's line of thought on Frances, apart from the fact that she had metamorphosed into a robin who sat on her gravestone, was that her separation from him and her change of name by deed poll had been temporary blips on the radar of their mutual happiness.

Finally, the officials approached Manny Fryde and received a terse reply. Kray took 'the very strongest possible objection that the remains of his late wife be removed from her grave or that any alteration be made to her memorial'. And there, however much

Home Office officials may have wished to the contrary, the matter and Frances Shea rested.

One early problem was who could be barred from visiting the Twins. A Home Office note dated 20 March 1970 reads:

> 'The problem of visitors to the Krays is a difficult one, the majority are suspect in some way or other but usually there is not a great deal of current intelligence about them.'

And even if there was, security was lax. Tommy Cowley had already visited Ronnie in Durham using the all-purpose name Smith.

A list of 50 people to be refused permission to visit was drawn up. It included possible helpers in any escape attempts, general supporters and others. The last category included the author John Pearson who, it was thought, would lose interest in them once his book was published. Wrong. Supporters included two priests, Father Foster and Father Richard Hetherington, along with 'one-armed Lou' Joseph, Auntie May Filler, Reggie's one-time girlfriend Carole Thompson and Connie Whitehead's wife, Patricia. However, by 1970 only the cat burglar Charlie Clarke remained on the barred list.

Their mother Violet was still campaigning for the Twins to be in the same prison, but that month Reg was moved from Parkhurst to Leicester and replaced in Parkhurst by his twin. Lobbied by her in October 1970, the National Council for Civil Liberties wrote to the Home Office taking up the Kray case:

'If there is to be a future for the Kray brothers, then it is important that this affection is not destroyed and that there is some hope of mitigating the inevitable deterioration which is bound to worsen as a result of a lengthy term of imprisonment.'

On 18 November the Home Office said there was no entitlement for the brothers to serve their sentences together. That decision had been made the previous year. There were many factors which had to be taken into consideration.[223] In fact the Home Office had no hard and fast rule about separating brothers in prison.

The next month there were threats to kidnap little Viscount Linley, the son of Princess Margaret, with suggestions that he would be held hostage until the Krays were released. In support of royalty, Reggie promptly went on hunger strike. Violet Kray wrote a 'mother to mother' letter of support to the Princess. Now Reggie fought with armed robber Pete Hurley in a quarrel over a doughnut and then with John Dudley, who was serving a life sentence for his part in the murder of three police officers near Wormwood Scrubs.

After the Special Wing at Durham had closed down, Ron's paranoid schizophrenia had recurred, and he was rapidly becoming out of control. Based on the hope they would have a moderating influence on each other, Reggie was transferred in February 1971 back to Parkhurst to join his twin.

Despite this, Ron was becoming increasingly disturbed and further out of control. Being together may have temporarily helped him, but in many ways it did not help Reggie. He attacked a man who was serving a sentence for manslaughter, with a bottle. Ron then tangled with a warder and received 56 days solitary confinement.

More serious were the injuries meted out to Anthony Seaward, then on remand in Brixton on fraud charges, which led to a three-year sentence. In April 1972 he was attacked and blinded after he had refused to leave a cell door open so another prisoner who had given evidence in the Kray case could be attacked. Seaward was jabbed in his eyes by Kray hirelings. He refused to name his attackers, and a year into his sentence he was paroled. No charges were brought and requests for an inquiry were rejected.[224]

The first serious step on the road to the Twins' beatification came with the initial serialisation in the *News of the World* followed by the publication of John Pearson's *The Profession of Violence* in November 1972. In fact, initially the Krays were not that pleased. Worse, Violet Kray, not realising that advances had to be cleared off, said she hadn't received any royalties. Over the months, however, when they discovered the status it had conferred upon them, the Twins changed their minds about the book, and in time it became the most read book in prison libraries and one of the most commonly stolen from bookshops.

But then came the problem of the prison reformer and general do-gooder Lord Longford, and Reggie's poetry. By 1973 Longford was telling the papers he believed the Twins had turned the corner. But in February that year, some of Reggie's sub-McGonigall poetry came to Longford's attention. Reggie was particularly fond of 'The Brooks', written almost immediately after he had been remanded in custody in 1968. It referred to his mother's house and he was exceptionally proud of the ending:

'Catch a glance while you may
Just like the rippling waters always moving
Spring is here but not to stay.'

Longford had not been allowed to take the poems out, but they were given to Violet who then handed them to him. There was confusion all round until Mark Carlisle, the then Home Secretary, explained to Longford that prisoners could have their work critically evaluated but could not publish it while serving sentences.[225]

By March that year Reggie was the one showing signs of stress and was described as 'tense and voluble'. Fed up with the same old faces, conversation and routine, both wanted to go on Rule 43, which provided separation from the general prison population. 'I doubt if their self-imposed isolation will last long', wrote the Governor on 13 March. On 22 March Ron was sent to the prison hospital when his mental condition deteriorated further. Reg remained on his self-imposed Rule 43.

In September 1972 Reg was in Parkhurst's Special Security Block (SSB) and his behaviour 'gave no cause for concern' but the troubles were expected to begin when he was placed in a 'normal location'. Unfortunately he had become friendly with a recent arrival 'whose influence on the wing is not a good one'. The Governor wrote, 'I do not see him as an inmate leader in a dispersal situation. He is not a strong personality.'[226]

On 17 April 1973 Ron was found in bed with another prisoner and was told that if it happened again he would be placed on Rule 43. Then at 9.15 a.m. on 22 May armed robber Royal Stuart Grantham, who had spent 16 months in Broadmoor, and who had tried to escape from Gartree for which he lost a year's remission, looked in on the Twins when they were in a cell together. At one time Grantham had been highly regarded by his fellow prisoners. Then he began to be seen as a grass and his status withered accordingly. A report of the incident read:

> 'What then transpired is not yet known but Grantham came out of the cell with severe cuts to the side of his face which required 36 stitches in his face and nine in his left hand, subsequently found to have been inflicted with a broken bottle.'

When warders entered the cell they found a naked Reggie (now transferred to the SSB) sitting astride Grantham and punching him. Other prisoners, including Neil George Adamson, then serving life with a minimum of 30 years for two murders, had joined in punching the bleeding Grantham while he lay helpless on the bed.[227] Once an incident is over, prisoners are usually unwilling to cooperate with the authorities both for their own safety and as a show of solidarity. But, not exactly in the spirit of prison *omertà* (the mafia code of honour), Ron said, 'He's an animal. He tried to hit me with a bottle, Gov, and before that he came in and poured a glass of my lemonade out.' In turn, Reg complained that Grantham used to read his letters.

Grantham, sensitive of his reputation as a grass, behaved rather better. He said not only would he not make a statement to the police, but he wanted to apologise to the Twins. There was clearly enough evidence against them to bring charges of grievous bodily harm, but the prosecution would have had problems. Apart from Grantham's lack of cooperation, it was thought other prisoners would lie on the Twins' behalf and that if a prosecution was brought not only would a judge not add to their sentences but their prison reputations would be even more enhanced. The Director of Public Prosecutions declined to lay charges and it was decided they should be sent before Visiting Magistrates, where they lost 28 days' privileges.[228]

That incident apart, by October 1973 Reg was once more regarded as the more stable of the Twins and something of a calming influence. That year, however, they were not recommended for downgrading. The Governor was told not to tell Ron 'unless he asks'.

By August that year they were both again becoming increasingly irritable and Ronnie was showing new symptoms of paranoia. There were suggestions they might be moved to C wing or even to the hospital, but there were fears they would exercise control of other inmates and also that they had the money to organise an escape.

In February 1974 Charlie had been allowed to visit his brothers. Strictly speaking he could have been banned because of his conviction, although this rule was often waived in the case of family members. Strictly it was unauthorized, because although a visit by Charlie had been mooted, there had not been actual Home Office approval. However, both Twins were now suffering from depression and were anxious about their 'present and future situation', and the prison doctors thought a visit from Charleie might be beneficial.

High-profile and good-looking male prisoners attract a great deal of what could be called 'fan mail' from women on the outside. Often, it is a case of the worse the offence, the more the interest. Generally, there are advantages for both parties. The women often carry a burning reformatory zeal, but are not obliged to face up to the reality of life with the man in question. Instead they are showered with letters, poetry and presents. Another benefit is that there is often no actual danger that the man will be let out for years to come and that dreams will turn into nightmares. If things do go wrong it is generally the woman who suffers.

In a number of cases, for better or worse, but usually for the latter, the correspondence and subsequent visits do lead to marriage. That is the benefit for the prisoner: a home to go to helps with the parole. Over the years the Krays had their fair share of women who for one reason or another wished to attach themselves to them.

Back in 1973 Essex girl Stella Burnette, now enamoured with Ron, was refused permission to see him. She told *The People*:

> 'I want him and am prepared to marry him no matter how long I have to wait. Apart from Ronnie's mother I am the only woman in the world who cares for him.'[229]

In July 1974 Ronnie was said to be helping a 30-year-old woman overcome her drug problem, writing to her twice a week. She had apparently met him before his arrest. 'I realised that he was shy with women. He didn't know how to communicate with them. But I think I was able to help him over that and I believe I got through to him.' He had bought her a hairdressing salon in Harrogate and she regarded him as a brother. She was now determined to kick her heroin habit so she could visit him.

Meanwhile, 'buxom blond bombshell' Christine Boyce was back on the scene and thought she had Reggie's 'licence to love'. She had left the country shortly before the trial. Reggie had given her permission to marry but didn't want her new husband to accompany her on prison visits, and expected her to be rid of him by the time he was released.[230]

In his cell Reggie had two Constable prints on the wall as well as a radio, record player and dozens of records. There was also a photograph of Christine Boyce and one of his ex-wife Frances. Frank Kurylo would later write that he believed Christine was the real love of Reggie's life, 'far above his love for Frances Shea', and that years into his sentence she was still writing to him.[231]

This was juxtaposed with the story of 40-year-old ex-barmaid Chloe, who told how Reggie 'misses his pint' and said that apart from his mother, she was the only woman who made 'the lonely visit to Parkhurst'.[232]

Even when the Krays were not putting themselves in the limelight, prison officers and other inmates were happy to pass on details of their moves to the newspapers. 'The crop-haired shaven-eyebrowed Straffen is their waiter and Dennis Stafford their cook,' wrote Dan Wooding.[233] John Straffen had killed two young girls in 1951. Reports that they did weight training three times a week and Reggie had taken up yoga were probably accurate.

In August 1974 they were still on the Special Wing and were described as withdrawn, spending most of their time in their cells. It was accepted that their prolonged stay in Special Security wings had caused personality damage. This situation did, however, have its benefits. They included showers and baths at any time, battery record players, inmates being able to cook for themselves and wearing some of their own clothes; they could write an unrestricted number of letters; they were allowed to receive extra-long fortnightly visits; and they enjoyed more frequent physical recreation. These privileges would cease on being moved back into the general prison population.

On 9 January 1975 the Twins were moved on, this time to C wing. There were, however, still vague fears they might try an escape.[234]

Two months later Dr Cooper, who had done so much to help prisoners in the aftermath of the 1969 Parkhurst riot, thought both the Twins should be moved to the psychiatric wing.

In July 1976, when both brothers were working as cleaners, it was reported that 'neither exerted themselves'. In November that year there were suggestions Reg could be promoted to a Category B prisoner; a report read, 'He is not prepared to accept he will be treated as any other life sentence prisoner and demands special privileges.' Unless there was a 'dramatic improvement, he will go to a dispersal prison'.[235]

Celebrities were beginning to campaign tentatively for the Twins' release. In 1977 a rock musical *England, England* by Snoo Wilson and Kevin Coyne portrayed the Twins as Jim and Jake. Bob Hoskins, champion of the West London villain, and fellow actor John Bindon, thought society owed them a debt:

'The ultimate paranoia is believing in your own myth then waking up one day and finding that it's true. We helped to create the Krays because we need our villains. We still do. They got to the top of their profession through sheer animal courage. They were modern-day gladiators.'[236]

In October 1977 they were moved back to the hospital wing but by now their Category A status was seen as symbolic. In October the next year Reg was saying he hoped to be released in five or six years but it was thought 'he is manufacturing some basis for hope (especially for mother) from an apparently hopeless situation'.[237]

In November 1979, there was some thought that Reg should go to Kingston Prison, a smaller, less pressurised establishment. It was hoped he might become an asset there by acting as a stabilising influence in the prison. However, a report in May 1980 suggested he had returned to his old ways and might act as a catalyst in the formation of a gang opposing other prisoners in Parkhurst's mainstream population. On 5 August 1980 another report thought he had been involved in drugs and would always be involved in some black-market operation:

> 'But that is the nature of the beast... he controls the fiddles and exerts considerable influence over other inmates. He has become far too sheltered at Parkhurst.'[238]

In June 1980 Reggie claimed he was happy to remain in the hospital wing in Parkhurst and wanted to give up his status as a gangster.

Meanwhile Ron's mental condition had deteriorated sharply. He was in solitary confinement for several months and his future wife Kate claimed he was naked except for a blanket for much of the time. The very humane Dr Cooper arranged for him to have a transistor radio.

On 25 July 1979 he was sent to Broadmoor, and never left.

CHAPTER 18
RONNIE KRAY IN BROADMOOR

If Ronnie did not at first live in the lap of luxury in Broadmoor, the high-security psychiatric hospital at Crowthorne in Berkshire, by the end of his life he certainly lived in some comfort and style. Known, in less kindly days, as the Broadmoor Criminal Lunatic Asylum, the old Victorian red-brick building at the end of a long driveway may have initially seemed forbidding with its reputation for a scary clientele, but Ronnie had his own single-bedded room with a separate lavatory, a stereo system, television and radio. He wore his own clothes. A chain smoker, said to smoke up to 140 cigarettes a day, he would sit by his bed and roll his own – 10 or 12 at a time. Safe in Broadmoor, and taking his medication, Ronnie was now effectively untouchable. In her book *Murder, Madness and Marriage,* his wife Kate Kray claimed that, at his peak, Ron was making £20,000 a year financing and advising on such diverse activities as robberies, counterfeiting, travellers' cheques and fake designer label clothes. After advising on one successful robbery of a jeweller in Brighton, he bought an interest in a wine bar in the town with his share of the proceeds. He splashed his earnings around on lavish presents for his gay friends – Kate claimed on one occasion she had to buy six Gucci watches for his lovers – and cashmere suits costing £800 for himself. 'It may be that if he is well enough to be the director of a company, he is too well to be in Broadmoor', one man complained ineffectually to the Home Office.

It had not always been peaches and cream. Kray was kept in isolation when he first arrived at Broadmoor on 25 July 1979, but shortly after his release into the main block he attacked another prisoner and was sent to the punishment block, the dreaded Norfolk House. On his release from the block he went to Somerset House and after 12 years there he moved to Henley Ward in a new block, Oxford House. His cell had an unbreakable window and he owned 14 shirts which he changed after every visit. Charlie, a fellow inmate, washed and ironed them and for his troubles was given a jar of coffee a week. Ron was allowed four hour-long visits a week and many of his visitors were East End friends who, according to Patrick McGrath, the son of one of the doctors:

> '...handed out liberal tips to patients left and right, and hopelessly disrupted the hospital's delicate internal economy. After they left, the staff would make the rounds of the wards, relieving disappointed patients of large quantities of cash.'[239]

They also settled his bar bill (for tobacco and non-alcoholic beer), which over time had been allowed to run to several hundred pounds.

On 5 August 1982 the Twins' mother Violet died. Over the years she had been a constant visitor, providing them with luxuries such as Brylcreem. She kept her cancer diagnosis secret from her sons right to the end, telling them she had been admitted to hospital for pneumonia. The Twins were allowed out of Broadmoor – Ron was the first ever – and Parkhurst respectively for her funeral a week later on 11 August. They met the coffin at the church, but care was taken that they were each handcuffed to large warders, so diminishing their physical stature. The funeral procession had started at Shoreditch and there were about 1,000 spectators. Mourners included two of the Nash brothers, Diana Dors and the boxer Terry Downes. There were over 300 wreaths which took 50 minutes to load into the cars, including from the train robber Buster Edwards, and a mound of chrysanthemums and lilies from 'all the boys in Parkhurst prison'.

The faithful Father Hetherington told the congregation that he had the greatest respect and affection for her. 'Among her qualities was loyalty, a loyalty to that which she held to be right, a loyalty to her family whom she loved, a loyalty to God'. The hymns 'The King of Love my Shepherd Is' and 'Abide with Me' were sung. There were unkind suggestions that old Charlie Snr was drunk and nearly fell into his wife's grave.

The *Sunday People* thought it was a 'Gangland Circus starring the Terrible Twins'. If, as people said, Violet was the only person of whom they were afraid, why did she not put her foot down more often?

After the service, Reggie kissed Leicester magistrate Dora Hamilton, who had announced she was going to write a book about Violet. Hamilton simpered, 'I managed to get a nice kiss from Reggie. They're always so affectionate, you know'. It was something that added fuel to the speculation she might be removed from the bench, with suggestions that her position as a magistrate was not compatible with her friendship with Kray. She changed her publishers but the book never appeared.[240] The *Sunday Express* thought, 'Another thing we could do without is female magistrates being kissed by Reggie Kray… the Kray twins went down the aisle like a pair of popes blessing the faithful.'

Next month Father Hetherington felt able to reveal that both were independently studying the Bible, often a helpful step on the way to parole, at least for Reggie. Better still, both had received certificates for 'understanding its meaning'.

While in Broadmoor Ronnie was alleged to have lived the life of an old-style mafioso to which he had aspired. It is said he had two people executed in London by hitmen and the only reason he did not put out a contract on his hated enemy Nipper Read is that he wanted to reserve the pleasure of killing him for himself. Kray had no time for Peter Sutcliffe, the Yorkshire Ripper. 'He's a nonce. I won't talk to scum like that who cut up women. He knows better than to even look me in the eye. If I had my way I'd deal with him properly. For good.'[241]

In due course he arranged for the Glasgow hardman Jimmy Costello, who was serving ten years for firearms offences, to slash Sutcliffe in Parkhurst Prison's hospital wing on 10 January 1983. The attack took place while Sutcliffe was getting water from a recess. Costello smashed him twice on the left side of his face with a broken coffee jar before Sutcliffe managed to push him away. One deep cut ran five inches from near his mouth to his neck, and another was two-and-a-half inches long, running from his left eye to his ear, requiring thirty stitches. Costello, who claimed Sutcliffe had attacked him, received a further five years.

Kray is also said to have listened to a plea in 1992 by Ann West, Anne Downey's mother, to have Myra Hindley harmed if not killed. Very much in the tradition of Vito Corleone, he refused, saying he could not have a woman, however evil, hurt.

Kray was apparently extremely polite with women. A man might, and Johnny Cardew did, get a slashing for saying he had put on weight, but when a woman told him, 'If you put on any more weight the next time we go out I'm not going to introduce you to any of these good-looking young boys' and patted his stomach, he merely simpered 'Bobby [McKew – the fraudster], tell her to leave me alone.'[242]

In 1985 Ronnie decided he should get married. Marriages or relationships with Broadmoor patients are fraught with difficulties on their release. A good example came in 1969 when Paul Beecham shot his father four times, his mother nine times and for good measure his grandparents, and ended up in Broadmoor, certified insane. There Rita Fry, a married member of Broadmoor's League of Friends, became attracted to him and on his release in 1979, her marriage now over, the cured Beecham moved in with her. It went well until 1997, when one of Rita's children called round and found Paul dead. Rita was nowhere to be seen. A month later an excavation of the patio unearthed her body. Beecham had killed her with a hammer before shooting himself.

There would be no question of Ronnie ever being released and now he settled on Elaine Mildener, often described as a rather homely divorced mother of two, to be his lucky bride. She began her relationship, as did many others, by being Reggie's pen friend before being moved on to his twin. The courtship was not without its problems and on Boxing Day 1984 Ronnie cut his wrists, something attributed to problems in his relationship with his fiancée.

Nevertheless, they married on 12 February 1985, the first wedding allowed in Broadmoor, and sold the story to *The Sun* for a reputed £20,000, for which the paper had its knuckles rapped by the Press Council. She was said to have put the money towards a house for her and Ronnie to live together when he was released. Kray spent the next year cultivating press interest in his new situation, even petitioning the Home Office to allow him to consummate the union. He wanted twins, he said. He believed that when, rather than if, he got out of Broadmoor, he would not live with his bride. He wanted to spend the rest of his life with Reg and to travel but, he added generously, she and her children could come and stay whenever they liked.[243] The attendant publicity was probably not what the new Mrs Kray wanted, and five months after the marriage she had ceased to visit him. Three years later, after he had instructed his then solicitor Stephen Gold to file a petition for divorce on the grounds of her desertion, Ronnie was able to sell that story to a tabloid. A decree was granted in May 1988.

On 6 November 1989 Ronnie married again. This time it was to 32-year-old divorcee Kathleen Anne Howard, who ran a kissogram girl agency. She was another who had first written a fan letter to Reggie after buying *The Profession of Violence* at a railway station.

Once more Reggie had passed her on to his brother. When David Bailey declined to be the wedding photographer, Lord Litchfield was paid £2,000 to take a picture of the happy bride. A white Rolls Royce provided transport to the hospital. Harrods provided the food for the subsequent wedding breakfast at the Hilton, Bracknell (Ron and Reggie *in absentia*) as well as the shellfish for Reggie's monthly visit to his brother in Broadmoor.

On 1 January 1990 *The Sun* reported Ron had bought Kate a £25,000 house near Broadmoor. He was said to be sick with worry that if her car broke down on the motorway she would be attacked. In turn Ron worried about catching Mad Cow Disease and Kate cheered him up by saying it would not matter, since he was mad already.

Not to be outdone, at the end of the month, Reggie was said to have bought a luxury six-bedroom house in Suffolk, complete with nine acres and a moat, from his old friend Geoff Allen, who had let him have it for £350,000, around £150,000 less than the going rate.

Less favourably, in the middle of the month there were suggestions in the press that Ronnie was under investigation for hiring rent boys in Broadmoor after two nurses claimed he had bribed a warder. Jimmy Savile, then heading a Broadmoor task force, was reported to have been informed.

Kate Kray was questioned over allegations of bribery. She explained that she employed two of the warders as chauffeurs. They had helped her and Ronnie and she was helping them. Four nurses were arrested and two were sacked. In her book *The Krays Free at Last,* she accepted she did in fact pay officers £500 to £1,000 or, if they preferred, gave them portable TVs or microwaves.

Kate then claimed that the next year, tired of Broadmoor, Ron put together a plot to be rescued as he travelled to Heatherwood

Hospital in Ascot for a hernia operation. Two American mafia hitmen were to be recruited, one to be dressed as a doctor and one as a porter, to kill his guards. He would then be put on a coach packed with old-age pensioners going to Kent for the day. From there he would be put on a cross-channel ferry and eventually be flown to Venezuela. She maintained the plot was aborted because Kray committed a cardinal gangland sin and lost his nerve.[244]

On 5 September 1992 Kate Kray was held on credit card offences in Debenhams. She had been using a stolen Diners Club card. Fined £240, she claimed she was now skint and living on £40 unemployment benefit. Ron was reportedly not pleased.[245] Nevertheless, he wrote as a preface to his 1993 book, 'Kate is my wife and we will never be parted. I have trusted her to help me tell the real story of the Krays today and she has.'

But the marriage did not last, and they were divorced in May 1994. Ronnie's petition claimed that Kate had committed adultery, breached matrimonial confidences, demeaned him and caused him distress by selling her story with photographs to *The Sun*. She had written a chapter entitled 'Sex and All That' in her book *Murder, Madness and Marriage* in which she detailed an affair she had.

Generally speaking his behaviour was good, at least until the summer of 1993 when he tried to strangle another patient, Lee Kiernender, who was annoying him. Kray, who had apparently been on reduced drug treatment, suddenly snapped and was pulled off by nurses before the unfortunate man went blue. It resulted in a loss of privileges and he seems to have been remorseful. 'I want to go on record as saying that this is the last act of violence Ron Kray will ever commit.' Note the third person speech.[246]

This was a bad time for him. He was unhappy with Fred Dinenage's book *Our Story*, claiming he had been misrepresented. Not all his troubles were of his own making, however. In 1994, 26-year-old Stephen Laudat stabbed 56-year-old Bryan Bennett to death at a Stratford day centre, believing he was killing Kray, something he described as 'a public service'. Laudat denied murder, but admitted manslaughter on the grounds of diminished responsibility and was sent to Rampton rather than to Broadmoor.[247]

On 15 March 1995 Kray complained of feeling unwell after breakfast. Despite writing to his friend Bert Rossi advising him on his diet – 'at one time he wanted me to take up a diet of garlic pills. Another time he said he was living off raw eggs and honey' – he was still chain-smoking.[248] A nurse thought he was having a heart attack – he had had a minor one in 1994 – and he was sent to Heatherwood Hospital, where he was treated for exhaustion and anaemia before being sent back to Broadmoor. That evening he complained of feeling weak and faint and was taken back to Heatherwood for tests. But the next day his condition deteriorated and he was sent to a specialist at Wexham Park Hospital, Slough, where he died at 9.07 the following morning. That morning, a gangland pal had told the *Daily Mirror* he did not think Ron Kray would last until Christmas. Reggie had phoned the hospital at 10 a.m. only to be told he had died an hour earlier. He had applied for leave to go and see him and had been refused.

Shortly before his death Ron had written Kate a nice little poem:

'No man knows me, only God can my mind see
And with a Big Sleep set me free.'

After the news of Ron's death his twin was placed in a cell with his friends Freddie Foreman and Joey Martin, receiving condolences from other inmates and drinking prison hooch. Foreman was given parole in time to be a pall bearer. Reggie had wanted Joey Martin to be one as well, but there was no release for him.[249]

As might be expected, tributes were mixed. *The Sun* was happy to record his dying words – echoing Edward G. Robinson's, 'Mother of Mercy, is this the end of Rico?' – as 'Oh God, mother help me.' Criminal turned criminologist John McVicar wrote in *The Times*, 'He sliced up more people than most normal people slice up Sunday joints.' Barbara Windsor took the opportunity to say she thought Reggie should be released. Charlie Kray said, 'He had principles all his life. All he ever tried to do was to keep boys out of trouble.'

Colin Fry, a Kray biographer, thought he had given away a million pounds to good causes, but he had kept £20,000 in the delusion he would one day be able to go on a world cruise.[250]

Nor was the inquest trouble-free. At the time, a coroner had powers to hold one when and where he liked, and the coroner for East Hampshire, Robert Wilson, decided to hold it alone in his own home in Waltham St Lawrence. In under five minutes he ruled that Ronnie had died from natural causes. Some thought it was not a valid inquest. Wilson was unrepentant, saying he should be congratulated because he had held it so speedily.[251]

Now was the time for the Twins to return once more to the East
End in triumph. On 28 March – the same day as the less well-attended
funeral of the serial killer Fred West – Ronnie's High Anglican funeral with a glass-sided hearse drawn by six black horses, followed by 25
black limos, saw a massive turnout.

Bouncers at the funeral home were organised by celebrity criminal Dave Courtney, and Ronnie's latest solicitor Mark Bloomfield was
also on the door. Courtney told the press, 'I see it as an honour. Losing
someone like Ronnie is like losing the monarch. To me Ronnie is now
lying in state.'[252] But, despite all Courtney's best efforts, it appears
that lines of cocaine had been smoked off the coffin as it lay at the
undertakers and someone had tried to set up a Ouija board to see if
it was possible to contact Ronnie. There were also suggestions that
when he was lying in his open coffin, a pair of earphones had been
put on his body. Later someone stole Ronnie's photograph from the
centerpiece of flowers in the cemetery. It was never recovered.

The funeral procession stretched from St Matthew's Church,
Bethnal Green to the Carpenters Arms, and the crowds that followed
the subsequent procession to Chingford cemetery was said to be over
a mile long, more than many a political demonstration.

Reggie's tribute, in red roses on white chrysanthemums, was
lettered 'To My Other Half'. Kate Kray's wreath was a heart pulled
in two composed of white and red carnations, with a note, 'Tears
in my eyes I can wipe away, but the pain in my heart will always
stay'. Other floral tributes included one from John Gotti of the
Gambino New York Family, and another from Danny Pagano of the
Genoveses. 'Black Widow' Linda Calvey, serving life in Holloway

for killing her lover Ron Cook, sent a floral boxing glove from her and the girls in H wing.

Inside the Order of Service was a message:

'We wish for only good to come from Ron's passing away and what is about to follow is our tribute to Ron. It is a symbol of peace that the four pallbearers will be Charlie, Freddie Foreman, Johnny Nash and Teddy Dennis; each one represents an area of London, north, south, east and west.'

Frankie Fraser had been invited to be a pallbearer but had declined, saying that as such a small man it would have appeared lopsided if he had been carrying the coffin with three six-footers. Instead he rode in a limo with Alex Steene, the boxing promoter. Reggie was brought separately by prison officers.

Hymns included 'Morning has broken' and 'Fight the Good Fight' and there was a recording of Whitney Houston singing Dolly Parton's 'I Will Always Love You' from the soundtrack of *The Bodyguard*. Publisher Robin McGibbon's wife Sue read 'Do not stand at my grave and weep', written by the American poet and florist Mary Elizabeth Frye. The service ended with a tape of Frank Sinatra singing 'My Way', itself well on its way to becoming the worldwide hymn of choice at any gangster funeral. A collection realised £850.

As the coffin was lowered, a World War Two Spitfire flew over the Chingford Mount cemetery, dipping its wings in tribute to a man his brother believed was the equal of Winston Churchill or the Duke of Wellington, if not both. Under Ronnie's name on his tombstone would appear the word 'Legend'.

At the wake the music was provided by 'Gary', who sang a selection of Sinatra favourites accompanied by backing tapes. When Tony Lambrianou approached him and asked him to sing 'New York, New York', Gary told him he had sung it three numbers ago and he thought he should wait a little while before he sang it again. Lambrianou merely said, 'Are you going to fucking sing it or not?' And so, sensibly, he did.[253]

It was a time for the renewal of calls for Reggie to be released. However, not everyone agreed. One man wrote:

> 'You as Home Secretary should have insisted this disgust-ing creature was interred in an unmarked grave within the precincts of the institution he finished his days.
>
> How on earth can the young and impressionable be convinced that crime does not pay when people of your standing in Government allow this circus to take place. The glorification of crime is not what I voted for.'

Unfortunately an incision at the hairline had been discovered: Ronnie's brain was missing. The 19th-century criminologist Cesare Lombroso believed that criminals' brains differed from those of 'normal' people such as barristers and judges. Over the years many of Lombroso's theories, including a belief that women with excessive pubic hair became prostitutes, have been discredited. Nevertheless when the autopsy was performed, his brain was removed in an attempt to establish whether any physical abnormalities had caused Ronnie's violent criminal behaviour. Or indeed if there was a tumour. Ron's brain weighed just over two pounds and showed signs of wastage. When he was buried it was still in a laboratory in Oxford.[254]

Now papers had a field day, with the *News of the World* displaying the tasteful banner headline 'The Great Brain Robbery' and going on to say, 'Docs have pickled Ronnie Kray's brain in a bottle – now his wife has half a mind to sue'. A campaign backed by another Sunday newspaper was sufficient to ensure that the brain was sent to Charlie Kray to be buried with its owner.[255]

Reggie never accepted the circumstances of Ronnie's death and shortly before he died it seemed he was considering calling for an inquiry. In a tape from prison he said:

> 'I wish to express doubt that my brother Ron Kray did not die from natural causes… There is a sequence of events which is unexplained – events which happened the day before he died and on the day of his death.'[256]

Nothing came of it.

Ronnie left an estate of approximately £10,000. He gave all his jewellery and personal belongings to his twin and the remainder was to be divided between Kate Kray, a family friend Anne Glew and his best man Charlie Smith, a double murderer who was eventually transferred to Maidstone psychiatric hospital, from where he escaped.

On 17 March 1997 a ceremony was held 'to try to help reconcile Ron with God and help him find peace', said the Reverend

Ken Rimini, vicar of St Matthews, Bethnal Green. The 40 or so celebrants included Dave Courtney. Another Spitfire flew past followed by a small plane bearing a banner with the words 'Ronnie Kray – Legend'. Frankie Fraser sent a telegram: 'Some they say are damned but Ronnie walks the streets of paradise now, his head held high and unashamed.' Reg Kray sent a tape: 'I asked Jesus how much do you love me? "This much," he answered and stretched out his arms and died. God bless, Reg Kray.'

On Ronnie's grave in Chingford Mount cemetery appears another short poem:

'The kiss of the sun for pardon
The song of a bird for mirth
One is nearer to God in a garden
Than anywhere else on earth.'

CHAPTER 19
SURVIVING RONNIE KRAY

In January 1981, nearly 15 years before his twin's death, Reg Kray was transferred without notice – a process prisoners call 'ghosting' – to Long Lartin in Gloucestershire. The move was not a success. As the year went on he found it harder and harder to cope with life there, and just before Christmas he cut both wrists with a safety razor in the Segregation Unit of the prison. He had been sent there the day before after quarrelling with his former friend, the Birmingham hardman Patsy Manning, then serving a sentence for a hammer attack on a nightclub bouncer. Kray had become convinced Manning was going to poison him. The wrist cutting was not considered a serious suicide attempt, but on 16 January 1982 he attacked Manning a second time and the next day he again cut his wrists with a safety razor. Once more the Governor thought that this was attention seeking.

In March he was disciplined after he threw a table at a television, and assaulted four members of staff and set fire to his prison hospital cell. Attitudes changed and there was now a fear of a real psychotic illness if he remained in a mainstream prison location. It was decided to ask Parkhurst if they would take him, and they agreed.

Unfortunately, in the short term, things did not improve. Back in Parkhurst, on 2 April he tried to cut his wrist with a broken spectacle lens. He was found when his cell was unlocked shortly before 7 a.m. with a two-inch traverse cut across his left forearm four inches above the wrist. When he was taken to the treatment room he threw a cup of tea over the warder and grabbed his tie. This time the Parkhurst medical officer believed it was a genuine suicide attempt. The medical report on him described him as 'depressed and appears to have lost hope' and the doctor was surprised at the deterioration in his mental condition from when he first went to Long Lartin.

He began to talk about Christianity, but the doctor was not convinced he was genuine. 'He is', said the report, 'extremely demanding and manipulative. Nevertheless the deterioration in his stability is now worsening over recent months.' He wanted to be moved to Broadmoor to be with Ronnie. One of the problems was that he had fallen out with a supportive inmate and he was having difficulties with another former inmate who was now allowed to visit him. It was thought that without help from other inmates he could not survive on a normal wing.

Reggie showed no signs of improvement in 1982 and was beginning to show serious signs of prison wear and tear. He had indeed not been able to cope with life on C wing in Parkhurst and had 'sought the sanctuary of the prison hospital'. In January another report told of a liaison which 'bordered on obsessional and might be based on a homosexual relationship'.

A year later, after his father's death on 31 August 1983, a report on Reggie, then in C wing, read:

'He is an arch manipulator of staff and has a few friends amongst his peers in the wing. He is tolerated by the gangsters and is disliked by some because of the company he keeps. These include the young-looking types of inmate who hero-worship him because of the gangster image of Kray. There are suspicions that the friendships of the young inmates are of a homosexual nature... he has not shown a genuine change of heart and will always remain a criminal who is prone to violence to achieve his grandiose schemes. He acts the role of 'Godfather' and has enlisted young inmates who are promised jobs on their discharge from prison.'

The next month the Assistant Governor wrote of Kray's relationship with a prisoner whom he introduced as 'family' as 'whilst not being overtly homosexual, certainly somewhat bizarre'.

'In summary he is a partly deaf, semi-illiterate, institutionalised 50-year-old who always accepts 'no' without question and is always polite, courteous and respectful to staff, and who is desperately trying to retain some dignity by maintaining a small, young group of prisoners around him with, apart from the one exception, noticeably less and less effect.'[257]

Now at last it was accepted he did not have the resources to effect an escape, and the Governor and staff continually tried to get him downgraded to a lesser category, a move which was regularly blocked by the Home Office.

Their father Charlie Kray Snr did not survive his wife for long. On 8 March 1983 Charlie Kray Jnr's son Gary found him collapsed on the stairs at Braithwaite House where they were both living. The Twins did not even ask to attend his funeral. Later they explained this, saying their father would not have wanted it.

Two years later in March 1985 the waxworks of the Twins were removed from the Chamber of Horrors at Madame Tussauds to make way for fresher figures and the Easter rush. Violet would have been pleased. She had regularly complained the effigies looked nothing like her boys.

It was about this time that Reg Kray began a long series of relationships, which at the time he denied were gay, with a number of younger prisoners. There was also speculation about his heterosexual love life, with a Maureen Cox gushing on the pages of the *Daily Mirror*, 'Reggie is writing me love letters. It's leap year next year and if I pop the question I think he may say yes'.[258]

In October 1986 the then real love of his life was 'jailhouse pup' Peter Gillett, a wannabee pop singer serving six years for possessing firearms and conspiracy to rob. Gillett denied he was having a homosexual affair with the lifer and Reggie was keen to emphasise that while he took Gillett breakfast in bed in his cell, theirs was a platonic friendship. 'We're not bent. It's like a homosexual affair without sex.' He was, he said, closer to Peter than he had been with anyone before including Frances. Among his many kindnesses, he arranged for a white Rolls Royce to collect Gillett from Parkhurst when he went on four-day home leave.

Kray and Gillett wrote songs together and he dreamed Gillett would give him his first No. 1 single:

> 'How stimulating if one day our lyrics could be heard in the vast Wembley Stadium, with the kids joyfully tapping their feet and clicking their fingers to one of our songs and recognising us as songwriters – then these austere days spent alone would really bear fruit.'[259]

It was not to be. On his release Gillett cut some records and appeared at Raquel's, the Essex disco infamous for the death of Leah Betts from an overdose of Ecstasy, but his career never took off. Joey Pyle, then a major force in the London underworld to whom Kray had recommended Gillett, was dismissive of his talents. 'At first I thought it a joke. The boy could hardly sing a note, there was nothing, no talent at all.'[260]

But by 1990 Kray had fallen out with his former protégé sufficiently to ask the actor Martin Kemp to hit him for real on the film set of *The Krays*, in which Gillett was an extra.

Reg Kray would remain in Parkhurst until February 1986 when there was another blot on his record. He claimed in *Our Story* that the authorities moved him so they could see how he handled a new environment and if this proved satisfactory, he would be transferred to a softer prison such as Maidstone or Nottingham. However, the Home Office records show that another lifer sustained a fractured cheekbone when he had been pushed down a flight of stairs by others acting on Kray's behalf. Kray was transferred to Wandsworth for

56 days as a punishment for 'disruptive behaviour and strong-arm tactics'. A Home Office memorandum of 14 February read:

> 'Information has been received from numerous independent sources (staff and inmates) that Kray, over a period of time, has been intimidating and bullying other inmates… security information in reports submitted since the incident have all indicated that Kray's behind-the-scenes behaviour has put many inmates on the defensive.'

It was thought several had armed themselves against 'possible assaults by Kray's front men'. He was therefore segregated under Rule 43 prior to the transfer to Wandsworth.

By the end of the year it was noted he had 'outstayed his welcome at Parkhurst' and other prisons were being canvassed. Of Maidstone it was said, 'I can see that the whole prison would revolve around him.' And as for Nottingham, at least two other lifers would have to move before Kray came. 'He has contracts on both', with an additional note, 'He is still a very dangerous man… frankly I would not trust him an inch.' And so the winner (or loser) in the raffle was Gartree in Leicestershire.[261]

From 1984 it had been clear that the Home Office had no intention of releasing Reg Kray in the foreseeable future. A memorandum set things out clearly:

> 'The expectation is that a prisoner in respect of whom a life sentence has been made with a minimum

recommendation will be detained for at <u>least</u> that period unless there are good reasons for doing otherwise. I hope this clarifies the situation.'[262]

The supposed love lives of the Twins still garnered regular newspaper interest. In August 1986 came the surprising news that Reggie was to marry BBC TV cashier Geraldine Charles. 'We are both wicked Scorpions. We have everything in common. He's an evangelist. I'm a Christian.' She told *The Sun* she wore black suspenders and stockings when she visited him in prison. She claimed she was prepared to wait for Reggie for as long as necessary, but ended up turning to Ronnie instead. This was all the more odd because by the next month Ronnie was involved with Kissogram girl Kate Howard.[263]

Reggie never learned that an unguarded remark to the press might become tomorrow's headline. In 1986 the journalist Paul Callan wrote an article entitled 'Why I murdered this man' in the *Daily Mirror* after speaking to Reggie. Reggie then wrote to the prison Governor complaining he had been misrepresented.[264] That year the authorities still regarded him as manipulative and believed he wielded considerable power. According to them, he had changed little during his sentence and was still seen as a risk to the public. In April 1987 a loyal Charlie disagreed, writing to Margaret Thatcher to say his brother had 'totally changed'.

In the mid 1980s the Kray bandwagon had really sprung into motion. There was more talk of a film to be made by Don Boyd, director of *Scum*, and in Richard Branson's Virgin Megastore there were Kray calendars (£2.99) with a picture of the Twins on every page and a caption reading 'Parole, it's about time'. There were also t-shirts at £4.99 with 25p royalties being paid to Charlie's company Krayleigh. The calendars were being marketed by Art Department, which operated out of a railway arch in Camberwell. Spokesperson Barry Porter said, 'We are trying to bring to public awareness the fact that the twins have been put away for 20 years when they didn't hurt a member of the general public'.

Kray memorabilia was stolen from Charlie's business partner in August 1986, but after a quiet word or two it was handed back. Charlie Kray, currently a music agent, said the money was going to charity and that he received hardly any from the sales. Fake shirts were also being made, but what was described as a 'polite word' on behalf of the brothers put a stop to that.[265]

Back in prison, in February 1986 it was noted that:

> '[Reggie] Kray is involved in every racket in the establishment, appearing a disruptive "Godfather". He is linked to strong-arming and the illicit brewing of alcohol. He has had a series of homosexual affairs with other younger inmates.'

Five months later in July 1986, after Kray had declined to be interviewed by staff and a local review committee member, the Parole Board knocked him back again until 1991. The Board thought he showed little insight into his problem and no remorse. They were right with the former. Over the years he consistently failed to see that he had to toe the line and do what the authorities wanted if he was ever to get out of prison. It was no use saying, as he did, that he would not see the appointed psychologist, but he wanted one of his own choosing. That was going to get him nowhere.

By July that year Reggie had been at Parkhurst for all but two years of his sentence and the Governor thought it was time he was moved. He had by now over 1,000 names and addresses on his record of letters and visits. How this had arisen no one seemed to know but, like Topsy in *Uncle Tom's Cabin*, 'it growed'. As a result he was being made to contribute £1 a week to the postage. Prisoners would buy food for him in the canteen and their relatives on the outside would be paid double. That September he was found with a small amount of cannabis, pethadine and other tablets.[266] That year at the Twins' request the sale of t-shirts at Virgin Megastore, now priced upwards of £5.99, were halted.

In January 1987 Reggie was finally sent to Gartree, but by that June he was already at odds with the staff. 'Kray does not cope with the prison regime, he gets other people to do it for him.' He was said to be fomenting trouble on the wing, 'especially where blacks are concerned', and 'to conclude I still feel he is a very devious and dangerous man who should not be trusted one inch.' Told he would have a review after 17 years, he replied, 'It's fucking not fair'.[267]

But over the next year he did better in Gartree and in a memo of 11 August 1988 it was suggested if he did well in Lewes for five years the Governor would recommend a Category C prison, perhaps The Verne in Portland, Dorset.

However, 18 months, later one view had changed. D.A. Brown, a senior Home Office official, wrote in a memo of 19 March 1990:

'All the indications are that he has not changed at all and beneath a façade of conformity he is still a subversive and pernicious influence.'

Reggie Kray had indeed moved to Lewes in 1989, where a report says that most of his time was taken up writing letters and books. It recommended he be regarded as a Category C prisoner. There had been problems over his relationship with a young lifer on C Wing, but this had cooled off. 'He intended to let his unofficial adopted son and his mother live in his home, but whether this is feasible remains to be seen,' wrote the officer realistically or cynically depending on one's viewpoint. He was also seen hanging around the door to A Wing speaking to young offenders. The next year it was reported he was sending and receiving 20 letters a day. The officer thought he was 'a likeable con'.

But there were troubles at Lewes where a firearm was found. No charges were brought and Kray denied any involvement, but in December 1990 after a short stay in Nottingham he was sent back to Gartree.

In January 1991 he refused to see a member of the Local Review Committee as a protest about still being held in a dispersal prison.

After his Parole Board Review in April that year he was returned to Nottingham.

'His Probation Officer [21 February 1991] doubts if he is repentant and thinks that his arrogance would make supervision difficult; that he intends to live in Sussex.'

It was reported in his parole board review that Reggie kept active mentally and physically because he wanted to maintain his celebrity status. Much of his time was spent dealing with his correspondence. Yet again he cannot have helped himself by refusing to be interviewed by the staff and a local review committee member. 'He has little insight and no remorse.' There would be no further review until 1995.

Apart from the regular campaigners, there was intermittent independent support for Reggie. In February 1991 one man wrote to the Home Office to say that he was a truly reformed character: 'God bless him. He was a victim also and still is a victim of circumstances. He is a man of honour and integrity.' But for every letter of support there was one explaining in simple terms why he should not be released. In 1999 one opposer wrote:

> 'They were no good. The money they had was money
> that decent people owned. These people were tortured for
> same. They should have hung years ago by their privates.'

In February 1992 Kray was sent to Blundestone, where he was still held in awe by other inmates. That year he was allowed to spend only £60 on presents for his friends, and was refusing to pay a £12,500 tax bill.

The author Peter Gerrard, who later collaborated on Reg Kray's *East End Stories*, visited him there and clearly found the regime allowed Kray a good deal of latitude. Kray had asked him to bring in brandy in a plastic bottle and Gerrard did this on a number of visits. During his first visit:

'We were constantly interrupted by well-wishers approaching the table to shake Reggie's hand or give him a hug and every one of them was received with the same patient and friendly demeanour. Autographs were sought, or thanks were given for looking after a certain person. It was obvious that Reggie had a great respect from all and for all.'[268]

But so far as his release was concerned, he was now thrashing about wildly. In July 1993 he told a Through Care officer, who would help him reintegrate in society if and when he was released, that on his release he wanted to go and live in Canterbury with a former professional landscape gardener, apparently a distant relation, and his wife, but he then changed his mind and said he would prefer to live in Northamptonshire.

Yet another report that year read, 'Because the events had no direct bearing on members of the public but was aimed at competitors, Mr Kray sees no real wrong.' Nevertheless, he was not seen as a potential danger to the community at large. It recommended he be moved to a Category C prison so he could be tested in less secure conditions.[269]

A probation report in September 1993 recounted three meetings with him; Reggie had halted the third because he 'didn't feel like talking'. He did not seem to want to have his early life probed. He showed no signs of remorse, arguing that his 'activities did not infringe the rights of the vast majority of the population'. As for the young men who surrounded him, he did tell the probation officer that it was his desire to use his position to 'deflect these young men from a life of crime'. There was another more positive report: 'It is difficult not to be struck by the vitality, energy and generally good humour displayed by Mr Kray.' He now had little or no contact with his 'adopted' son Bradley Lane, a 10-year-old boy from Doncaster who had changed his name to Kray. The report also said that 'in the past 18 months he has started to look old'.

He was transferred to Maidstone in March 1994. Concerned about security in his new prison, he was extremely apprehensive about the move, and wrote for help to his friend John Heibner, who had been there since 1989. He wanted everything to be sorted out before his arrival – allocation on Heibner's wing, a cell next door to him, a wing cleaner's job – and Heibner arranged all these for him.

But he still could not keep his head down. He and Ron were adamant Myra Hindley should not be released. Reggie wrote to *The People* that year on his personalised notepaper, citing the case of his friend Joey Martin, who had been convicted in 1965 for killing a man in an armed robbery and was not whining about his sentence.[270] Nevertheless in November 1994 he was finally downgraded to Category C status.

Julian Broadhead, a probation officer experienced in dealing with lifers, thought:

> 'Everyone knew it was going to be forever. The risk factor
> in releasing him would have kept him in but he and his
> friends and supporters made it easy for the Home Office
> to do just that. Every time he made the newspapers, every
> time there was another book about or by him, every time

there was a demonstration or petition on his behalf, every report that he was running businesses from prison, the cell door became ever harder to unlock.'[271]

Two years later he was described as 'manipulative and wielding considerable power'. He had, said the report, changed little during his sentence and was still a risk to the public.

He was still not cooperating over his interviews for parole. He declined to go to Wayland, a Category C prison near Thetford in Norfolk, or to be interviewed by the local probation service and a psychologist.

A report dated 21 December 1995 explained that Reggie had not been released because 'he has little insight into the reality of his offending and as such he remains a risk'. He also had an alcohol problem: the authorities knew he was drinking illicit hooch and he said he intended to stop. Nor could he stop writing to the papers.

In November 1996 Reggie told the *Daily Mirror*'s Jeff Edwards that he was having a homosexual affair with Bradley Allardyce, then serving 12 years for armed robbery. 'The best way to describe our friendship is that he is like a son to me.' Allardyce had just married Donna Baker in a ceremony in the prison with Kray as his best man. Reggie had introduced her to Allardyce after she began writing to and then visiting him in prison. Kray gave him a gold identity bracelet inscribed, 'Goombah – my son'. Allardyce said he hoped to be out the next year and settle down. 'I wouldn't want to do that if I was gay, would I?'[272]

As the years went by it became clear that former friends and lovers were preparing to sell their stories to the newspapers along with his sometimes explicit letters to them. Rumours swirled that he had been pestering young prisoners he fancied, but in an attempt to shut down potential blackmailers Reggie struck first and admitted in a letter to the *Sunday People* that he was bisexual, blaming it on 26 years in prison. Now he persuaded the prison doctors to have him tested for AIDS.[273]

As with the killings of Cornell and McVitie, what Ronnie did yesterday, Reggie had to do tomorrow. Once Ronnie had married, it was Reggie's turn to consider matrimony. It might also help his next parole application. First into the tabloid pages was the model Maureen Flanagan. The feisty Flanagan had known the family since cutting Violet Kray's hair every Thursday.

At first she thought the proposition a reasonable one, but soon changed her mind, when she realised Reggie really only wanted her to run around asking people for money. When she turned him down, Flanagan was afraid he would take the news badly, but he merely said, 'Okay, then,' and changed the subject.[274]

Next came Gill, whom he called 'Brown-Eyes', while she referred to him as Rabbit. Sadly it turned out that Miss Right was in fact already Mrs Right, with a husband called Andy.

Sandra Wrightson came along a few years later, already married to Peter. She said that Kray fantasised she might like a three-in-a-bed with Kray and cellmate Kevin Bulmer. 'I reckon that you and Kevin should have sex. I'm sure you would like him once you get to know him.' She also allowed him to grope her through her blouse and he wanted her to fondle him through his undone trousers. As a result, her marriage broke down. At Kray's insistence she housed an ex-con for three months. When she finally asked her unwanted lodger to leave, Kray was furious. 'I have given up my life for Reggie Kray,' she said mournfully.[275]

Finally however, some brightness came into Reggie's life. He met Roberta Jones, the daughter of a Lancashire schoolteacher who had died when she was twelve. She had a degree in English Literature and was the director of a successful business. She first met Reggie when a business colleague asked if she would take over the publicity for a video of Ronnie's 1995 funeral, and she visited Kray in Maidstone with Maureen Flanagan as guide. Later she wrote:

> 'It wasn't love at first, no chemistry or flying sparks. I thought he was interesting, but what was most fascinating was how he had managed to survive that long in jail without going completely mad.'[276]

And still the 'Release Reggie' campaign toiled on – an earlier one in 1993 had resulted in a 10,000-signature petition being sent to Downing Street. Sidelined was the actress Patsy, daughter of Reggie's old friend Jimmy. Her then-partner Liam Gallagher had told her not get involved with the Krays because it might spoil his image. On the plus side was the fact he had been given £100,000 by Karl Compton, who had served four and a half months for a glassing in a Blackpool pub. Crompton had then won £11 million on the lottery and shared some of it with Reggie. Kray had promised to give it all away to old people and children's charities, but instead apparently gave his prison friend Allardyce over £50,000. In April 1997 he disassociated himself from a play *Inside the Firm* based on the book by Tony Lambrianou, which was touring small theatres.

Meanwhile his relationship with Roberta Jones deepened. He telephoned her as soon as she had returned home after her first visit, and from then on bombarded her with calls, letters and requests for her to visit him. Reluctantly she gave him her office telephone number on the promise that he would only telephone in an emergency, but emergencies seemed to happen on a daily basis. As the months progressed it became clear that, after the death of his twin, he was more and more dependent upon her. In May 1997 he was granted permission to marry her in Maidstone. She gave up her directorship and went to live near the prison.

It was quite natural he should want to do something special for his wife to be, but it was equally natural for the authorities to think he was thumbing his nose when on the wedding eve he organised a laser light display on the prison walls. Perhaps it was coincidence, but a condition was imposed that the wedding photographs were to remain in Crown Copyright and they were not released to the Krays for eighteen months.

In August 1997 at long last he was moved to C wing at Wayland; it had a reputation for violence – Reggie had been told black prisoners would try to steal his jewellery – and the prison regime was much harsher than Maidstone.[277] Roberta took a flat in Norwich to be near him. Although there were mainly short-term prisoners, visits were three a month instead of six and there were other restrictions on dress. On the other hand, telephone calls seemed to be limited to the credit on the telephone card, and he rang Roberta several times a day. He had trouble settling down there; he was still drinking prison hooch and failing to conform to Wing discipline. If drinking prison liquor was a bar to parole, however, then few prisoners would ever achieve it.

With the 30-year minimum tariff coming to an end, Reggie Kray was still in a Category B prison. The staff at Wayland were relatively busy preparing reports, but Reggie Kray was still not helping himself. Initially he had been placed on report on four occasions for refusing to work but now he was on a cleaning job 'where he, or others for him, do a reasonable job'. The report went on to say that he was well behaved and polite, if manipulative. Kray's extramural business activities continued. A second-hand car agency run for him had failed, but now there was talk of a scaffolding business. He was still receiving strong East End support from showbusiness celebrities such as Barbara Windsor and Leslie Crowther, but the report's writer wondered if this would continue after his release.[278]

In March 1998 the Parole Board knocked him back again. He had had generally favourable reports from the staff at Wayland but there was the caveat that he had not really been there long enough for a thorough assessment, something which was hardly his fault. He and Roberta took this hard; it was not his choice that his transfer from Maidstone had taken so long.

Again, it cannot have helped that the next year the Krays' tills were still ringing, with a 1999 calendar on offer for £6.95, a key ring with two hands shaking, and a flying jacket priced at £49.95.[279] The Free Reggie Campaign received a boost when Roberta went on Sky Television to plead his case, and the next day a friend flew a light aircraft over the prison with a banner reading 'Reg Kray Political

Prisoner 1968-1998'. It was yet another gesture unlikely to endear the prisoner to the authorities.

If he thought Jack Straw, the Home Secretary, would never free him in ordinary circumstances, he was probably correct. After the Parole Board had turned him down and before the next hearing in 2000, the prison psychologist expected him to have satisfactorily completed a long list of assessments, including: Intelligence Test (WAIS III); Enhanced Thinking Skills (ETS); Semi-Structured Interview; Social Response Inventory; Mini Situations Inventory; Personality Questionnaire; Interpersonal Reactivity Index; and eight others. If he completed those successfully he would then be placed on a group work programme and have to show he was applying these skills before being considered for an open prison.[280]

Meanwhile he was denied what was called 'town leave' in which he would have gone to Norwich for the day accompanied by a prison officer, a precursor of home leave. Crowd control was one of the reasons cited. But now there was a steady groundswell of press opinion in his favour, including Simon Heffer in the *Daily Mail*, and opinion polls in various papers overwhelmingly supported his release. In the end, however, the Parole Board never heard his final application.

Then came what must have seemed the great betrayal. Freddie Foreman appeared on a television documentary to tell of his and Reggie's involvement in Frank Mitchell's escape and death, not long before Reggie's scheduled parole hearing on 10 January 2000. It has never been satisfactorily explained why he acted in this way. Roberta Kray hints at jealousy, though why Foreman should be jealous of a man locked up for 30 years is difficult to fathom. Perhaps even more damaging was a programme that March featuring Dave Courtney, which seemed to depict him smuggling secret recording equipment into Wayland. Courtney claimed it was a practical joke, but it cannot have helped Kray.

The next Kray to die was Charlie. Throughout his time in prison on drugs charges, he had consistently maintained his innocence. In October 1999 he wrote to the wife of one East End friend, 'you know many people who know me and they know I've never seen a drug in my life – in fact it is well known I'm anti-drug and always have been.'

Charlie had thought 'I've never been ill in my life,' but he developed pneumonia while at Frankland prison. A few days out of the prison hospital, he was transferred to Parkhurst, 'all in a big rush. I don't know why, but there you are.'[281] After a stroke earlier that year, he now suffered a heart attack. Earlier Reg had been allowed to visit him in Long Lartin, but now on 18 March he was taken from Wayland under strict security to see Charlie in Parkhurst. He left just after eight after the van had been examined by a sniffer dog; they stopped at Winchester for lunch and arrived at 3 p.m. He stayed with Charlie for 45 minutes and remained at the prison, visiting him in the local hospital morning and afternoon. An application for Charlie's compassionate release had been made earlier but, while the Home Office was waiting for a report from a consultant surgeon at St Mary's Hospital, Newport, Charlie died on 4 April 2000 with Diane Buffini at his bedside.

The cracks which had existed between the brothers throughout their lives, particularly after Charlie had tried his hopeless scam over the film profits, were finally papered over. Charlie had hoped his would not be a celebrity funeral but, as in his life, Reggie's wishes prevailed and his funeral was masterminded by his younger brother.

The funeral cars were overflowing with flowers, one in the form of a broken heart from Diane Buffini which read, 'To my darling Charlie, with my eyes wide open, am I dreaming, can it be time?' A boxing ring of flowers from his brother read, 'Dear Charlie, rest in peace, Love Reg and Ron' and three-foot high red boxing gloves made out of chrysanthemums were sent from his friends on C Wing in Parkhurst. On one side of the hearse that would carry Charlie's body were the words 'GENTLEMAN' and on the other side 'CHARLIE' was spelled out with white carnations.

Once again the funeral in East London was policed by bouncers in black overcoats and sunglasses. This was quite apart from the actual police presence, which was said to have cost £2 million. Hells Angels provided security and notable guests included Frankie Fraser, Freddie Foreman – seemingly forgiven over his television gaffe – and John Pearson, who had done so much to create the Kray legends. This time the address was given by Father Ken Rimini, who told the congregation, 'It is not up to any of us here today to pass judgment on Charlie, now that he stands before a far greater jurisdiction than any judge on earth.' Hymns again included 'Fight the Good Fight', 'Morning has Broken' and 'Abide with Me'. Recordings of Celine Dion and of Shirley Bassey singing 'As Long as He Needs Me' were played. Ronnie had had 26 Daimlers in his cortège. It was down to 12 for Charlie, which, of course, was nine more than most people can summon.

On the way to the cemetery Reggie was hailed as the legend he had become. Caps were raised, children ran beside his car and after he had laid a wreath on his wife's grave, there was a cry for three cheers for him. He held up his handcuffed hand in recognition and disappeared back to Wayland prison.

By the time of Charlie's death, however, Reggie was seriously ill himself, his constitution ruined by years of prison hooch. He had claimed he had suffered from stomach pains for the past two years if not more. He had been told there was no question of cancer and had been treated with milk of magnesia. Now he did have cancer of the bladder, which moved inexorably to his bowel and then spread further. In the second week of August 2000 he collapsed in his cell and was rushed to hospital, where a large tumour was removed from his bowel. A second operation followed. His condition was being monitored by the Home Office and it was clear 'in no circumstances could he tolerate prison conditions'. After a great deal of lobbying by his solicitor Trevor Lynn, on the Friday afternoon before the August Bank Holiday came the announcement that the Home Secretary had decided to release him as an act of mercy. A note in his file reads that 'it is preferable he is released before he dies'. There were, however, conditions. He was not to leave the Norfolk and Norwich Hospital without prior permission from his probation officer.

He stayed nearly a week before he was well enough to be discharged, but it was only a matter of time. The manager of the Town House Hotel in Norwich offered him the honeymoon suite overlooking the river at £35.50 a night. Roberta and his last prison lover Bradley Allardyce discussed funeral arrangements with him there. His stay in the suite had not been well received by two honey-mooners who had actually booked it. By the time they were due there he was too ill to be moved and they had their bill remitted. Roberta told the reporters crowding the bar:

> 'I read to him and we'd listen to the radio. Friends came for dinner. He drank a weak Scotch looking out over beautiful scenery. And at last we slept in each other's arms.'

Visitors included Frankie Fraser and there was just time for one last interview, given by Reg to his old friend Bill Curbishley, manager of The Who and brother of Alan, the very successful boss of Charlton Athletic. The interview was controversially sold to the BBC for £280,000. In it Kray unrepentantly told his faithful public:

> 'It is very difficult to apologise in some cases but not in others, but I suppose I've been a bit too violent over the years. I make some apologies about it but there again there is little I can do about it now so again, it's no good reflecting back, it's pointless, negative.'

He also spoke about another killing, thought by Nipper Read to refer to Mad Teddy Smith. There was, however, a word of advice for today's youth:

> 'Prison life is a waste of time. I get letters from all over the country and I advise kids, it's very difficult when kids

have nothing to do and no money and all kinds of social problems out there, so it's easier to say than it is done, but speaking from my heart to them I would like to see them stay out of prison – some will make it, some won't.'

Kray also spoke of the murder of McVitie. 'I didn't like the fellow McVitie. He did everything wrong. He was very uncouth, he was loud and aggressive... a vexation to the spirit.' He said McVitie had 'pushed' him into the murder and that on the night he had 'a lot of frustration in me and anger, probably more anger that night than any other night of my life'.

Reggie's friend Wilf Pyne telephoned Foreman to tell him that it seemed that Reggie was dying and they had better come soon. Roberta tried to cancel Foreman's visit but he came nevertheless, with Joey Pyle and Johnny Nash. They found Allardyce stroking his thigh in the Norwich honeymoon suite while Allardyce's wife, Donna, looked on and Roberta mopped his brow. When a doctor came in to see Reggie they went to the hotel bar until Wilf Pyne told them they could come back.

Roberta Kray says that as Reggie was dying, Freddie Foreman locked himself in the bathroom and the others were banging trying to get him out. She thought they'd come to reclaim him as their own. Foreman claims he whispered, 'Time to let go, son,' or words to that effect, to the last of the Krays, and had then locked himself in the en-suite while the others alternated between banging on the door and returning to the bedside to be in at the death.

Foreman poignantly described and re-enacted the scene in a conversation with Tony Lambrianou in *Getting it Straight*:

'He gasped his last fucking gasp for air and that was the old fucking death rattle then you know. And I went straight to the bathroom and Wilf came over and said, 'He's dead,' and I said, 'I know he's dead.' Course, I got a little bit emotional and then I went back out into the room and Roberta sat down on the bed and was crying, having a little sob over there. And we just came down and went to the bar.'[282]

Reggie Kray left an estate of rather under £210,000. On 6 September while in the Norfolk and Norwich Hospital he had written a will leaving his wedding ring, gold cross and gold boxing gloves with chain to Roberta. His Omega watch went to his friend Bill Curbishley; Allardyce had his 'Legend' brooch; Donna had his gold pendant engraved with Ron's picture. As for the residue, Roberta was to receive 80%, another prison friend 8% and Bradley and Donna 12% between them. There was a caveat that if the Allardyces published any personal letters before or after his death or contacted the media to sell his story without the trustees' permission, then their gifts were forfeit.

There was an additional clause. 'I direct that all persons attending my funeral do so on a happy note and express only happiness at the time of my demise.' This may have been slightly ambiguous and certainly did not turn out to be the case.

But first there was the ultimate betrayal by Bradley Allardyce. Unable to keep his hands off spare cash and unaware of the provisions of the will, he had taken a picture of Reg with an oxygen mask in the hospital and passed it on to the newspapers. At first he denied it, then denied he had received money, and finally admitted his deceit.

On 11 October 2000 Reggie Kray, the last surviving brother, was buried in what would be called Kray Corner at Chingford cemetery. In contrast with his brothers' funerals it was a relatively quiet affair, albeit with a modest 18 limousines following the six black horses which drew the hearse covered in wreaths bearing words such as 'Respect', 'Free at Last' and 'Reg Beloved'. One in the form of a red cushion showed two clasped hands and the motto 'Reunited Again'. The hearse slowed in tribute in Vallance Road and then drove to St Matthew's Church. Only about 3,000 of the estimated 100,000 turned out to watch. Two Kray funerals in one year was one too many for the East End faithful.

Many old-timers stayed away. They included Tony Lambrianou and Freddie Foreman, who instead kept an appointment at Scotland Yard to discuss his apparent admissions over the Mitchell killing. Foreman claimed Reggie had asked him to be a pallbearer but Roberta had decided otherwise. In fact, of the real old timers, only Frank Fraser, for whom there was generous applause from the crowd, could be spotted in the church.

Taking the service were the Reverends Allan Green and Ronald Vaughan together with Dr Ken Stallard, the Free Church minister from Oxford. During the ceremony Donna Allardyce read a little poem:

'It broke our hearts to lose you but you did not go alone.
A part of us went with you the day God called you home.'

There was a tribute from his solicitor Mark Goldstein, who described Reggie as 'A man of honour' and 'a 20th century icon'. Dr Stallard, who told the congregation he was not going to talk about Reggie's crimes, instead described Kray's repentance. 'There were tears in my eyes when I said to him, 'Reg do you repent of those things you have done?' It was almost as though I should not have asked such a stupid question, as he said 'of course, of course'. Stallard then went on, saying in Mockney how Kray had told him, 'I wanna be a Christian. But I don't want anybody to fink I done it just to influence people and get parole.' Stallard added in his tribute, 'This rare bird has flown his cage'.[283] The congregation again sang 'Morning has Broken', 'Fight the Good Fight' and 'Abide with Me'.

The body was taken to Chingford, where locals visiting graves were turned away by security men wearing red armbands embroidered with RKF (either 'Reggie Kray's funeral' or 'Reggie Kray forever') as the great man was finally laid to rest.

It had been hoped that a Spitfire would fly past, but the weather was bad and the pilot never took off. Old-time villain Albert Chapman threw a rose on the coffin on behalf of Tony Lambrianou and Foreman.

After Charlie's funeral there had been a big wake held at the Horn of Plenty in Stepney, and the landlord Paul Jonas brought in the food for another wake.[284] It was cancelled by Roberta but others still went there.

Naturally there were long obituaries and assessments in the newspapers, with a notable exception being *The Times*. When asked why, the obituaries editor remarked obliquely, 'We don't do obituaries for gangsters unless they go on to run countries.'[285]

Given that Charlie's son Gary was already dead, with Reg's death so ended the legitimate male Kray line. For all practical purposes, however, 'Those were the Krays.'

Possibly not, however.

CHAPTER 20
THE END OF THE LINE

Was the death of Reggie really the end of the male Kray line?

In his unpublished memoir, his cousin Ronnie Hart claimed that Reggie Kray fathered three illegitimate children and forced another girlfriend to have an abortion.

If it is accepted, however, that Nancy Kray/Grey is Charlie's daughter, then there is still the female side of the family. Nancy married Norman Jones from a well-known North London family. She had three sons, one of whom, Jamie, became a successful apprentice jockey, riding 15 winners mainly on the all-weather tracks, until he was involved in a very bad fall in a five-horse pile up at Kempton Park on 30 July 2008. He broke three vertebrae and never returned to the track.

The next year another son, 24-year-old Joseph Jones, and his stepfather Norman were convicted of the murder of traveller John Finney, whom they were alleged to have tortured and killed, believing he had stolen their drugs.

Around 7 p.m. on 29 February 2008 Finney, a scrap metal dealer, was kidnapped from his Mitsubishi Pajero at Park Farm in Northaw, near Potters Bar in Hertfordshire, and driven at gunpoint to an industrial unit in Hitchin. Two weeks later his naked remains were found behind a garage block in Wilbury Way which had been rented by the Joneses. His buttocks had been slashed and his head and hands cut off. They were never found. His Mitsubishi was found at Park Farm with a window smashed and with Finney's mobile on the front seat. The van in which he was abducted was found burned out but John Finney's keys were still inside.

In March Joseph Jones went to Malaga with his girlfriend and Norman followed him three days later. They were arrested on 1 May and returned to England, where they stood trial at St Albans Crown Court in February 2009.

The prosecution claimed the Joneses had cleaned the unit twice but left traces of Finney's blood on the wall. Part of the evidence against Norman Jones was that his Range Rover had been seen on CCTV on the night of the killing, but he maintained that the vehicle had not been moved that night from a gated community in North London. Other damning evidence was said to be a threatening telephone call and another call from Norman Jones' pay-as-you-go near the murder scene. There was also a suggestion the pair had made a dry-run the day before Finney's abduction.

In a cut-throat defence Joseph Jones, who claimed all he had done was act as an obedient son and had been manipulated by his father, claimed he was playing poker on the night of the murder. Norman Jones said he had never met Finney. Shortly after the murder a man committed suicide, and the Joneses claim that he was the real killer.

Both men received life sentences, Joseph with a minimum of 30 years and Norman a minimum of 33. Sentencing them, Mr Justice MacDuff, who said he nearly wept when reading the victim impact statements, told the Joneses:

> 'You are both evil men with nothing to commend you. You committed a meticulously planned murder. You decided summarily to execute a man who you thought rightly or wrongly, probably wrongly, had crossed you. You have both lied in a breathtaking way to this court to save your skins. It is difficult to comprehend how evil you are. You lack any semblance of humanity.'

Their appeals were dismissed but Norman Jones, in particular, maintained his innocence, and a website arguing his case was set up on his behalf in January 2012.

The next year Joseph Jones was alleged to have taken part in a racially motivated attack when a black prisoner was hit with billiard balls wrapped in a sock. The *Daily Star* reported enthusiastically that only a few weeks earlier Jones had begged the then Home Secretary not to allow him to die in prison.[286]

When Nancy Grey was last heard of, she was running market stalls in the Home Counties.

CHAPTER 21
WHO DID THEY REALLY KILL?

In his deathbed interview, Reggie Kray hinted at one more murder. In turn his biographer Colin Fry said he thought there were about 30, including Ernie 'Mr Fixit' Isaacs, shot inside his flat in Shoreditch on 24 May 1966; their sometime driver Jack Frost; an old Richardson man, Billy Stayton; and their friend and letter writer Mad Teddy Smith. Bodies were jammed in oil drums and dropped in a hole. In Essex there was, Fry said, a garden centre which 'has difficulty in planting deep-rooted trees'.[287]

John Pearson, and indeed a number of people after him, has it that the Krays killed Frost, a victim of the 'mini-cab call in the night', then said to be in vogue: 'Cab, sir.' 'I haven't ordered a cab.' The target was hustled in and that was the last anyone saw of him. Pearson wrote:

'The comradeship within the Firm was not improved when two of its members disappeared after trouble with Ronnie. One was his driver, a talkative young man called Frost… To this day, Frost [remains] on Scotland Yard's missing persons list.'[288]

Later Pearson wrote:

'The great [Scotland Yard] investigation, for all its
thoroughness, seemed to have missed the biggest crimes…
there was no hint of what happened to Jack Frost.'

Frost had disappeared after the murder of his friend McVitie because
it was thought the Twins feared he might inform on them. But like the
death of Mark Twain, Frost's demise had been greatly exaggerated.
In fact he had merely travelled north, and he resurfaced many years
later in the East End.[289]

The second potential victim was Firm member Mad Teddy Smith,
who disappeared after the Frank Mitchell escape. He was certainly
still around on 11 October 1966 when he refused to give evidence for
the prosecution in the D.S. Leonard Townshend bribery case. He was
almost certainly alive at Christmas that year, writing drafts for Mitchell's
letters to the press. There have been continuing stories that Smith had
been killed in a quarrel with Ronnie over a rent boy at Steeple Bay in
Essex. In *Notorious*, John Pearson says Kray friend Wilf Pyne told him
that Ronnie had told him that sometime in April 1967 he had broken
Smith's neck in a headlock, over 'trouble with a boy'.[290]

However in his 1974 book *Buller*, Henry Ward claimed that, well
after the Kray trial, he had met Teddy Smith in a cinema queue in
Leicester Square and Smith told him he had managed to break away
from the life.[291] But there were other stories that he had left England.
Albert Donoghue said he had heard Smith had gone to Australia
and died there of natural causes. This story was confirmed by Micky

Fawcett, who wrote in *Krayzee Days* that Smith had died in 2014 or 2015 in Australia. Other stories have him dying there a decade earlier aged 74.

However, the former Flying Squad officer John Rigbey maintained he had been told by one of a family of North London brothers and by Kray associate Leslie Berman that whatever anyone said, Smith had indeed been killed in Steeple Bay.

In 2002 Reg Kray's prison boyfriend Peter Gillett appeared on the Channel 5 documentary *The Krays: Their Empire Behind Bars* to say:

> '16 years ago Reg burdened me with the secret of this other murder he did. It was a young gay boy. He was disgusted with himself for realising that he enjoyed that sort of thing, and he shot the kid.'

Another unlikely suggestion has been that Ronnie Kray, while in custody, organised the murder of the flamboyant solicitor David Jacobs, whose showbusiness clientele included Liberace. One of the first male solicitors to wear makeup in court, on 15 December 1968 Jacobs was found hanged in his garage at home in Hove, Sussex. The story goes that he had refused to help in the Krays' defence against the Cornell and McVitie murder charges, and this was retribution. There was no evidence to support this but, as has been said on many occasions, this should not be allowed to get in the way of a good story.[292]

More interesting is the murder of 42-year-old professional criminal Ernie Isaacs, a self-styled Prisoners' Welfare Officer who covered his illegal activities by street trading. A gunman was lying in wait for Isaacs when he arrived at his basement flat at Penn Street,

Shoreditch on the night of Tuesday, 24 May 1966. The killer fired five times, hitting Isaacs with four of the shots. The fifth hit the skirting board. He was probably killed with one of his own guns, a Webley or Enfield service rifle, which the killer knew would be in the flat. A .38 revolver of the type which fired the bullets was missing, and a .9mm Luger was found wrapped in a piece of cloth in the piano. His body was found by his live-in girlfriend when she woke at around 5 a.m. She told the police she had heard nothing unusual during the night.

There was no question of robbery. Isaacs had £215 in cash and £200 in bonds on him. There was, however, a wide variety of potential suspects. Isaacs was a violent man whom his former wife described as 'a vicious man who would hold a grudge forever'. The word in the underworld was that the killer had been Reggie Kray but once again there was no real evidence against him.

The police looked closely into Isaacs' relationship with the Krays and the Richardsons. He had been a friend of George Cornell and after that man's death he had made no secret of the fact he believed the Krays had done it. The police decided that they had no hard evidence against the principal suspects and that in any event Isaacs was so disliked, any of a number of people could have killed him. Years later an Anthony Patrick Austin confessed, saying the Krays had paid him £500 and he had thrown the Luger pistol he had used into a nearby canal. A short investigation showed he had been in prison at the time of the killing. He was now in Rampton secure hospital.[293] The file remains open.

People can agree on only one thing concerning the death of Freddie Mills, one-time light heavyweight champion of the world and a hugely popular television celebrity. And that is that on the night of 25 July 1965, he was found shot in the eye in his car parked in Goslett Yard at the back of his club, Freddie Mills' Nitespot, on the Charing Cross Road, which he ran in partnership with Andy Ho. Many other questions arise: was it suicide or murder and, whichever was the case, why? Why would Freddie, one of the most popular figures of his day in sport, want to kill himself? Why would anyone want to kill him? Nevertheless, it is a death to which the Krays' name has become linked over the years.

There have been many suggestions, some more improbable than others, why Mills was killed with a faulty rifle which he had borrowed from a fairground stall holder the previous week: he was in all sorts of personal trouble and had been liquidating his properties in South London – by the time of his death he was almost bankrupt; he was killed to prevent him informing on a homosexual ring; he could no longer go on paying protection money to the Krays or the Richardsons or the Chinese; the Chinese wanted his club to distribute drugs; his club was haemorrhaging money; his partner was stealing from him; he was being blackmailed over a homosexual relationship; he had been arrested for importuning and could not face the scandal; he was the murderer Jack the Stripper. These point to suicide, but yet another suggestion is that he was killed by Mafia hitmen on the orders of Meyer Lansky because he was trying to blackmail boxing promoter and Mafia associate Benny Huntsman for the £2,500 needed to keep the Nitespot open, by threatening to expose the Mafia takeover of gambling in London.[294]

In 2002 the old Soho figure Bert 'Battles' Rossi, then in his 80s, who had served four years with Frank Fraser for the attack on Jack Spot, may have provided the solution. He knew Ronnie during a period in prison and he claimed that, after his release, over a period of time he acted as their unofficial adviser. Then, in July 1965, Ronnie told him that Andy Ho wanted Mills out of the club and that there was money in it for them if they got him out. Rossi told Ronnie he didn't think it was a good idea. Freddie wasn't going to take any nonsense from them and he'd have hit them. 'Then they'd have had to up the ante so to speak and maybe it would have got out of hand.'

He agreed however to see Freddie, whom he knew. 'I said that his partner had gone to people in the East End and I said, 'Your back's to the wall. Give a little or there'll be trouble.' I left him in an uncertain state of mind'.

Rossi told Ronnie Kray to leave things alone for four or five days. Then if Mills said he was prepared to go, Kray could tell the Chinese it was down to him and he would get the credit. Rossi remembered saying to Kray, 'If need be, do what you have to do':

> 'But I didn't want any part of it. Five, six, seven days later, all of a sudden he's dead in the car. I went to Ronnie and asked what he'd done. Ronnie said it was nothing to do with them and I said, 'Are you sure?' And I believed him when he said he hadn't.'

But why, given all their protestations of devotion to boxing in general and Mills in particular, would the Krays even entertain going against him? Rossi's answer was simply that it was business. There was money in it.[295]

After Nipper Read arrested the Krays he began to inquire into Mills' death, touring the West End and speaking to the usual characters. All he could get was, 'Oh guv, you know better than that.' One man said, 'We don't make examples of other people. If somebody don't pay we break his legs, not somebody else's.'

Read later wrote:

> 'Nothing would have given me more pleasure than being able to show that Freddie had not committed suicide. In those days there was much more of a stigma attached to the act than there is today. Moreover, if I could link the Krays to it, my investigation would have a major boost. It would have been beautiful to have tagged this murder to them.'[296]

But the most sensational claim of all came from Bradley Allardyce, when he was released after serving his nine-year sentence for armed robbery. He told the *News of the World* that Reggie's first wife Frances had not committed suicide and in fact Ronnie Kray had killed her, forcing her to take an overdose.[297] Reggie, burdened by this information, had told Allardyce when they were in the cell reminiscing.

> 'I was sitting in my cell with Reg and it was one of those nights where we turned the lights down low and put some nice music on and sometimes he would reminisce. He would get really deep and open up to me. He suddenly

broke down and said "I'm going to tell you something I've only ever told two people and something I've carried around with me" – something that had been a black hole since the day he found out. He put his head on my shoulder and told me Ronnie killed Frances. He told Reggie what he had done two days after.'[298]

Scotland Yard was said to have been investigating the allegation which, in one form or another, had been floating around the East End for a number of years. Given that everyone concerned was dead, it would seem to have been an interesting if less than profitable exercise.

Then in 2015, at the time of the release of the film *Legend,* in which Tom Hardy appeared as both Twins, an even more outrageous allegation was made in a new documentary *Krays –Kill Order.* It claimed that Violet Kray had a hand in Frances' death because she was pregnant and she did not think her daughter-in-law would have been a suitable mother.[299]

CHAPTER 22
WHERE HAVE THEY ALL GONE?

What happened to them all? Many disappeared into anonymity and what Mandy Rice-Davies called the 'one slow descent into respectability'. Others only gave up crime when their legs ran out of steam.

As for those on the side of the angels, beginning at the top, Judge Melford Stevenson would tell fellow members of the Garrick Club that Ronnie Kray had said only two truthful things during the trial. The first was that he, Melford, was biased and the second was that prosecutor Kenneth Jones was indeed 'a fat slob'. Stevenson went blind and died in November 1994. Ronnie was pleased with the blindness, attributing it to a curse put on the judge by Dot Brown and commissioned by him.

After Stevenson's death, the ever-generous-spirited defence lawyer John Platts-Mills wrote to *The Times*:

> 'Contrary to general belief, I had a most friendly relation-
> ship with Melford. The only unkindness that I can lay
> at his door, and this was a gross injustice, was trying
> the Kray twins for the murders of Cornell and McVitie

together when there was no common feature except that the victims had both died. My judgment of the case was that if Melford had tried the murders fairly, both Twins might well have got off but for Stevenson's bias.'

He also wrote:

'While defending Ronnie Kray at the Old Bailey in 1969 I found him to be a most kindly and thoughtful client. I told Melford out of court that Ronnie was probably a nicer chap than I was. I am not surprised to learn that Melford cribbed this remark and made it his own.'[300]

Of the prosecutors, in 1974 Kenneth Jones was appointed a High Court judge. On the bench he generally displayed a kindness to defendants, particularly women who had met with family difficulties. In October that year, he discharged a woman who had killed her totally blind and practically deaf daughter, who had no real hope of life, saying, 'I regard this as an extreme case even amongst exceptional cases...' Professional criminals, child molesters and terrorists received no such help.

Junior prosecution counsel in the first Kray trial John Leonard also went to the High Court bench. A most amiable man, he was pilloried in the press when, in what was called the Ealing Vicarage case, he passed a lenient sentence for the rape of the vicar's daughter. He later described it as a 'blemish – I make no bones about it'. He retired as his eyesight began to fail, and died in 2002.

Fellow prosecution counsel James Crespi ruined his chances of a seat on the High Court Bench by marrying a much younger nightclub hostess, a union which lasted only a few weeks. He was later injured in the IRA bombing of the Old Bailey and joked he believed that had he not been in the way, much of the building would have been destroyed. At least he had the distinction of having his own chair at El Vino's, the barristers' evening watering hole in Fleet Street. He died in 1991.

Some of the defence lawyers including Desmond Vowden were appointed to the bench. Platts-Mills would certainly not have wanted an appointment, but some of the others might. He went on to have repeated clashes with Stevenson, notably in the so-called Angry Brigade trial – a group of anarchists convicted of a series of bomb attacks between 1970 and 1972 – when he alleged the police had planted his client's fingerprints on a compromising exhibit. Stevenson became so angry he ordered Platts-Mills to forfeit a portion of his fees, a decision smartly overturned by the Court of Appeal, which ruled he had no authority to make such a ruling.[301]

Platts-Mills' junior in the case, Ivan Lawrence, went on to have a successful career both at the bar and in politics as the Conservative MP for Burton. Among his more famous defences, after that of Ronnie Kray, was of the serial killer Dennis Nilsen. In his political career he was chairman of the Home Affairs Select Committee and an influential figure on the Eurosceptic wing of the party, also instigating the National Lottery with a Private Member's bill. In retirement he wrote his memoir *My Life of Crime*.

Sir Lionel Thompson continued to live a louche life, sueing, in something of a role reversal, a woman to whom he had given £15,000 to invest. He was disbarred after receiving a six-month suspended sentence at Lewes Crown Court for fraud. Upon his death in 1999, his baronetcy died with him.

As for the Krays' solicitors in the trial, Manny Fryde suddenly left the country on an evening flight after receiving advice from a leading QC. He lived in Majorca for several years. Ralph Haeems qualified in 1973 and went on to run the largest criminal practice in London. He employed both former police officer Sid Rae and George Stanley as his managing clerks, and they worked for him until they were well into their 80s. Stanley, who for a time had been the brains behind the East End firm of Lesser & Co, was reputed to have been a paymaster to wives of members of the Great Train Robbery.[302] A heavy smoker all his life, Haeems died in March 2005 after heart surgery.

The pill provider, stitcher-upper and much-loved Dr Morris Blasker died on 28 December 1974, aged 70, after being taken ill suddenly in his surgery on the Isle of Dogs. In 2010 a new riverside road was named 'Blasker Walk'. A campaign in his name to raise funds for kidney machines for the Royal London Hospital was established. Fund raiser Daisy Woodward said at the time, 'I did not have to ask for money. It just came in from people who lived on the Island or had moved away. Word had got around and that was enough'.

Perhaps because of his earlier refusal to join the Flying Squad, Nipper Read never quite received the recognition due to him. Instead of rising to the top of the Metropolitan Police he became Assistant Commissioner of the Regional Crime Squad. After his retirement he advised on security for the National Gallery and became chairman of the British Boxing Board of Control as well as Vice President of both the World Boxing Council and the World Boxing Association. He received the Queen's Police Medal.

John Du Rose later wrote his memoirs *Murder was My Business*, in which he claimed to have solved the Jack the Stripper murders. In his chapter on the Krays he does not mention informer and prosecution witness Alan Bruce Cooper. In his memoir *The Sharp End*, Frank Cater told how he traced Lisa the nightclub hostess.

After retiring from the Met, Read's principal aide Henry Mooney, who worked so hard to convince the barmaid at the Blind Beggar that it would be safe for her to give evidence, qualified as a solicitor and set up a small practice in West London.

Trevor Lloyd-Hughes, Nipper Read's DC, who died in 1986 aged 52, fell from grace after his death. He had been the note-taker on behalf of Commander Bert Wickstead in the so-called 1977 Epping Forest Murder Trial, in which North London faces Bobby Maynard and Reggie Dudley were sentenced for the murders of two other North Londoners, Billy Moseley and Mickey Cornwall, for reasons which were never explained. Their convictions were quashed in 2002 when Lloyd-Hughes's written statements were deemed to be unreliable. The principal evidence against them had been that during a series of interviews they and other defendants had made ambiguous comments which led to their convictions. After a long-running campaign for their release, in July 2002 the Court of Appeal quashed the convictions on the grounds that Lloyd-Hughes could not possibly have written down the statements at the speed he was said to have done. Wickstead was also dead by this time.

Of the women who brought the Twins down, Carol Skinner died from cancer. 'She never recovered from that night,' said her friend Jenny King. Patricia Kelly the barmaid remained in constant fear of the Twins and their followers until the time of Ronnie's funeral. As for Lisa Prescott, the nightclub hostess, she headed for Australia with her boyfriend after the police bought them a van and put them on the Cross-Channel ferry. Trevor Lloyd-Hughes received a postcard from Turkey, but Read never heard from them again. In fact she returned to England, married and had a family. In 2014 a play by Camilla Whitehill, *Where Do Little Birds Go*, based on her role in the case, was performed at the Camden People's Theatre. The title was taken from the song sung by Barbara Windsor in Lionel Bart's first musical *Fings Ain't Wot They Used T'Be!*

Frankie Shea bitterly regretted his sister's marriage to Reg Kray. In 2002 he gave an interview to the *East London Advertiser* headed, 'I spurned gay Reg so he wed my sister in revenge'. He committed suicide on 5 August 2011. He was in the last stages of cancer of the larynx. In Freddie Foreman's *Running with the Krays*, Frank Kurylo claims that Ronnie tried to rape Frank Shea and that he should have told his sister. There are also unverifiable stories that Frank Shea slept with both the Twins.[303]

Just in time for the release in 2015 of the film *Legend*, Frances Kray's niece, also Frances, put in her pennyworth. Her recollection is that, far from the image of the retiring girl we have been led to believe, her aunt was indeed a wild child, who was well capable of dealing with Reggie and outshone Barbara Windsor. Pre-echoing Jack McVitie's words at the fatal party – 'Where's the birds?' she said Frances, on a trip to Africa, had more or less leaped off the plane, calling out, 'Where's the hashish?' Her niece had read diaries to back up her claims but thought it better they remain private. She and her daughter had been so annoyed at the film that to prevent them leaving early, they had taken off their shoes. As the niece was only four at the time of her aunt's death, her recollections may not be wholly reliable.[304]

Those who had helped the police in their inquiries could expect a helping hand in return. In October 1972 Leslie Payne, defended by Platts-Mills, was convicted at the Old Bailey for conspiracy to pervert the trial of five defendants charged with handling stolen cars. Read, called to give evidence, said that Payne had played a substantial part in breaking the Krays, but nevertheless he was jailed for five years.[305]

As for the defendants, Albert Donoghue fared well for a time:

'Nipper came to see me in Maidstone and said three months had been taken off my sentence and he was there to take me home. I went first to Peckham and then to Edenbridge in Kent.'[306]

There he lived incognito, listening to stories from men who claimed to have been in the Blind Beggar the night Cornell was shot. 'I asked if they knew Albert Donoghue and if he'd been there that night. "Oh yes," they'd say.' Then he heard someone was making inquiries about him in Peckham and thought it would be only a matter of time before he was traced. Although none of the immediate Kray team were left, Donoghue feared the hangers-on might try and make a name for themselves. He and his family then went to live near High Wycombe.

On 8 September 1970 Donoghue, together with his friend Tommy Herbert, was joined in the Railway Tavern, Rotherhithe by two men, one of whom was the killer and eventual supergrass Billy Amies. Later, while they were in a car together, Donoghue noticed Amies was about to draw a knife on him and in the ensuing struggle, Amies was cut in the face. Donoghue went straight to the police and appeared in court the next morning. Since it would seem he had a perfectly good argument of self-defence, Donoghue rather curiously pleaded guilty, telling the court, 'I know there is someone after me. I know they are trying to get me and I am scared that if it is the Krays there is going to be one bang.' Read again appeared in mitigation and Donoghue was fined £20.[307]

He then changed professions from house-painting to house-breaking, burgling middle class homes. It was an occupation he explained as, 'I'm sorry to say, I went astray again.' Donoghue claimed he burgled houses at the rate of one a fortnight for two years until he was caught. Nipper Read sent Frank Cater to his trial to provide much-needed mitigation. And Donoghue received a sentence of 30 months' imprisonment. He was released in 12 and took up industrial painting for a living. He also wrote two books about his time with the Twins.[308] In 2004 he suffered a major stroke and was confined to a wheelchair. He died aged 80 in April 2016.

The fraudster Charlie Mitchell, who told Read there was a contract on him, did not fare so well. The story in the underworld is that he had had his head trapped in the door of a car and was dragged along the road but the prosecution's case was, more prosaically, that he had been shot at near his home in Ellerby Street, Fulham.[309]

Mitchell reportedly died in Spain after being attacked in a bar near Marbella. A notice was put by his grave, 'Do not walk on the grass'.[310]

George Osborne, who had been kind enough to shield Ronnie in the Podro trial and helped get him out of the mental hospital, died in Brighton in 1968. He had a heart attack while swimming but the underworld story was that he had been poisoned. Another to die in Brighton was the reputed killer of Frank Mitchell, Alf Gerard, allegedly after eating a lobster, but more prosaically from cirrhosis of the liver. In 1980 he died in the flat of his great friend Jerry Callaghan, who also died in Brighton in 2013.

The other Osborne, Colin 'Dukey', the Krays' armourer, was found dead on Hackney Marshes on 1 December 1980. Earlier that year he had put together a scheme importing drugs from Pakistan which all went wrong when, in October, one of the team members 'Silly' Lennie Watkins shot and killed a customs officer, Peter Bennett.

There are various versions of Osborne's death, who was wanted both by customs officers and associates of Watkins. One is that he committed suicide, another that he died from a drug overdose or a heart attack, possibly during questioning by his former colleagues over the whereabouts of the drugs and their proceeds. Whichever is correct, it is probable he died at the flat of bank robber Ronnie Cook, the lover of the Black Widow Linda Calvey. It was thought his body had been put in a freezer while a decision was made about its disposal. Watkins later received life imprisonment for killing Bennett, and committed suicide in prison after an abortive escape attempt. Another allegedly on the importing team was Freddie Foreman, who was acquitted of Bennett's murder.

In January 1977 the Twins' friend, property dealer Geoffrey Allen, the 'Michelangelo of Arson', was found guilty of swindling insurance companies of more than £300,000 after fires at Briggate Mill in Norfolk and Shortgrove Hall near Saffron Walden. He received seven years at Norwich Crown Court and died in late 1992. At one time he had been suspected of involvement in the Great Train Robbery. He had also been dubbed 'The Godfather', a soubriquet which appeared on his gravestone in the village cemetery following his 25-year career in crime. Another property he owned, Gedding Hall, was later bought by Rolling Stones' Bill Wyman.

Connie Whitehead, perhaps the best businessman among them, opened a club and then a wholesale liquor business. In one of the wheels which continue to turn in the East End, he bought the Norseman Club in Canning Town, once owned by fearsome Firm member Alfie Gerard.

Ronnie Hart was said to have tried to commit suicide in Norwich and later to have gone to Australia. John Dickson became a successful businessman. After his release Ian Barrie disappeared from the criminal scene.

The Lambrianou brothers went different ways. Tony Lambrianou served out his sentence and, forgetting his grounds of appeal, took to lauding the Twins. Always a handsome man, he and Freddie Foreman appeared in advertisements for a London shirt makers and collaborated on the book *Getting It Straight*, in which they reminisced over their lives and crimes. He died in 2004. On his release his elder brother Chris became involved in charity work. He did not entirely disown his old friends and in December 2014 he was seen at the funeral of Mad Frank Fraser. Both brothers wrote books about their time with the Firm.

Ronnie Bender 'never put himself about', as one East End face described it. Bender had been a stevedore and 'although he mixed with heavies he was really a straight man'. Nevertheless he was alleged to have ruled Chelmsford jail after he was transferred there in 1970, running card schools and having a doorbell over his cell. It was alleged he advised and helped prisoners and warders alike and maintained a stock of cigars and brandy. Bender's rule ended when he was transferred after a fire broke out at Chelmsford. By the time of his release he was semi-institutionalised and effectively became a recluse, dying in 2004 aged 66.

Freddie Foreman continued in his role as one of the most feared of London criminals. After the Security Express robbery in 1983, then the largest of its kind, he went to Spain, living on the so-called Costa del Crime near Marbella. He was later sentenced to nine years for receiving part of the proceeds of the robbery.

On 10 January 1999 Foreman had rather disgraced himself in the eyes of some members of the criminal fraternity after his ill-judged television appearance around the time of Ronnie Kray's parole hearing. Mad Frank Fraser roundly condemned him for this apparent betrayal and the two old men scuffled in a Hampstead coffee shop. Despite his confessions Foreman was never charged over the murders or his claim that he had intimidated witnesses in the Cornell murder. In 2018, a rather anodyne video *Freddie* featured him declining to explain exactly what happened to Mitchell's body and a number of other things. His son Jamie has appeared in a number of films and, for a time, was Derek Branning in the television soap *East Enders*.

In January 1970 the fraudster Bobby McKew went down again, this time for five years and a fine of £10,000 for conspiracy to flood the continent with forged Swiss franc notes. On his release McKew went to Majorca, where he was involved in what was euphemistically called 'transport work'. He later published a bestselling novel, *Death List*.

After his release, George Ince and Dolly Grey continued to live quietly in the East End. Dolly became increasingly fragile and, confined to a wheelchair, died in 2017. The short, balding Harry 'Hate-em-all' Johnston, who had attacked Ince in prison over his affair with Dolly, died following a heart attack.

Micky Fawcett followed the Rice-Davies path to respectability. After initial resistance from the British Boxing Board of Control, he was eventually granted a licence and became a successful trainer before writing his memoir *Krayzee Days*.

So far as the various Lords, knights and MPs were concerned, after his involvement with the Krays ended, Lord Effingham became an associate of a travel agency and regularly appeared in the House of Lords to claim his daily fee, usually without speaking. He died aged 91 on 22 February 1996. He had no children and the title passed to his nephew.[311]

In 1967 Lord Boothby married again, this time to a Sardinian, Wanda Sanna. He was 67 and she was 30 years younger. 'Don't you think I'm a lucky boy?' he called to bystanders outside London's Caxton Hall. He died in July 1986 aged 86. His efforts to have himself made a Companion of Honour had failed.

In 1969 Dickie Hart's widow Eileen married Stanley Naylor, who later received 12 years for his part in the Tibbs-Nicholls families feud.[312]

On the plus side, however, the old Spot man Gerry Parker can still be seen most weekdays breakfasting in Claridges.

And the Krays' 'boys'? Peter Gillett never made it as a singer and was convicted with Joey Pyle in 1992 for a drug conspiracy, receiving five years. He was again convicted, this time in May 2002, when he was given a conditional discharge after swallowing a bag of heroin when the police searched his house. He was in a coma for seven days.

The next year Gillett did a great service to the art world and at the same time increased Reggie's iconic status. Reggie's art work was so highly regarded it had become worth faking. After Gillett's intervention, three watercolours for sale by the Cambridgeshire auctioneers Cheffins were withdrawn. They included a beach scene and a nude, apparently signed by Kray, and with his prison number, and were set to fetch at least £500 each. A third piece, *Girl Bathing*, was said to be a homage to *The Tub* by Degas. Gillett, explaining his good deed, said of his former lover, 'Reg was far too idle to paint much. There are a lot of forgeries out there. He was an egomaniac. If he had been that good he would have let everybody know.'[313]

He was back in the news in April 2014 when the drum-playing Joanne Dunmore, who lived next door to him in Littlehampton in Sussex, was given an interim ASBO over allegations of racially aggravated harassment. Gillett told the newspapers that compared with Dunmore, Peter Sutcliffe, the Yorkshire Ripper, was 'a saint'.[314]

Another of Reggie's prison 'sons and lovers' Bradley Allardyce demonstrated that those who believe prison will cure criminality are likely to be sadly disabused. After Reggie's death he went to Spain where he opened a gay bar in Altea, but in 2002, a few days after house hunters Anthony and Linda O'Malley were kidnapped and murdered, he closed everything up and returned to England.

The O'Malleys had been lured to a villa by Venezuelan brothers-in-law Jorge Real Sierra and Jose Velazquez Gonzales. Mrs O'Malley was bound and held hostage in the cellar while her husband was forced at gunpoint to empty their bank account with a series of card transactions for cash and goods. They were then killed. Sierra and Gonzales were sentenced to an aggregate of 116 years in prison. In 2006 Sierra wrote to a civil rights lawyer protesting his innocence and trying to lay the blame on Allardyce.[315]

In January that year the bisexual Allardyce told a BBC reporter, 'I am openly admitting for the first time that we [he and Reggie] had a sexual relationship, as much as it was against my will and he knew it was against my will.' But he added somewhat ambiguously, 'There is not one day I would change with mine and Reggie's relationship.'

By 2005 Allardyce was back in serious trouble. The money left him by Reggie brought no happiness. His wife Donna had gone and now a David Fairburn became involved with Amy, sister of Allardyce's girlfriend Tracey Cooper. The relationship turned sour and Allardyce, along with Shane Porter and Wayne Turner, attacked Fairburn, stabbing him in the heart. They were all jailed for life with a recommendation they serve a minimum of 18 years.

Ronnie and Lord Bobby's lover Leslie Holt died in September 1979 after a botched operation to remove disfiguring warts on his hands and feet. It had been carried out by Dr Gordon Kells, a former lover who used to inform him when wealthy patients would be away from their homes. In September 1979 Kells gave him a dose of Methohexitone 10 to 20 times higher than recommended. Pathologist Ian West told the inquest it was a totally inappropriate procedure to perform without an assistant present. Kells was acquitted of both murder and manslaughter at the Old Bailey when he explained that at the time of the operation he had been suffering from the effects of a car accident.[316]

Bobby Buckley, who went to prison for four years following an unsuccessful bank raid in Hackney in 1966, died from a drug overdose in the 1970s. His wife Monica, Ronnie's confidant, remarried.

As for the Richardsons, the brothers became estranged after Eddie was sentenced to 35 years following a conviction in 1990 for involvement in a £70 million cocaine and cannabis heist. He was released after 12, bringing his total number of years served to 23. A talented artist, he also wrote his memoirs. Charlie Richardson died in September 2012. Frank Fraser, who gave evidence at the Kray trials, wrote a number of books and became something of a minor celebrity. He died in 2014.

The property dealer Peter Rachman died at the age of 42 following a heart attack on 29 November 1962. Two years earlier he had married his long-standing girlfriend Audrey O'Donnell, but he continued his relationship with Mandy Rice-Davies and a number of other women including the nightclub hostess Christine Keeler. Rachman was buried in the Jewish cemetery at Bushey. He left an estate valued at under £10,000 but the bulk of his property was said to have passed prior to his death to the money lender and Kray associate Tony Schneider.

What about the Kray hangouts? The Carpenters Arms in Cheshire Street has changed hands several times and is now a gastro pub. Previous owners made much of the Kray relationship and claimed the bar had been made out of coffin lids. The Blind Beggar, the location of the first sermon delivered by William Booth of the Salvation Army, became a stop on the tourist tours of criminal London. At one time it was owned by the former England football captain Bobby Moore.

Opened in 1874, the nearby Grave Maurice, where Nipper Read first saw Ronnie Kray in 1964, became a wine bar during the gentrification of the East End, but finally closed its doors in 2010 and was converted into a Paddy Power betting shop.

The Green Dragon in Aldgate passed through a number of hands. At one time it was owned by Kray associate, Bill Ackerman and run by Sammy Lederman. On 2 June 1969 an armed robbery took place in the club in which a gambler was shot. In the spring of 1975 there were a number of shootings at the club, culminating in what was seen as the contract killing in July of 32-year-old West Indian Lowell Lawes, shot when two masked gunmen opened fire while he was playing double rummy. Both the gunmen had northern accents. Georgie Plummer, the one-time boyfriend of Blonde Carol Skinner, had tried to intervene to prevent the shooting. No prosecution followed.

Esmeralda's Barn became the site of the five-star Berkeley Hotel, described as 'Contemporary Chic in Knightsbridge'.

The Stowe Club was taken over by some of the Nash brothers and Mickey Bloom. The one-time manager, cat burglar Charlie Clarke, was murdered in Kent on 10 March 1989 at the age of 71.

Clarke had been known as a police informer for some years and on one occasion had set up Lenny 'The Governor' McLean to be given a bad beating and strangled with chicken wire. McLean escaped and Clarke was obliged to pay him substantial compensation. It appears that Clarke surprised a youth, Shane Keeler, during a burglary, and was stabbed in the neck.

In January 2009 an auction of Kray memorabilia in London fetched an amazing £100,000 plus. In a second auction, a police photograph of them in their teens realised £7,500 against an estimate of £100. In May 2014, letters from Reggie to his wife Frances and notes she made about their relationship made a total of just under £8,000 at Gorringes auction house in Sussex, which had held regular sales of Kray memorabilia.

CHAPTER 23
THE KRAY LEGACY

What legacy, if any, did the Twins leave, and why do they remain in the public eye today?

Part of their appeal was that they were twins. From the time of Greek and Roman mythology, twins have always held a special interest in folklore, history and romantic literature – they often become separated, or one is good and one is evil. With the exception of June and Jennifer Gibbons, catatonic female twins who committed arson in 1982, in British criminal history the Krays were unique. Indeed examples of twins, let alone identical twins, who are such high profile criminals are not exactly common worldwide. As a result opportunities for sociological studies are limited and should therefore be grasped.

Then there has always been the fascination with the East End. There may have been more riots, freaks, bodies or slashings *per capita* in Elephant and Castle, Kings Cross or Paddington, but none of these areas has held the criminal cachet as the East End.

There was of course Jack the Ripper, about whom over 500 books have been written. Another possible identity was revealed in 2015.

Between the wars the East End was regarded by the middle classes as dangerous, and as evidence, police only patrolled the area in pairs. Just as their New York counterparts did in pre-war Harlem, 'society' in white tie and tails would end an evening slumming at Charlie Brown's Railway Tavern in the East India Dock Road, where gentlemen would be taken behind a curtain to be shown exotica and erotica. Everyone could boast the next day of their bravery in surviving the encounter.

Earlier there had been the Ratcliffe Highway Murders, the Dock Strikes, the Elephant Man Joseph Merrick, born in Leicester but exhibited in the Mile End Road, the Sydney Street siege, and later the long-running myth of how the East Enders linked arms and repulsed Oswald Moseley's Blackshirts. Perhaps it is because the very word East carries with it the spice of the Orient.

In fiction, Dickens' *The Mystery of Edwin Drood* opens in an East End opium den, and in Conan Doyle's Sherlock Holmes story *The Man with the Twisted Lip*, the title character disappears in a den in Limehouse; Sax Rohmer's Fu Manchu used the East End as his base for his plans to corrupt the western world.

The rise of the Krays coincided with the rejuvenation of the area after heavy bomb damage in World War Two. The Theatre Royal, Stratford, re-opened. An interest in working-class culture developed nationwide. For the first time, members of the working class could be seen on the screen and in print as heroes or anti-heroes. Prior to the war and immediately after, working-class heroes were mostly of the comic variety – Stepin' Fetchit in America; George Formby, Tommy Trinder, Norman Wisdom and Gracie Fields are good examples in the UK. They might still get the man or the girl at the end of the film, but they were never in competition with David Niven. Now, with Joe Lampton, John Braine's anti-hero from *Room at the Top*, Alan Sillitoe's *Saturday Night and Sunday Morning* and so-called kitchen-sink dramas such as *The L-Shaped Room*, working-class people, unmarried mothers, gays and black men were treated as real people and not simply as ciphers or figures of fun. The first British film with a black actor in a starring role was Basil Dearden's 1950 *Pool of London*, in which Earl Cameron has a tentative relationship with Susan Shaw. The trend stuttered on from there.

The general consensus is that the Twins were practically innumerate, illiterate and not particularly intelligent. And worse, they were deaf to sound advice. The old-time villain Bert Rossi, who died in 2017, wrote:

> 'If I were Tony Mella [the Soho club owner], with the way he mangled up words, I'd say I think they were 'unmentorable', if there is such a word. Goodness knows I and others tried hard enough. They had good people around them as well, people who knew what they were doing. People like Leslie Payne and Freddie Gore who were two of the best Long Firm fraudsmen of the time. But did the Twins learn how it should be done? No, of course they didn't. Would they even listen? No, of course they wouldn't.'[317]

Respect is a crucial word in the vocabulary of the villain, and the Krays put themselves out to create an image, even if it was a very different one from reality. This doubtless contributed both to their fall and subsequent phoenix-like rise. They were keen to portray themselves as charity workers, presenting prizes at amateur boxing events, promoting wrestling tournaments and raffling useless racehorses. A trawl through the *East London Advertiser* over the period produces numerous references to them as local and successful businessmen, but a really sensible criminal would remain unknown to the public. Before the era of Billy Hill and Jack Spot in the late 1940s and early 1950s, traditional criminals did not try to rise above their primordial station and mix with their betters. Spot and Hill were good copy for rival newspapers. Later Spot would attribute his downfall to his craving for publicity. The same could be said for the Twins. They simply got above themselves.[318]

The interest and debate about their sex lives explains some of the fascination surrounding the Twins. Were they heterosexual, bisexual or gay? Is there any truth in the suggestion the Twins had incestuous sex together? According to author John Pearson, Ronnie confessed that for some time, fearful of outsiders discovering their sexuality, this was the case. Whether this involved anything more than teenage mutual masturbation, who can actually say?[319]

Ronnie's predilection for good-looking young men is well documented. And a boy had to be careful if he turned him down. It has been claimed he was turned off women after he once woke to find the girl he had slept with had started to menstruate.[320] Other rumours suggest he deflowered the daughter of a woman who had worked in Esmeralda's Barn on her 16th birthday, and then regularly had sex with both her and her mother. There are other stories that he said women 'smelled and gave diseases'.

Reggie's sexuality appears much more complex. He clearly liked having women about him, but whether he had sex with them is another matter. Reg claimed he only became bisexual after many years in prison, but there were persistent suggestions his marriage to Frances was never consummated. His one-time friend Micky Fawcett recalled how he was invited by Reggie to a threesome with a gorgeous girl, but they all lay like logs throughout the night.[321]

Certainly in 1965 a waitress from Poplar brought a paternity suit against Reggie, claiming he was the father of her baby girl. Her claim was dismissed for lack of corroboration, 'as I knew it would be,' said Kray. But there have been suggestions Reggie paid the girls to bring these suits against him, thereby confirming his heterosexuality.

In March 2001 a woman claimed she was the result of a fling between Reggie and a cabaret dancer at the Double R club in 1958. She went on to say that her son was the spitting image of Reggie.[322] Kray would later use the claim as evidence that his marriage to Frances had been consummated.

Does it matter? Perhaps not as much in these more liberal times, as much as in the days when they were kings of a section of the East End. For a start, homosexual acts short of buggery, whether in private or in public, were punishable by up to two years' imprisonment, and they were regularly handed out. The sentence for homosexual buggery itself until 1860 was the death penalty, and still carried life imprisonment. In the 1960s in the milieu in which they flourished it mattered a great deal, as to a lessening extent it does in sport today. To admit to being gay meant peer derision and with it the loss of face.

On 12 February 1988 an unkind doggerel was felt-tipped onto Frances' grave:

> 'There once was two brothers named Kray
> Who were both mad, perverted and gay
> Ron was a rascal who loved a young arsehole
> From 16 to 60, they say.'

Were they really as powerful as has been made out since their imprisonment and deaths? On a personal note, by the time of their arrests I had established a practice dealing with serious criminal cases in North London, but because of the insularity of the various suburbs, I had actually never heard of them. They were obviously known to East Enders but west of Aldgate, they would have been unrecognised by the general public. However, the appalling details of the McVitie and Cornell murders appealed to an audience devoted to the *News of the World*. George Orwell had written of *The Decline of the English Murder* but here was proof that it was alive and well. With those lurid details, and the swingeing sentences they received, they began to be noticed by a much wider public.

After their imprisonment Bert Wickstead cleared up the Dixon brothers, who were running a small protection gang, and with that there was no comparable gang in London for the next seven years. Then other families sprang up in South London and over the years they became much more organised and much more violent.

The Twins were not bright, they were impatient, they had no foresight and they craved recognition and adulation. Sensible gangsters swimming in the relatively small pool of East End crime do not go about squiring fading Hollywood stars and over-the-hill boxers in a blaze of publicity. Their other big mistake was committing murder for personal rather than business reasons. The Krays were never even in the class of the Richardsons, and they would not have survived 24 hours among today's gangs.

Now, some 60 years after they began their rule of the East End, there are two very different schools of thought about them. There is the idea of the Twins acting as modern-day Robin Hoods, making the streets safe for women and children and only stealing from fellow criminals or from those who had acquired their wealth under dubious circumstances. As for the deaths, well, they had merely exterminated parasites such as Cornell and McVitie. Even a man whom they had ruined and left penniless thought well of them, saying to Nipper Read, 'They're such nice fellas.' Ronnie's counsel Platt-Mills thought him 'a kindly and most thoughtful client'.

On the other hand, Gerry Parker, the old time Spot man, thought:

> 'What the Twins did was out of order; fucking outrageous. They were bullies leaning on small shopkeepers, people struggling to make a living. No question of that.'[323]

And set alongside that are the opinions of the bank robbers of the time, who despised them, seeing them as nothing more than thieves' ponces and bullies. One bank robber said:

'There really is a load of shit talked about them. They ran the East End but they never ran the West End. If they'd come near us they'd have been seen to. Of course they protected clubs. There's a lot of weak people in this world. They never had the arsehole to rob for themselves. Are they nice people? Well, tell me if this is nice. You get a young boy come into the club with his girlfriend. He's got a load of cigarettes to sell. They take the cigarettes, never pay him and he ends up getting shafted up the arsehole. Is that nice?'[324]

Take your choice. After all, 'Those were the Krays'.

ACKNOWLEDGEMENTS

My thanks are due first to Dock Bateson without whose support this book would never have been completed. Then in strictly alphabetical order thanks are due to the following, as well as to those who have asked not to be named.

The late Mickey Bailey, the late J.P. Bean, Michael Bekman, Keith Bottomley, Duncan Campbell, the late Clive Coleman, Jonathan Davics, the late Stan Davis, Carrie de Silva, the late Ronnie Diamond, Micky Fawcett, the late Frank Fraser, Adrian Gatton, Jeffrey Gordon, the late Ralph Haeems, Michael Hallinan, Ron Historyo, Sir Ivan Lawrence Wayne Lear, Barbara Levy, Cal McCrystal, the late Henry Mooney, Gerry Parker, John Pearson, Lilian Pizzichini, William Powell, Pam Randall, Nipper and Pat Read, Jamie Reid, the late John Rigbey, the late Norbert Rondel, Mark Roodhouse, the late Bert Rossi, Charles Taylor and Ajda Vucicevic. In addition, my thanks go to the staff of the British Library, the Tower Hamlets Local History Library & Archives, and the National Archives at Kew.

SELECTED BIBLIOGRAPHY

Bronson, C., *The Krays and Me*, John Blake, London, 2007.

and Richards, S., *Legends*, Vol. 1, Mirage Publishing, Gateshead, 2003.

Bryan, E. and Higgins, R., *Infertility: New Choices New Dilemmas*, Penguin, London, 1995.

Cabell, C., *The Kray Brothers: the image shattered*, Robson Books, London, 2002.

Campbell, D., *That was Business, This is Personal*, Secker & Warburg, London, 1990.

Carr, G., Barker, J. and Christie, S., *The Angry Brigade: A History of Britain's First Urban Guerilla Group*, Gollancz, London, 1975.

Cater, F. and Tullett T., *The Sharp End*, The Bodley Head, London, 1988.

Cole, P. and Pringle P., *Can you Positively identify this man?* Andre Deutsch, London, 1974.

Collins, D., *Nightmare in the Sun*, John Blake, London, 2007.

Crowther, E., *Last in the List*, Basset Publications, Plymouth, 1988.

Davidson, E., *Joey Pyle*, Virgin Publishing, London, 2003.

Dickson, J., *Murder without Conviction*, Sidgwick & Jackson, London, 1986.

Donoghue, A. and Short, M., *The Krays' Lieutenant*, Smith, Gryphon, London, 1995.

With a Gun in My Hand, Blake's True Crime, London, 2008.

Du Rose, J., *Murder Was My Business*, W. H. Allen, London, 1971.

Evans P. and Bailey, D., *Goodbye Baby and Amen, A Saraband for the Sixties*, Corgi Books, London, 1970.

Fawcett, M., *Krayzee Days*, Pen Press, Brighton, 2013.

Ferris, P. with McKay, R., *The Ferris Conspiracy*, Mainstream, Edinburgh, 2001.

Fido, M., *The Krays Unfinished Business*, Carlton Books, London, 1999.

Fineman, B., *Original Motor Mouth*, John Blake, London, 2015.

Flanagan, M., *One of the Family*, Arrow Books, London, 2015.

Foreman, F., *Running with the Krays*, John Blake, London, 2017.

with Lisners, J. *Respect*, Century, London, 1996.

and Lambrianou, T., *Getting it Straight*, Pan Books, London, 2001.

Fraser, F., *Mad Frank*, TimeWarner Books, London, 1995.

    Mad Frank and Friends, Warner Books, London, 1999.

Fry, C., *The Krays: the Final Countdown*, Mainstream, Glasgow, 2001.

Gold, S., *Breaking Law*, Bath Publishing, Bath, 2016.

Green, S., *Rachman*, Hamly Paperbacks, Feltham, 1981.

Greig, G., *Breakfast With Lucian: A Portrait Of The Artist*, Jonathan Cape, London, 2013.

Hamilton, L., *Branded by Ronnie Kray*, John Blake, London, 2002.

and Cabell, C., *Getting away with Murder*, John Blake, London, 2006.

Hebdige, D., *Kray Twins: study of a system of closure*, University of Birmingham, 1974.

Hyams, J., *Frances: The Tragic Bride*, John Blake, London, 2004.

Keeler, C. with Thompson, D., *The Truth at Last*, Sidgwick & Jackson, London, 2001.

Kray, C., *Me and my Brothers*, Grafton, London, 1997.

Kray, K., *Murder, Madness and Marriage*, Blake Publishing, London, 1994.

    The Krays: Free at Last, Blake Publishing, London, 2000.

Kray, Reg, *A Way of Life, His Final Word*, Sidgwick & Jackson, London, 2000.

with Peter Gerrard, *Reg Kray's East End Stories*, Sphere, London, 2010.

Kray, Reg and Ron, *Our Story*, Pan Books, London, 1989.

    Villains we have Known, N.K. Publications, Leeds, 1993.

Kray, Roberta, *Reg Kray: A Man Apart*, Sidgwick & Jackson, London 2002.

Kray, Ron and Dineage, F., *My Story*, Pan, London, 1993.

Lambrianou, C., *Escape from the Kray Madness*, Sidgwick & Jackson, London, 1995.

Lambrianou, T., *Inside the Firm*, London, Smith Gryphon, London, 1991.

Lewis, D. and Hughman, P., *Most Unnatural: an Inquiry into the Stafford Case*, Penguin, Harmondsworth, 1971.

Mason, E., *The Inside Story*, Pan Books, London, 1994.

Massingberd, H. (ed), 'Sir Melford Stevenson' in *The Very Best of the Daily Telegraph Books of Obituaries*, Pan Books, 2001.

Morton, J., Gangland, Macdonald, London, 1992.

    East End Gangland, Warner Books, London, 2000.

    Gangland Soho, Piatkus Books, London, 2008.

SELECTED BIBLIOGRAPHY

Bert Battles Rossi, National Crime Syndicate, Los Angeles, 2017.

and G. Parker, *Gangland Bosses*, TimeWarner Books, London, 2005.

Mrs X., *The Barmaid's Tale*, Little Brown & Co, London 1996.

O'Leary, L., *Ronnie Kray, a man among men*, Headline, London, 2000.

O'Mahoney, B., *Wannabee in my Gang? From the Krays to the Essex Boys*, Mainstream, Edinburgh, 2004.

Pearson, J., *The Profession of Violence*, Pan Books, Grafton, London, 1985.

The Cult of Violence, Orion Books, London, 2001.

Notorious, Century, London, 2010.

One of the family, Century, London, 2003.

Pim, K., *Jumpin' Jack Flash*, Jonathan Cape, 2016.

Platts-Mills, J., *Muck, Silk and Socialism: recollections of a left-wing Queen's Counsel*, Wedmore, Paper Publishing, 2002.

Raymond, D., *The Hidden Files*, Little Brown, London, 1992.

Read, L., *Nipper, The Man who Nicked the Krays*, Future Paperbacks, London, 1992.

Scala, M., *Diary of a Teddy Boy: A memoir of the long sixties*, Sitric Books, Dublin, 2000.

Scott, P., *Gentleman Thief*, Harper Collins, London, 1995.

Stafford, D. with Hildred, S., *Fun-loving criminal: the autobiography of a gentleman gangster*, John Blake, London, 2007.

Sturley, L., *The Secret Train Robber*, Random House, London, 2015.

Teale, R., *Bringing Down the Krays*, Ebury Press, London, 2014.

Thompson, D., The *Hustlers*, Pan Macmillan, London, 2012.

Mafialand (previously *Shadowland*), 2011, Mainstream, Edinburgh.

Thorpe, D.R., *Supermac: The Life of Harold Macmillan*, Chatto & Windus, London, 2010.

Tremlett, G., *Little Legs, Muscle Man of Soho*, Unwin Hyman, London, 1989.

Webb, B., *Running with the Krays*, Mainstream, Edinburgh, 1993.

Ward, B. with T. Gray, *Buller*, Hodder & Stoughton, London, 1974.

'Blood Brother', *Time Out*, 30 April-6 May 1962.

Boyle, S., 'My strange romance with Charlie Kray', *The Express*, 11 January 1998.

Callan, P., 'Why I murdered this man', *Daily Mirror*, 29 May 1986.

Campbell, D., 'Krays myth of keeping East End Safe debunked by hench-man', *Guardian*, 3 June 1995.

Clydesdale, L., 'Roberta Kray on her life as a gangster's widow', *Daily Record*, 13 October 2009.

Dalrymple, J., 'The Krays I knew (and they're still as stupid as ever)', *Daily Mail*, 24 June 1997.

Earl of Mountbatten, *Report of the Inquiry into Prison Escapes and Security*, HMSO, 1966.

Edwards, J., 'I'm glad he's dead', *Daily Mirror*, 18 March 1995.

Fortune, N., 'The East End after the Krays,' *Time Out*, 12, 19 January 1973.

Gayford, M., 'The Naked Truth', *Sunday Times Magazine*, 2 September 2018.

Hebdige, D., 'Kray Twins: a study of a system of closure', University of Birmingham, Centre for Contemporary Studies, 1974.

Hughes, S., Troup, J. and Lazzeri, A., 'The Reggie they spoke of in church, all love and Christianity, was not the Reg I knew', *The Sun*, 12 October 2000.

Jenks, C. and Lorentzen, J.L., 'The Kray Fascination', *Theory, Culture and Society*, August 1997.

Jones, D., 'The Great Kray Lie Yet again', *Daily Mail*, 2 September 2000.

Kray, Roberta, 'Best of Times, Worst of Times', *Sunday Times Magazine*, 9 April 2006.

Lowe. R., '"Evil" father and son will spend life behind bars for John Finney murder', *Times-Series.co.uk*, 18 May 2009; Daily Star, 12 May 2013.

McCrystal, C., 'Glad to be Kray', *The Independent*, 1 April 2001.

McGurran, A., Rock, L. and Swain, G., 'Reggie Kray 1933-2000. He wanted a statesman's funeral but all he got was a freak show full of has-beens', *Daily Mirror*, 12 October 2000.

Mangan, W., 'Reggie Kray's wife was a drug taking wild child', *Daily Mirror*, 8 September 2015.

Morton, J., 'A very personal practice', *New Law Journal*, 13 March 1987.

Oakes, P., 'Goings On', *Sunday Times*, 14 August 1977.

Payne, Professor J. P., 'A Queer Affair', *The History of Anaesthesia Society Proceedings*, Volume 34, Proceedings of the Summer Scientific Meeting, Grangewood Hotel, Grange-over-Sands, 2-3 July 2004.

Pearson, J., 'The Gangster and the Peer', *Independent on Sunday*, 15 June 1997.

'Ronnie, Reggie and Me', *Esquire*, January 1999.

Pringle, P., 'The case they had to drop', *Sunday Times*, 17 May 1970.

Rawlings, S., 'Ron killed Reg's wife', *News of the World*, 13 January 2002.

Sellars, K., 'Fun Lovin' Criminals', *Esquire*, November 1999.

Sengupta, K. and Mellor, J., 'The £39m cocaine scam that gave Kray's life story a surprise ending', *The Independent*, 21 June 1997.

Taylor, P. and White, S., 'Evil Ronnie did this to the Ripper', *News of the World*, 27 August 1995.

'Raving Ron's Deadly Escape Plot', *News of the World*, 3 September 1995.

the gentle author, 'Billy Frost, the Krays' driver', *Spitalfields Life*, 24 February 2010.

'Lenny Hamilton, Jewel Thief', *Spitalfields Life*, 1 September 2010.

Wooding, D., 'The Krays: Kings and their prison courtiers', *People*, 30 June 1974.

'I've got Reggie's licence to love,' *People*, 7 July 1974.

NOTES

1   *Daily Express*, 25 February 2001.

2   James Morton, *Gangland 2*; Dennis Stafford had a long criminal career, mainly as a long-firm fraudster and later in the celebrated Stafford-Luvaglio case of January 1967 in which Angus Sibbett, the manager of a gambling club in Newcastle, was killed. Both Stafford and Michael Luvaglio were convicted and a long campaign began to clear their names. Eventually after they were paroled Stafford told the *News of the World* that, in fact, he but not Luvaglio had killed Sibbett. He later retracted this, saying he had confessed only for the money. He resumed his life as a conman. Dennis Stafford, *Fun-loving criminal: the autobiography of a gentleman gangster*; David Lewis and Peter Hughman, *Most Unnatural*.

3   Nat. Arch. Crim 1/2064

4   Ronald Hart, unpublished manuscript; John Pearson, *Infamous Twins;* Anthony Nutting, *Gordon: Martyr and Misfit.*

5   William Hugo Kline was born in 1866 in Bochum, Prussia. He came to England some time before 1911, working as a strongman and wrestler on the Music Halls. He died in 1957 in Kensington. Reg Kray, *Born Fighter,* pp. 22-23.

6   Charlie Kray, *Me and My Brothers*, pp. 32-34.

7   Reg & Ron Kray, *Our Story*, p. 24.

8   Martin Fido, *The Krays Unfinished Business*, p. 104.

9   Back in 1952 they managed to stay out for a few months, sometimes staying at Dickie Morgan's home, sometimes with David Levy, one of a large family from Mile End, sometimes under the protection of Tommy Smithson in billiard halls in Soho, until they were arrested for desertion and assault back in Hackney on 19 January 1953 when they claimed they had merely pushed a police officer out of their way. On 26 February, again at Thames Magistrates' court, they each received a month for assaulting the officer. In fact the assault on PC Roy Fisher, who was off sick for three days, had occurred back on 29 October when he had tried

to arrest them then. *Inside the Kray Family*, p 114.

10   Charlie Kray, *Me and My Brothers*, p.41.

11   Conversations with SD, 29 October 2009, 24 October 2013; Henry Ward with Tony Gray, *Buller.*

12   John Pearson, *The Profession of Violence*, p. 87.

13   Conversation with JM.

14   Henry Ward, *Buller,* pp. 150-151.

15   *The Times*, 6 September 1956.

16   Nat Arch. MEPO 2/9753; Laurie O'Leary, *Ron Kray: A Man among Men*, p. 117.

17   Nat. Arch. MEPO 2/9753; Reg Kray, *Born Fighter*, p. 57.

18   Billy Webb, *Running with the Krays*, pp. 101-2.

19   Reg Kray, *Born Fighter*, p. 56.

20   Reg Kray, *Born Fighter*, p. 58.

21   Dick Hebdige, *The Kray Twins: a Study of a System of Closure.*

22   Conversation with JM, 4 November 2014.

23   Reggie Kray, *Born Fighter*, p. 139.

24   MEPO 2/11410. Dawood received three years on 7 February 1969. For some years afterwards he claimed he had been the victim of a police trap.

25   On 1 July 1962 the 19-stone Paul, apparently once a small-time wrestler probably working for independent promotions, was killed by his brother Bernard after he had gone berserk after a party at the remote Creeksea Ferry Inn at Rochford, Essex, which their mother managed. He knocked her to the ground. It was then Bernard went for the shotgun and shot his brother in the stomach. He was charged with manslaughter but the magistrates refused to commit him for trial and he was discharged. *Southend Standard*, October-November 1962; Reg Kray, *Our Story*, p. 121.

26   Reg Kray, *Born Fighter,* pp. 67-8.

27   Charles Bronson, Steve Richards, *Legends*, Vol. 1, p. 74.

28   John Pearson, The *Cult of Violence*, pp. 55-57.

29   Reg & Ron Kray, *Our Story*, p. 32; Charlie Kray, *Me and My Brothers,* p 66.

30   Nat. Arch. MEPO 2/10075.

31   Charlie Kray, *Me and My Brothers*, pp. 84-7.

32 Nat. Arch. Crim. 1/3142; MEPO 2/10075.

33 Conversation with JM, 17 April 2015; Nat. Arch. MEPO 2/11386.

34 Leslie Payne, *The Brotherhood*, pp. 16-18.

35 *Evening News*, 27 September 1963.

36 Eric Mason, *Inside Story*, pp.170-171.

37 Albert Donoghue, *The Krays' Lieutenant*, p. 49; Conversation with JM, 7 September 2012.

38 It was a time of sieges. In March that year James Baigrie killed himself in a van in Earl's Court during another siege. He had escaped in October 1983 from Edinburgh's high security prison during a life sentence for shooting a barman in the back. He had been on the run for 16 months.

39 *The Times*, 4 April 1959.

40 Conversation with JM, 16 August 2007.

41 John Dickson, *Murder without Conviction*, pp. 1-6.

42 George Tremlett, *Little Legs: Muscle Man of Soho*; Frank Fraser, *Mad Frank's London*, pp. 58-9. For more about Smith generally see Mrs X, *The Barmaid's Tale*.

43 Conversation with JM, 27 May 2015.

44 Conversation with JM, 7 September 2012.

45 Conversation with JM, 22 May 2017. Sir Eric Miller, once head of the public company Peachey Property Corporation, committed suicide on the Jewish Day of Atonement, Yom Kippur 1977 while under investigation for fraud. Doubts have been raised about the circumstances of his death, with some suggesting he may have been murdered.
A leading member of an early neo-Nazi National Socialist Movement, on 25 January 1967 Colin Jordan was sentenced to 18 months in prison at Devon Assizes for a breach of the Race Relations Act 1965 by circulating material likely to cause racial hatred. He died in 2009.

46 Conversation with JM, 17 April 2002.

47 Conversation with JM, 10 April 2015.

48 Conversation with JM, 24 October 2013.

49 Conversation with JM. In 2002 Mickey Bailey recalled the Pelliccis: 'Terry's dead now. He was very friendly with the Twins but Nevio's still alive. There was better service in both of them than in the Savoy, and

the cooking was better. Everything was clean, freshly cooked and you couldn't fault it. There's a mention of them in Egon Ronay. At dinner time there'd be roast beef and potatoes or steak and kidney pudding. It was a proper Italian-run caff that served English food.'

50 Henry Ward, *Buller*, pp. 175-6.

51 Reg Kray, *Villains we have Known*, p. 41; John Pearson places the shooting in the Green Dragon Club; *Profession of Violence*, p. 208.

52 Conversation with JM.

53 Albert Donoghue, *The Kray's Lieutenant*, p. 51.

54 'Scotch' Jack Buggy, who had served a nine-year sentence for wounding, was shot and killed in the club in May 1964 when he went inquiring about the disappearance of Great Train Robber Roy James's share of the money. It was run by a serious player 'Franny' Daniels, an old Jack Spot man, who was later acquitted of Buggy's murder. Donoghue, *The Kray's Lieutenant*, p.51. For an account of the career and death of Buggy, see Leonard Read, *Nipper*.

55 Conversation with JM,

56 Ronald Hart, Unpublished MS.

57 Eric Mason, *The Inside Story*, pp. 184-5.

58 Conversation with JM, 17 March 2015.

59 Ronald Hart, Unpublished MS.

60 Foaled in 1958, before it was sold to the Krays, Solway Cross came second twice as a two-year-old and in 1962 was third in two Selling Hurdles, the winner of one of which fetched only 380 guineas. It last ran that year at Windsor, where it finished down the field at 20-1.

61 Conversation with JM, 27 April 2015.

62 Sally Green, *Rachman*, pp. 166-168.

63 Ronald Hart, Unpublished MS.

64 Leslie Payne, *The Brotherhood*, p. 66.

65 Min Scala, Diary *of a Teddy Boy*, p.60.

66 Kieron Pim, *Jumpin' Jack Flash*, p 94.; Min Scala, *Diary of a Teddy Boy*, p. 69.

67 Nat. Arch. KV 2/2387; National Archives of Australia.

68 Conversation with JM, 19 March 2015.

69 Nat. Arch. MEPO 2/10075.

70   *Evening Standard*, 22 February 2010.

71   Geordie Greig, *Breakfast With Lucian: A Portrait Of The Artist*.

72   Charlie Kray, *Me and my Brothers*, p. 82; Tony Lambrianou, *Inside the Firm*, p. 110.

73   the gentle author, 'Lenny Hamilton, Jewel Thief', *Spitalfields Life*, 1 September 2010.

74   John Pearson merely has Hamilton branded on both cheeks. Ron Kray, *My Story*, p. 50; Leslie Payne, *The Brotherhood*; Joe Lee and Rita Smith, *Inside the Kray Family*; Micky Fawcett, *Krayzee Days*; Lennie Hamilton, *Branded by Ronnie Kray*.

75   Min Scala, *Diary of a Teddy Boy*, pp. 62-64.

76   BW Conversation with JM, 14 April 1995.

77   Nat. Arch. MEPO 2/10937 [Closed].

78   Kate Kray says she was told on good authority that in fact it was Ronnie who had shot Teddy Berry. *The Twins: Free at Last*, p.8.

79   Nat. Arch. PREM11/4698; The Times, 1 August 1964. §

80   Conversation with JM 25 January 2019.

81   John Pearson, *Notorious;* D.R.Thorpe, *Supermac, The Life of Harold Macmillan*.

82   Nat. Arch. LO 2/708.

83   Rees-Davies had been involved in an attempt to buy off the exceptionally beautiful club hostess Christine Keeler to stop her giving details of her affair with MP John Profumo. He offered £500 and thought he had been successful but unfortunately wires were crossed and she had wanted £5,000. As a result Rees-Davies was adversely named in the subsequent Denning Inquiry into the affair. His 'punishment' was that his application to become a Queen's Counsel, something normally immediately granted to a barrister MP, was delayed for several years.

84   PREM 11/4689

85   Conversation with JM, 26 January 2009.

86   *The Times*, 28 July 1959.

87   'The Charitable Life of the Brothers Kray', *Sunday Times*, 9 August 1964.

88   Nat. Arch. MEPO 2/10763.

89   Nat. Arch. MEPO 2/10763.

90 Leonard Read, *Nipper*, p. 89.

91 ibid pp. 92-3.

92 *Sunday Times*, 28 December 1969.

93 Conversation with JM, 4 July 2013.

94 Nat. Arch. MEPO 2/10763; *The Times*, 14 May 1971.

95 Nat. Arch. MEPO 2/11462.

96 Conversation with JM 25 January 2019

97 Frank Fraser, *Mad Frank's London*, p. 74.

98 Leonard Read, *The man who nicked the Krays*, p.103; Jimmy Evans, and Martin Short, *The Survivor;* Freddie Foreman & Tony Lambrianou, *Getting it Straight*, pp. 65-6.

99 Leonard Read, *The Man who Nicked the Krays*, pp 102-3.

100 *The Times*, 11 February 1965.

101 Nat. Arch. MEPO 2/10763. Police report. para 140.

102 Reg Kray, Born *Fighter,* p. 93.

103 Lewis Chester and Cal McCrystal, 'The Long Hard climb from Bethnal Green', Sunday *Times,* 11 April 1965.

104 *Daily Express*, 30 April 1965.

105 *Daily Express*, 8 June 1967; Daily *Mirror*, 14 June 1967.

106 Unpublished MS by Hart.

107 'The Kray Brothers: Reg, Charlie, Ron', *London Life*, 27 November 1965; Ronald Hart, unpublished MS.

108 Nat. Arch. Crim 1/ 2589; *The Times*, 26 May 1955; 'A sordid story of the slums', *East London Advertiser*, 27 May 1955.

109 Reg Kray, *Born Fighter*, p. 95.

110 the gentle author, 'Lenny Hamilton, Jewel Thief', *Spitalfields Life*, 1 September 2010.

111 Mrs X, *The Barmaid's Tale*, p. 42.

112 MEPO 2/10933.

113 For an account of the Hennessey family see J.P. Bean, *Over the Wall*, Ch 17.

114 Nat. Arch. DPP 2/4156; *The Times*, 25 May 1966.

115 In 1969 Hart's widow Eileen married Stanley Naylor who later received 12 years for his part in the Tibbs-Nicholls families feud. Naylor's son, Lennie, was himself shot and killed at his home in Istead Rise on 19 April 2001. In 1996 he had been cleared of a charge of attempted mur-

der when the victim of a machete attack in Canning Town refused to give evidence. He had also served a seven-year sentence for drug dealing. See James Morton, *Gangland Today*.

116 Micky Fawcett, *Krayzee Days*, p. 136.

117 the gentle author, 'Billy Frost, The Krays' Driver', *Spitalfields Life*, 24 February 2010. In *Born Fighter* Reg Kray says that when he and Ron were in Brixton awaiting trial on the Hide-A-Way club charges Cornell slightingly told a member of the Firm, 'The King is Dead'.

118 Conversation with JM, 27 May 2015.

119 Andrews had his leg amputated following the shooting and was later fitted with a false leg. He died from cancer shortly afterwards. Henry Mooney, unpublished MS 2001.

120 Micky Fawcett, *Krazy Days*, pp. 137, 145-6.

121 Nat. Arch. MEPO 2/11297.

122 Mrs X, *The Barmaid's Tale*, pp. 44-5.

123 Brian McConnell, *The Evil Firm*, p. 82. As another example of the various stories about the Twins, in his unpublished memoir Ronald Hart says that they moved into a flat in the Lea Bridge Road found for them by the 'Cat Man' Charlie Clarke. The early incumbents were Hart, Ronnie and Reggie, Ian Barrie and Ronnie's boyfriend 'Little Billy'. Later Donoghue joined them.

124 Mrs X, *The Barmaid's Tale*, p. 54; Albert Donoghue, conversation with JM, 7 September 2012.

125 Paul Ferris, *The Ferris Conspiracy*, pp, 56-7. The Glasgow police kept more or less continuous observation on Thompson and there was a note that on 27 July 1964 Albert Dimes and Frank Fraser had been there to see him. In April 1965 Thompson had stayed a fortnight at a boarding house in Clacton run by a 'Big Mac' McGregor.

126 Charlie Richardson, *My Manor*, p. 182; Robert Parker, *Rough Justice*. Roy Hall, later convicted at the so-called Torture Trial, was sentenced to 10 years. The prosecution's case was that he had manned a hand-cranked generator originally designed for sending out SOS signals from aircraft which was used to torture those who had displeased Charlie Richardson.

127 Conversation with JM, 7 September 2012.

128 Nat. Arch. DPP 2/4223; *Daily Mirror*, 6 August 1966.

129 In 1959 Roberts and an accomplice had posed as tax inspectors to gain entry into the home of an elderly man. Once inside the man was bound and robbed and beaten about the head with a glass decanter. When Roberts was captured and tried for the crime the judge, Mr Justice Maude, sentencing him to seven years, told him, 'You are a brutal thug. You came very near the rope this time. It is to be hoped you do not appear before us again.' His victim, who never recovered from his injuries, died one year and three days after the attack. Under the law at the time, had he died two days earlier, Roberts could have been tried for his murder. He was finally paroled for the murder of the police officers in 2014.

130 Ronnie Kray, *My Story*, pp. 40-42.

131 Reg and Ron Kray, *Our Story*, p. 78.

132 Nat. Arch. MEPO 3/3140.

133 The Earl of Mountbatten, *Report of the Inquiry into Prison Escapes and Security*, 1966, para. 155.

134 In *Born Fighter* Reg Kray says it was Alf Donoghue and a Joe Williams who went to collect him, p. 110. Quite why this is so is difficult to understand. It can hardly be to protect Teddy Smith who had disappeared over twenty years earlier. In *Our Story* the men are Donoghue and Smith.

135 Leonard Read, Nipper, *The Man who nicked the Krays*, p. 314.

136 Nat. Arch. Crim 1/4903.

137 Conversation with JM, 14 January 2015.

138 Nat. Arch. MEPO 2/10680.

139 MEPO 2/10680.

140 Freddie Foreman and Tony Lambrianou, *Getting it Straight*, p. 77.

141 ibid.

142 Conversations with the author. For other accounts of Gerard see Marilyn Wisbey, *Gangster's Moll*, and Freddie Foreman's *Respect* which has a long account of Gerard's brutal treatment of his dog.

143 Nat. Arch. J 82/1335.

144 Conversation with JM.

145 Nat. Arch. Crim 1/4903.

146 Nat. Arch. MEPO 2/11386.

147 In the 1990 film *The Krays* he was played sympathetically by Tom Bell which reinforced the image of a rather weedy character. Freddie Foreman and Tony Lambrianou, *Getting it Straight*, p.101.

148 Frank Fraser, *Mad Frank*, pp. 155-157.

149 House of Commons Debate, 10 December 1959 vol. 615 cc. 896-906. McVitie was also said to have thrown a girlfriend out of his car. He claimed they were arguing when she fell against the door which opened.

150 Bobby Cannon was no relation of the West London Cannons. Ronald Hart, unpublished MS; *Albert* Donoghue, *Gun in My Hand*, p. 171.

151 Conversation with JM, 28 December 2012.

152 Ronnie Hart, Unpublished MS; David Jones, 'The Great Kray Lie Yet again', *Daily Mail*, 2 September 2000.

153 Conversations with JM, 2002-2015.

154 *News of the World*, 16 March 1969.

155 Leonard Read, *Nipper, The Man who nicked the Krays*, pp. 133-4.

156 For the Jack the Stripper case see Chapters 21-22. Between 1944 and 1948 Haigh, who was known as the acid bath murderer, poisoned a number of mostly elderly people and then dissolved their bodies in acid. Unfortunately for him, an identifiable gallstone survived the acid and he was convicted and hanged in 1949.

157 John Du Rose, *Murder was my Business*, pp. 126 *et seq.*

158 Leonard Read, *ibid* p.144.

159 Conversation with JM, 16 April 2015.

160 Leonard Read *Nipper, The Man who Caught the Krays*.

161 Lennie Hamilton, Branded; Leonard Read, *ibid*, p 146.

162 Nat. Arch. MEPO 2/10935.

163 Nat. Arch. Assi. 84/170; 94/48.

164 Gemma Mullin, 'The Kray Twins were both GAY', *Mail Online*, 26 July 2014.

165 Conversation with JM, 7 September 2012.

166 Colin Fry with Charlie Kray, *Doing the Business*, Ch. 10.

167 Nat. Arch. MEPO 2/11101.

168 Frank Illiano was reputed to be one of the men who shot Albert Anastasia in the Park Sheraton Hotel in New York on 25 October 1957. Illiano died of natural causes in 2014 aged 86. He had lived for many years with a bullet in his head fired by a sniper as he stood by a hot dog stand in 1974.

169 John Pearson, *The Cult of Violence*, p. 133.

170 Nat. Arch. MEPO 2/11101.

171 Leonard Read, *ibid*, pp. 177-158.

172 In *Murder without Conviction*, John Dickson writes that Reggie Kray did indeed go to see Cooper but this is certainly not correct. *Crime of the Krays Omnibus*, pp. 139-140.

173 Kate Kray, *The Krays, Free at Last*, p. 15.

174 Leonard Read *Nipper, The Man who Caught the Krays*.

175 Chris Lambrianou, Escape *from the Kray Madness*. Tony Maffia was a friend of the safebreaker and prison escaper Alfie Hinds whom he helped to escape from the Law Courts in 1957. Maffia gained his nickname because of the amount of stolen goods he hoarded. On 27 May 1968 he was shot dead in Essex. Stephen Jewell from Manchester was convicted of his murder on a 10-2 majority decision. He has continually protested his innocence. James Morton, *Gangland*.

176 Leonard Read, *Nipper, The Man who Caught the Krays*, pp. 172-5.

177 Leonard Read *Nipper, The Man who Caught the Krays*.

178 Conversation with JM, 16 September 2009.

179 Leonard Read *Nipper, The Man who Caught the Krays*.

180 Laurie O'Leary, *Reg Kray: A Way of Life*, pp. 8-9.

181 Nat. Arch. MEPO 2/11411. His employers did not prosecute Terence Hart after he agreed to repay the money on a weekly basis.

182 Chris Lambrianou, *Escape from the Kray Madness*, pp. 150-151.

183 Nat. Arch. DPP 2/4583; Robert Teale, *Bringing Down the Krays*.

184 Hugh Massingberd (ed), 'Sir Melford Stevenson', *The Very Best of the Daily Telegraph Books of Obituaries*, pp. 31-34.

185 Conversation with JM, 4 February 2014.

186 Leonard Read *Nipper, The Man who Caught the Krays*.

187 HO 3336; 11 December 1968.

188 Nat. Arch. Crim. 8/39.

189 Nat. Arch. Crim. 1/1543

190 Chris Lambrianou, *Escape from the Kray Madness*, pp. 160-161.

191 Reg & Ron Kray, *Our Story*, p. 98.

192 Nat. Arch. Transcript of Summing up, J 82/1332.

193 Nat. Arch. J 82/1328.

194 John Platts-Mills, *Muck, Silk and Socialism : recollections of a left-wing Queen's Counsel*, pp. 469-471.

195 Nat. Arch. J 82/1330.

196 Quoted in Ernest Millen, *Specialist in Crime*, p. 260.

197 Eric Crowther, *Last in the List*, p. 231.

198 John Platts-Mills, *Muck, Silk and Socialism: recollections of a left-wing Queen's Counsel*, pp. 469-471.

199 *People*, 23 March 1969.

200 Nat. Arch CRIM 1/1400.

201 Nat. Arch. Crim. 1/5350.

202 Nat. Arch. MEPO 2/4588.

203 Reg Kray, *Born Fighter*, p.111.

204 Nat. Arch. J 82/1338.

205 Nat Arch, J 82/1312.

206 Nat. Arch. J 82/1312.

207 Nat. Arch. MEPO 2/11386; Peter Pringle, 'The case they had to drop', *Sunday Times*, 15 May 1970. On 18 February 1971 Derek Higgins was arrested and charged with burglary and handling stolen property value £20,000 in Harrogate. He had been involved in trying to recover paintings stolen from a Joan Wright. That case was dropped in November that year. *The Times*, 30 November 1971.

208 Nat. Arch. MEPO 2/11386.

209 Nancy is also reported in *The People* newspaper in June 2004 to have wanted Charlie Kray's body exhumed so that DNA tests could prove if he really was her father.

210 Charles Bronson, *The Krays and Me*, p. 120.

211 *The Times*, 29 July 1974.

212 Conversation with JM, August 2012.

213 *The Sun*, 31 October 1989. For a full account of the death of Barbara Gaul and her husband's activities see James Morton, *Gangland*.

214 *The Times*, 25 November 1981.

215 Sheron (sic) Boyle, 'My strange romance with Charlie Kray', *The Express*, 11 January 1998; 'Why did a former girl guide fall for a villain?', *Sunday Express*, 1 March 1998. Charlie Kray with Robin McGibbon, *Me And My Brothers*, pp. 282-283.

216 Bernard O'Mahoney, *Wannabee in my Gang?* , p. 157.

217 Frank Fraser, Mad *Frank and Friends*, p. 229.

218 Kim Sengupta and James Mellor, 'The £39m cocaine scam that gave Kray's life story a surprise ending', *The Independent*, 21 June 1997.

219 Nat. Arch. HO 336/869.

220 ibid.

221 Convicted in 1965, between 1960 and 1963 Copeland murdered three men, two in Derbyshire because they were gay, something he said he hated. His third victim was a 16-year-old boy in Germany whom he killed after watching the boy have sex with a girl.

222 Nat. Arch. HO 282/66.

223 Nat. Arch. HO 336/872.

224 Nat. Arch MEPO 26/329 [Closed].

225 Nat. Arch. HO 336/696.

226 Nat Arch. HO 336/715.

227 On 11 May 1970, 32-year-old Adamson received two life sentences with a 30-year minimum recommendation after being convicted of the murder of a policeman and a night-watchman during a botched safe-blowing expedition at Farsley, Yorkshire on 15 February that year. Nat. Arch. DPP 2/4817.

228 Nat. Arch. DPP 2/5288.

229 *People*, 14 April 1973.

230 *People*, 7 July 1974.

231 Freddie Foreman with Frank and Noelle Kurylo, *Running with the Krays*, p. 131.

232 Dan Wooding, 'I've got Reggie's licence to love', *People*, 7 July 1974.

233 Dan Wooding, 'The Kray Kings and their prison courtiers', *People*, 30 June 1974. He was sent to Broadmoor the next year and, during the few hours he was at liberty when he escaped, he killed another girl. This time he was deemed sane and sentenced to death, commuted to life imprisonment. He died still in prison in November 2007.

234 *Mirror*, 21 January 1975; *Guardian*, 29 January 1975.

235 Nat Arch. HO 336/722.

236 Philip Oakes, 'Goings On', *Sunday Times*, 14 August 1977.

237 Nat. Arch. HO 336/715.

238 Nat. Arch. HO 336/713.

239 Patrick McGrath, 'I grew up in Broadmoor', *Daily Mail*, 7 September 2012.

240 Daily Star, 29 March 1995.

241 *The People*, 19 March 1995.

242 Douglas Thompson, *Hustlers*.

243 Reg and Ron Kray, *Our Story*, p. 138.

244 Taylor, P., and S., White, S., 'Raving Ron's Deadly Escape Plot', *News of the World*, 3 September 1995.

245 *Daily Mirror*, 9 October 1992.

246 *East London Advertiser*, 10 June 1993.

247 *The Independent*, 17 December 1994.

248 James Morton, *Bert Battles Rossi*, Ch. 9.

249 Laurie O'Leary, *Reg Kray, A Man Apart*, p. 269.

250 *The Times, Daily Express, The Sun, Daily Mirror*, 18-21 March 1995.

251 *Daily Mirror*, 21 March 1995.

252 *Daily Star*, 29 March 1995.

253 Conversation with JM, 19 March 2015.

254 *The Independent*, 5 June 1997.

255 For an account of solicitor Stephen Gold's efforts to find out why the brain had been removed and his other dealing with the brothers, see Stephen Gold, *Breaking Law*.

256 *Mail on Sunday*, 20 February 2000.

257 Nat. Arch. HO 336/736. In this chapter all probation, special and medical reports appear in HO 336. In particular his parole reports appear in HO 336/734, 736, 738.

258 *Daily Mirror*, 29 December 1983.

259 Reg Kray, *Born Fighter*, p. 158.

260 Earl Davidson, *Joey Pyle*, p. 246.

261 Nat. Arch. HO 336/713.

262 Nat. Arch. HO 336/733.

263 *Sunday Express*, 11 August 1986; *The Sun*, 1 September 1986; *Sunday Mirror*, 9 July 1989.

264 Paul Callan, 'Why I murdered this man', *Daily Mirror*, 29 May 1986.

265 *Sunday Times*, 21 December 1986.

266 Nat. Arch. HO 336/714.

267 Nat. Arch. HO 336/731, Report of 26 June 1987.

268 Reggie Kray and Peter Gerrard, *Reggie Kray's East End Stories*, p. xviii.

269 Nat, Arch. HO 336/746, Report 7 September 1993,.

270 *The People*, 14 August 1994.

271 Conversation with JM, 20 September 1996.

272 Jeff Edwards, 'I'm not Reggie GAY'. *Daily Mirror*, 22 November 1996.

273 *Sunday People*, 8 October 2000.

274 Maureen Flanagan, One *of the Family*, p. 291.

275 Chris Tate, 'My Jailhouse gropes with Kinky Kray', *News of the World*, 19 December 1993.

276 Roberta Kray, 'Best of Times, Worst of Times', *Sunday Times Magazine*, 9 April 2006.

277 Roberta Kray, *A Man Apart*, p.193.

278 Nat. Arch. HO 336/746.

279 'Guess who's out to make a killing this Christmas?' *News of the World*, 22 November 1988.

280 Roberta Kray, *A Man Apart*, pp. 274-5.

281 Letters to PB, dated 4 October 1999.

282 Freddie Foreman and Tony Lambrianou, *Getting it Straight*, pp. 360-361.

283 Aidan McGurran, Lucy Rock and Gill Swain, 'Reggie Kray 1933-2000. He wanted a statesman's funeral but all he got was a freak show full of has-beens', *Daily Mirror*, 12 October 2000; Simon Hughes, John Troup and Antonella Lazzeri, 'The Reggie they spoke of in church, all love and Christianity, was not the Reg I knew', 12 October 2000.

284 Freddie Foreman and Tony Lambrianou, *Getting it Straight*, pp. 364-366.

285 *Daily Express*, 12 October 2000.

286 Rebecca Lowe., '"Evil" father and son will spend life behind bars for John Finney murder', *Times-Series.co.uk*, 18 May 2009; *Daily Star*, 12 May 2013.

287 Sarah Arnold, 'Krays killed 30', *News of the World*, 1 April 2001.

288 John Pearson, *The Profession of Violence*, p 249.

289 the gentle author, 'Billy Frost, the Krays' driver' in *Spitalfields Life*, 24 February 2010; Conversation between Lennie Hamilton and Billy Frost, YouTube.com.

290 John Pearson, *Notorious*, pp. 224-5.

291 Henry Ward, *Buller*, p. 205.

292 Mick Brown, 'The Mystery of David Jacobs The Liberace Lawyer', *Daily Telegraph*, 2 June 2013.

293 Nat. Arch. MEPO 2/10937.

294 Douglas Thompson, *Shadowland*, pp. 197-201.

295 James Morton, *Fighters*, pp. 285-287.

296 Nipper Read, *The Man who Nicked the Krays*, p. 187. For a full analysis of Mills' death see James Morton, *Fighters*, Ch. 21.

297 *News of the World*, 13 January 2002.

298 'Kray "murdered brother's wife"', *BBC News*. 12 January 2002.

299 Stefan Kyriazis, 'Legend shocker – BOTH Krays were bisexual and their MUM had Reggie's wife killed', *Express*, 10 September 2015.

300 Letter to *The Times*, 8 November 1994.

301 Gordon Carr, John Barker, Stuart Christie, *The Angry Brigade: A History of Britain's First Urban Guerilla Group*.

302 Lee Sturley, *The Secret Train Robber*; Conversations with author, July 2011; *Daily Mail*, 14 May 2009.

303 Freddie Foreman, *Running with the Twins*, p. 130; *Herts and Essex Observer*, 14 May 2013.

304 Warren Manger, 'Reggie Kray's wife was drug-taking wild child', *Mirror*, 8 September 2014.

305 *The Times*, 24 October 1972.

306 Conversations with JM.

307 *Evening Standard*, 9 September 1970. Billy Amies served his short sentence and died outside London according to one East Ender of natural causes, whatever that may mean in the circumstances.

308 Albert Donoghue and Martin Short, *The Krays' Lieutenant; With a Gun in My Hand*.

309 *The Times*, 23 July 1975.

310 Carrie de Silva, conversation with JM, 10 August 2018; Derek Raymond, *The Hidden Files*, pp. 311-313.

311 Nat. Arch. BT 226/4826; *The Times*, *The Guardian*, 1 March 1996.

312 James Morton, *Gangland Today*.

313 *Daily Mail*, 11 May 2013.

314 See also 'The New Face' in Duncan Campbell, *That was Business, This is Personal.*

315 Danny Collins, *Nightmare in the Sun. Mirror*, 27 January 2005.

316 Professor J. P. Payne, 'A Queer Affair', The History of Anaesthesia Society Proceedings, Volume 34. Proceedings of the Summer Scientific Meeting, Grangewood Hotel, Grange-over-Sands, 2-3 July 2004.

317 James Morton, *Bert Battles Rossi*, p. 91.

318 Dick Hebdige, *Kray Twins: study of a system of closure.*

319 John Pearson, *Notorious*, p. 38.

320 Bobby Teale, *Bringing Down the Krays*, p. 53.

321 Mickey Fawcett, *Krayzee Days.*

322 Mike Hamilton, 'I'm Reggie Kray's "secret daughter"', *Sunday Mirror*, 11 March 2001.

323 Conversation with JM, 23 March 2017.

324 Conversation with JM, 6 June 1991.